THE DATA PROTECTION DIRECTIVE AND MEDICAL RESEARCH ACROSS EUROPE

Data Protection and Medical Research in Europe: PRIVIREAL

Series Editors:
Deryck Beyleveld and David Townend
PRIVIREAL, Sheffield Institute of Biotechnological Law and Ethics

PRIVIREAL (Data Protection and Medical Research in Europe) is a European Commission funded project examining the implementation of Directive 95/46/EC on data protection in relation to medical research and the role of ethics committees in European countries. PRIVIREAL members and authors are experts in their fields from each country, and the project is co-ordinated by Professor Deryck Beyleveld, Faculty of Law, University of Sheffield.

The PRIVIREAL series consists of five separate volumes following the development of the PRIVIREAL project, from first assessments of the implementation of the Directive and its impact on medical research, to consideration of the role of research ethics committees and data protection in practice, leading to recommendations and suggestions to the EC on the implementation of the Directive and the remit to be given to RECs to protect research participants' rights.

The information collected in this series provides a valuable resource for those involved with data protection, medical research, and how they interact. The volumes work to present a comprehensive view of current proceedings right across Europe, including both New Member States and Newly Associated Member States.

Other titles in the series

Implementation of the Data Protection Directive in Relation to Medical Research in Europe
Edited by
D. Beyleveld, D. Townend, S. Rouillé-Mirza and J. Wright
ISBN 0 7546 2369 6

Privacy in Medical Research
Recommendations for Interpretation and Action
Edited by
Deryck Beyleveld and David Townend
ISBN 0 7546 4351 4

The Data Protection Directive and Medical Research Across Europe

Edited by

D. BEYLEVELD, D. TOWNEND, S. ROUILLÉ-MIRZA
AND J. WRIGHT
Sheffield Institute of Biotechnological Law and Ethics

ASHGATE

Published by
Ashgate Publishing Limited
Gower House
Croft Road
Aldershot
Hants GU11 3HR
England

Ashgate Publishing Company
Suite 420
101 Cherry Street
Burlington, VT 05401-4405
USA

Ashgate website: http://www.ashgate.com

British Library Cataloguing in Publication Data
The Data Protection Directive and medical research across
    Europe. - (Data protection and medical research in Europe)
    1. European Union. Directive 95/46/EC on Data Protection -
    Congresses 2. PRIVIREAL Project - Congresses 3. Medicine -
    Research - Law and legislation - European Union countries -
    Congresses 4. Medical records - Access control - European
    Union countries - Congresses 5. Privacy, Right of - European
    Union countries - Congresses 6. Data protection - Law and
    legislation - European Union countries - Congresses
    7. Medical policy - European Union countries - Congresses
    I. Beyleveld, Deryck
    344.4'041

Library of Congress Control Number: 2004111852

ISBN 0 7546 2367 X

Printed and bound in Great Britain by TJ International Ltd, Padstow, Cornwall

Contents

List of Contributors

Deryck Beyleveld PRIVIREAL Director and founder of the Sheffield Institute of Biotechnological Law and Ethics based in the Department of Law at the Sheffield University. He obtained his chair in 1995 and is an internationally acclaimed jurist and moral philosopher.

Carlos María Romeo Casabona PRIVIREAL member for Spain, Director of the Inter University Chair BBV Foundation-Provincial Government of Biscay in Law and the Human Genome and editor of *Law and the Human Genome Review.*

Mette Hartlev PRIVIREAL member for Denmark and Associate Professor in the Faculty of Law at the University of Copenhagen. She is currently Vice-Chairman of the Danish Council of Ethics and chaired a Government Committee on informed consent in biomedical research.

Lasse A. Lehtonen PRIVIREAL member for Finland and Assistant Professor and Administrative Chief Physician at the Helsinki University Central Hospital, Laboratory Services.

Herman Nys PRIVIREAL member for Belgium, Professor of Law at KU Leuven, Guest Professor, Université Catholique de Louvain, and Professor of International Law, University of Maastricht. He is editor of the *International Encyclopaedia of Medical Law,* and a member of the Belgian Advisory Committee on Bioethics.

Stefano Rodota PRIVIREAL member for Italy and President of the Italian Data Protection Commission. He holds a chair of Civil Law at Rome 'La Sapienza' University Faculty of Law and currently chairs the European Working Party which includes representatives of Data Protection Authorities.

Ségolène Rouillé-Mirza PRIVIREAL co-ordinating co-worker, Avocat, qualified Lawyer for the French Legal System.

David Townend PRIVIREAL co-ordinator, member of the Sheffield Institute of Biotechnological Law and Ethics, and is Sub-Dean for Postgraduate Studies in the Faculty of Law at the University of Sheffield.

Jessica Wright PRIVIREAL co-ordinating co-worker and Doctoral student at the Sheffield Institute of Biotechnological Law and Ethics.

Foreword

Today, fundamental advances in medical science have extended the possibilities for and expectations of medical practice to extraordinary levels. Within this field, as in all other areas of commerce, culture and society, technology offers limitless possibilities of data processing adding to the potential for developing new medical research, diagnostic procedures, treatments and benefits for all. At such times the vulnerabilities of individuals can be most at risk. The development of a coherent and effective ethical and legal framework within which the individual can receive appropriate protection must be made alongside the advances. Such ethical and legal developments must be independent and carefully reasoned to justify any slowing of the undoubted benefits that science and technology bring to the many, but they are essential to safeguard the individual.

PRIVIREAL has the opportunity to make such an independent investigation through the opportunities provided by the Fifth Framework programme of the European Commission's research programme, and especially through the initiative and vision of the Science and Society directorate within the Commission. We are particularly grateful to Drs. Rhoda, Salvi, Sachez, and Pitkanen in the Science and Society Directorate for their enthusiasm and encouragement in developing PRIVIREAL, and especially to Drs. Sachez and Pitkanen for their work as project managers within the Commission.

The coordination of PRIVIREAL has been undertaken in the University of Sheffield in the Sheffield Institute of Biotechnological Law and Ethics (SIBLE), and particularly in the School of Law. Without the confidence and commitment to the project shown by Professor John Birds, Head of the School of Law, we would not have been able to undertake the project, and certainly not to integrate the Newly Associated States into the programme at its earliest stages. We are extremely grateful to him.

Throughout PRIVIREAL, and especially before permanent staff could be appointed, a small number of people within the School of Law have worked with us on the project. Their work enabled us to establish the framework of the project and then to maintain it on a strong footing. We are very grateful to them: they are Marie-Jo Goode, Anna Greene, Joy Pierson, Sebastian Sethe, Susan Wallace, David Moxon, Jane Miller, and Rebecca Wong. We are also blessed to have in SIBLE a number of very strong and capable students reading for the MA in Biotechnological Law and Ethics. They often join in SIBLE projects, and some— Daniel Byrne, Adrienne Hunt, Chantal D. M. Gill'ard, Maria del Mar Gonzalez, Christian Lopez Silva, and Fang Wang—worked for PRIVIREAL on the preparation of comparative tables and in compiling information for reports to assist us.

Concerted Action projects bring together those who are experts into one place for short times to share ideas and information. Quiet efficiency in the arrangements and a warm welcome ensure that the meetings can be their most fruitful, and we were served very well in Sheffield. The first PRIVIREAL workshop was held at Stephenson Hall in the University of Sheffield. We thank Alan Walker and his staff, and also Brenda Styran and the staff of the Cutlers' Hall where we enjoyed the Conference Dinner, for their hospitality. Mrs Carol Heathcote, the PRIVIREAL secretary, produced excellent work dealing with the enormous task of arranging the travel for all the delegates (from each of the EU member countries, Norway, and from the Newly Associated States), caring for them while they were in Sheffield, and, perhaps most importantly, maintaining friendly and enthusiastic links with them throughout the project. We owe her the greatest debt of thanks.

We are very grateful to those who have helped in the production of this book. In Sheffield, we are grateful to both Rosemary Gumbley and Matthew Wisbey, the PRIVIREAL (NAS) secretaries, who joined the project after the first workshop and have assisted with the production of the copy for publication. We are also enormously grateful to John Irwin, Alison Kirk, Pam Bertram, and their colleagues at Ashgate for their patience and encouragement in developing the books in this series.

Concerted Actions would be nothing without the network of participants, members of the project who give their time to share their research, discuss new perspectives, and forge new understandings. The PRIVIREAL network is remarkable not only because of its coverage—having representation from all the Member States—but also because of the quality and enthusiasm of the members. It is a great pleasure and privilege working with the network, many members of which are contributors to this book, and are central to the success of PRIVIREAL. We are enormously grateful to them all.

Deryck Beyleveld
David Townend
Ségolène Rouillé-Mirza
Jessica Wright

Sheffield, 2004

PART I
INTRODUCTION AND
KEYNOTE PAPERS

Chapter 1

Introduction

Deryck Beyleveld, Ségolène Rouillé-Mirza, David Townend
and Jessica Wright

The papers in this volume contain keynote papers given at the first workshop of the EC funded 5th Framework Programme concerted action project, 'Privacy in Medical Research and Law' (PRIVIREAL) (PL QLRT-2001-00056), which took place at the University of Sheffield from 9–12 January 2003. The volume also contains an overview of Directive 95/46/EC on Data Protection, with special emphasis on provisions with implications for medical research, and a report on the implementation of this Directive in the EU Member States and the Newly Associated States (NAS), the majority of which are now EU members, again with special emphasis on medical research. This report was compiled from papers prepared by experts in the countries concerned who are partners in the PRIVIREAL project (with the exception of Cyprus and the Slovak Republic, on which information was not received). These papers are published in a separate volume. It is appropriate for this project to maintain the distinction between pre-2004 Member States and the group formerly known as the NAS because the duties in relation to the implementation of the Directive are different between the two groups. The term 'NAS' is therefore used to indicate Bulgaria, the Czech Republic, Cyprus, Estonia, Hungary, Latvia, Lithuania, Malta, Poland, Romania, the Slovak Republic, and Slovenia; 'EU Member States' refers to pre-2004 Member States.

Aims of PRIVIREAL

Protection of privacy of subjects in medical research depends as much on ethics review as on data protection law, but little is known about how this interacts with implementation of Directive 95/46/EC to protect privacy. PRIVIREAL brings together experts on relevant law and on ethics review of medical research from across all the EU Member States (except Luxembourg, which is nevertheless covered) and Norway (like Iceland and Liechtenstein, a member of the European Economic Area but not the EU, but which has agreed to be bound by Directive 95/46/EC) as well as the NAS, to evaluate the interaction between implementation of the Directive and research ethics review in protecting Directive rights of research subjects, with a view to making recommendations to the Commission about how to optimize the protection provided by research ethics review (taking into account the background EU and domestic legal and ethical culture/s).

To carry out these aims, PRIVIREAL has three phases. In the first phase, leading to the first PRIVIREAL workshop, what the partner countries have done, or plan to do, to implement Directive 95/46/EC in relation to medical research is ascertained, and the adequacy of this is evaluated in relation to the requirements of the Directive. This volume and its companion present the results of this phase. In the second phase, which led to the second PRIVIREAL workshop (Helsinki from 14–17 August 2003), the remit and practice of ethics committees reviewing medical research (RECs) in relation to legal requirements generally and those of data protection law, in particular, were ascertained. In the third phase, which is the concern of the final PRIVIREAL workshop (Coimbra in July 2004), the protection of privacy of medical research subjects resulting from domestic implementation of Directive 95/46/EC together with the remit and practice of RECs to protect data protection rights of medical research subjects will be evaluated in the context of domestic legal and ethical culture in relation to the objectives of Directive 95/46/EC, and recommendations will be made to the European Commission about what it might do to better protect privacy of medical research subjects where protection is judged to be inadequate. The results of the second and third phases will also be published by Ashgate Publishing Ltd.

Methodology of PRIVIREAL

The primary source of data is reports by experts in the partner countries. However, central to the project is a website (http://www.privireal.org). This contains relevant legislation and guidance on the topics of relevance to the project, with as much as possible being made available in translation to English as well as the original language. To assist with the second and third phases of the project, there is a questionnaire for RECs that can be completed on-line in English, French or German. There is also a public discussion forum in addition to sections that can only be accessed by the partners. The website is complementary to the published volumes, and readers of the volumes are invited to consult the website and use it actively.

The workshops have been only open to partners of PRIVIREAL. The purpose of the first two workshops was primarily to enable partners to discuss summaries and analyses of the material they submitted which form the basis of the reports prepared for the first two phases by the co-ordinating team. The purpose of the third workshop is to discuss and prepare recommendations for the European Commission. The first two workshops also provide for keynote papers given by invited partners or by persons from outside to discuss controversial, but crucially important, topics for the relevant phase of the project. These papers do not represent a consensus among the partnership. They are merely the views of their authors. Only in the recommendations will concerted statements and judgments (where possible) be made.

Chapter 2

An Overview of Directive 95/46/EC in Relation to Medical Research

Deryck Beyleveld[1]

Introduction

This chapter outlines the provisions of Directive 95/46/EC with the use of personal data for medical research centrally in mind. The Directive makes no specific mention of medical research and, consequently, it contains no provisions for medical research as an explicitly delineated category. However, at times, the Directive refers to medical purposes (though medical research is not explicitly listed under this category) and there are provisions relating to the use of data relating to a person's health. It also refers to the use of personal data for scientific research or statistics. Consequently, this overview is an analytic construction from these related provisions together with any other of the Directive's provisions that could apply to medical research, including those of a wholly general nature that apply to any processing of personal data.

The overview that follows represents my personal view, rather than the collective view of the participants in the PRIVIREAL project. It is presented here for the benefit of the general reader and also because it might assist in understanding the questions that participants were asked to address for the purpose of gathering the information for the comparative analysis presented in Chapters 10 and 11.

Objective of the Directive

The purpose of Directive 95/46/EC is to enable the free flow of personal data from one European Union (EU) Member State to another for the purposes of the internal market by ensuring that fundamental rights and freedoms of individuals (in particular, privacy) are safeguarded (see Recitals 3 and 10 and Article 1(1)) and a high level of equivalent protection of these rights and freedoms is ensured in all the Member States (see Recitals 7 and 8). The Directive gives substance to and amplifies the fundamental rights and freedoms contained in the Council of Europe

---

[1] Privireal Co-ordinator.

Convention of 28 January 1981 for the Protection of Individuals with regard to Automatic Processing of Personal Data (see Recital 11). Since at least the *Second Nold Case (Case-4/73)* [1974] E.C.R. 507, the European Court of Justice (ECJ) has recognized, at least in principle, that violation of fundamental rights as fundamental principles of EC law (in which are included the fundamental rights and freedoms of the European Convention on Human Rights (ECHR) of the Council of Europe [which is alluded to in Recital 10]), is sufficient to invalidate at least *secondary* Community Acts.[2] However, despite the fact that a commitment to fundamental rights and freedoms has subsequently been enshrined in Article 6 of the Treaty of European Union (the 'Treaty of Maastricht'), it must not be forgotten that the EU does not have competence to legislate for fundamental rights and freedoms *for their own sakes*. The legal basis of EC law generally lies in the aim of constructing a single European market (and the legal basis of the Directive lies specifically in the aspect of the single market referred to as 'the internal market'). Thus, the competence of the EU to legislate to protect fundamental freedoms and rights only arises for the reason that this protection is deemed necessary for achieving the purposes of the single market. For this reason (as well as for the reason that the Directive is concerned in its attention to fundamental rights and freedoms not only to protect privacy but all fundamental rights and freedoms to the extent that they may be interfered with in the use of personal data)[3] it can be misleading to refer, as is often done, to the Directive as 'the Privacy Directive'.

Article 1(2) asserts that Member States shall not restrict or prohibit the free flow of personal data between themselves for reasons connected with the protection of fundamental rights and freedoms. However, this does not mean that the Directive is essentially concerned with legislating a balance between fundamental rights and freedoms and economic objectives of the internal market (let alone that the purpose of free flow between Member States overrides all considerations of fundamental rights and freedoms). Instead, adequate safeguarding of fundamental rights and freedoms must be viewed as a condition of the free flow of personal data, in line with which Article 1(2) signifies, primarily, that if a Member State (A) implements the Directive correctly then another Member State (B) may not restrict or prohibit the flow of personal data from B to A because B does not consider the level of protection for fundamental rights and freedoms provided by A's implementation to be adequate (see Recital 9). Presumably, it also means that if B does not consider that A provides the protection required by the Directive, then B may not restrict or prohibit the flow of personal

---

[2] Manfred A. Dauses, 'The Protection of Fundamental Rights in the Community Legal Order' (1985) 10 *European Law Review* 398–419, at 407, argues (on the basis of Articles 53 and 64 of the Vienna Convention on the Law of Treaties 1969, according to which any treaty is void if it violates a peremptory norm of general international law) that, in theory, violation of at least some fundamental rights is sufficient to invalidate even the European Treaty itself. However, it must be remembered that the ECJ has no jurisdiction to rule on the validity of the Treaty (see Article 234 EC (ex Article 177)).

[3] This is because the words 'in particular privacy' in Article 1(1) mean 'especially privacy' not 'only privacy'.

data from B to A on that ground either (but should refer the matter to the Commission or the ECJ). This, however, is not to say that the Directive is not concerned with a balance between economic objectives and the protection of fundamental rights and freedoms. However, such a balance is best viewed, in my opinion, as 'internal' to the activity of protecting fundamental rights and freedoms rather than as signifying a conflict between the protection of fundamental rights and freedoms as such and other factors. This is because to view the matter 'internally' is to observe that, e.g., Article 8(1) (the right to private and family life) of the ECHR may be derogated from in terms laid down by Article 8(2) ECHR, and relevant considerations include the economic well-being of the country, and may include economic objectives more generally to the extent that they serve, e.g., the fundamental rights and freedoms of others, or the public interest. To view the matter 'externally', on the other hand, requires the objectives of the internal market to be seen as in conflict with the entire framework set up by, e.g., Article 8(1) *together with* Article 8(2), which is both unnecessary and not consistent with the concept of a *fundamental* right or freedom.

Definition of Personal Data and Scope of the Directive

The Directive defines personal data as any information relating to an identified or identifiable natural person ('data subject') (see Article 2(a); Recital 26), and this includes 'sound and image data relating to natural persons' (see Recital 14). An identifiable person is, in turn, defined as a person who can be identified directly or indirectly from the data in conjunction with other factors (see Article 2(a)) 'likely reasonably to be used' by any person (see Recital 26—which also specifies that codes of conduct under Article 27 may provide guidance about when data have been rendered anonymous).

Recital 26 states that the principles of data protection (see below) apply to all personal data (within the scope of the Directive), but that they do not apply to data that have been rendered anonymous so as to render the data subject no longer identifiable (i.e. that has rendered the data non-personal). That data remains personal if *any person* is reasonably likely to be able to identify the data, seems to imply that data are not to be considered anonymous for the purposes of processing by a data controller (whom Article 2(d) defines as any person or body (private or public) that individually or jointly determines the purposes and means of processing) who cannot identify the data subject directly or indirectly from the data if any other person is reasonably likely to be able to identify the data subject directly or indirectly. If so, the circumstances in which data may be considered anonymous are extremely limited. However, precisely when data may be considered to be rendered anonymous and whether (and to what extent) processing of data in anonymous form that has been collected in personal form falls under the

Directive are highly controversial matters. (Anonymization is discussed in Chapter 4—and see also Deryck Beyleveld and David Townend 2004.[4])

'Natural person' is not defined. However, by stating that national legislation concerning the processing of personal data relating to legal persons is not affected by the Directive, Recital 24 suggests that a natural person is a person who is not a legal person. Processing of personal data covers anything that can be done with personal data automatically or manually (see Articles 2(b) and 3(1); Recital 27). However, the Directive only covers manual processing if the data are part of or intended to be part of a 'filing system' (see Article 3; Recital 15), which is defined as a 'structured set of personal data which are accessible according to specific criteria' (see Article 2(c); Recitals 15 and 27). Member States may define these criteria (see Recital 27). The Directive also does not cover processing of personal data for purposes that fall outside of the scope of EC law or processing by a natural person for purely personal or household purposes (see Article 3(2); Recitals 12, 13 and 16).

Situations in which Member States must apply their national law implementing the Directive are specified in Article 4 (and see Recitals 18–21).

Limits on Member States' Discretion in Implementing the Directive

Member States have a degree of discretion as to the conditions of lawful processing under national law. However, this discretion is limited by Articles 6–21, with which national laws must be compatible (see Article 5; Recital 22). Implementation may be by means of a general law or different laws for different types or 'sectors' of processing (see Recital 23).

Principles of Data Protection

Article 6(1) (see also Recital 28) lays down five principles of data protection, which are that personal data must be

-   processed fairly and lawfully (see Article 6(1)(a));
-   collected for specified, explicit and legitimate purposes (which, according to Recital 28, must be determined at the time of collection of the data) and not further processed in a way incompatible with those purposes (see Article 6(1)(b)) as originally specified (see Recital 28);
-   adequate, relevant and not excessive in relation to the purposes for which they are collected/further processed (see Article 6(1)(c));

---

[4] Deryck Beyleveld and David Townend 'When is Personal Data Rendered Anonymous? Interpreting Recital 26 of Directive 95/46/EC' (2004) 6 *Medical Law International* 2: 73–86.

- accurate and, where necessary, kept complete and up to date (see Article 6(1)(d));
- not be kept in a personally identifiable form for longer than necessary for the purposes for which they were collected or (compatibly) further processed (see Article 6(1)(e)).

Article 6(2) requires Member States to impose responsibility for compliance with the data protection principles on the data controller (see also Recital 25).

Regarding the 2nd principle, further processing for historical, statistical and scientific purposes is not incompatible provided that Member States provide appropriate safeguards (see Article 6(1)(b)), which 'must, in particular, rule out the use of the data in support of measures or decisions regarding any particular individual' (see Recital 29). Regarding the 5th principle, for these purposes and under appropriate safeguards, personal data may be kept for longer than necessary for the purposes for which it was originally collected (see Article 6.1(e)).

The 1st principle can be viewed broadly or narrowly. Viewed broadly, for processing to be lawful, all the requirements of the Directive imposed on processing must be complied with. Thus viewed, compliance with the 2nd, 3rd, 4th and 5th principles is necessary to satisfy the 1st principle, as is compliance with Articles 7–21. Viewed narrowly, only some of the requirements for lawful processing under the Directive as a whole are requirements for lawful processing in relation to the 1st principle specifically, and the wording of Recitals 30–36 (in particular, Recital 31) suggests that these are the requirements of Articles 7 and 8, while Recital 38 suggests that the requirements of Articles 10 and 11 are the Directive's specific requirements of fair processing.

However, whichever way the matter is viewed, satisfaction of the conditions specified under Article 7 'Criteria for Making Data Processing Legitimate' and Article 8 'Special Categories of Processing' (see below), cannot be taken to be sufficient to render processing lawful under the Directive as a whole. Articles 6–21 all set (where applicable, given the nature of the personal data and processing, and taking into account exemptions) requirements that are hurdles to be overcome to render processing lawful. For processing to be lawful under the Directive as a whole, all the applicable hurdles must be overcome.

Necessary Conditions for Legitimate Processing of Personal Data and Sensitive Personal Data

Article 7 (see also Recital 30), which applies to all personal data, can be satisfied in six different ways

a. by obtaining the unambiguous consent of the data subject, 'consent' being defined by Article 2(h) as 'any freely given specific and informed indication of his wishes by which the data subject signifies his agreement to personal data relating to him being processed'; or

b. if processing is necessary to perform or enter a contract to which the data subject is party; or

c. if processing is necessary to comply with a legal obligation of the data controller; or

d. if processing is necessary to protect the vital interests of the data subject (which Recital 31 reveals to be interests 'essential for the data subject's life'); or

e. if processing is necessary in the public interest or in the exercise of official authority (in relation to which Recital 32 states that national legislation may determine who the controller performing a task carried out in the public interest should be); or

f. if processing is in the legitimate interests of the controller or recipients of the data (unless protection of the fundamental rights and freedoms of the data subject is overriding) (with Recital 30 explaining that Member States may specify when this condition is satisfied).

With regard to Article 7(e) and 7(f) at least, Article 14(a) (see also Recital 45) specifies that these conditions may not be appealed to unless the data subject is given the opportunity to object on compelling legitimate grounds, *unless* 'otherwise provided by national legislation'.

Article 8 applies to what Recital 34 calls 'sensitive categories' of personal data, which Recital 33 characterizes as 'data which are capable by their nature of infringing fundamental freedoms or privacy'. Article 8 specifies such data as 'revealing racial or ethnic origin, political opinions, religious or philosophical beliefs, trade-union membership, and . . . data concerning health or sex life'. Article 8(1) *prohibits* the processing of such data, *unless* certain conditions are satisfied (see Article 8(2)(a)–(e) and 8(3)–8(5); and Recitals 33–36). For the purposes of processing data concerning health, the most relevant are

Article 8(2)(a)   with the 'explicit consent' of the data subject (see also Recital 33) (which is not defined in the Directive) (unless national law does not permit the prohibition to be lifted by the data subject's consent); or

Article 8(2)(c)   where processing is necessary to protect the vital interests of the data subject or another person where the data subject physically or legally cannot give consent; or

Article 8(2)(d)   the processing is of data manifestly made public by the data subject or that is necessary to establish, exercise or defend a legal claim; or

Article 8(3)   where the processing is necessary for the purposes of 'preventive medicine, medical diagnosis, the provision of care or treatment or the management of health-care services, and where those data are processed by a health professional subject under national law or rules established by national competent bodies to the

> obligation of professional secrecy or by another person also subject to an equivalent obligation of secrecy' (see also Recital 33); or

Article 8(4)   subject to suitable safeguards (which, according to Recital 34, must also be specific) specified by national law or the decision of the Supervisory Authority in the substantial public interest (which decisions must, per Article 8(6), be notified to the Commission) (with regard to which Recital 34 identifies scientific research and government statistics as an important reason of public interest that might justify processing of sensitive categories of data). (The concept of 'public interest' in the Directive is discussed in Chapter 7.)

Article 8(7) provides that Member States must determine when personal data may be processed employing a national identification number or any other identifier of general application.

Because Article 7 applies to all personal data, it is obvious that it is necessary for the processing of sensitive personal data that at least one condition from Article 7 as well as one condition from Article 8 be met. However, it is also obvious that meeting some of the conditions in Article 8 will automatically meet a condition in Article 7. So, for example, meeting the condition of explicit consent in Article 8 will also meet the condition of consent in Article 7.

Nothing in the Directive states explicitly that any condition in Article 7 takes priority over any other; and the same must be said about the conditions in Article 8(2). Nevertheless, it is arguable, at least where the processing of sensitive personal data is concerned, that the conditions in Article 8(2) and those in Article 7 are not entirely open alternatives. This is because the European Court of Human Rights (whose judgments, while not binding on the European Court of Justice, are taken very seriously by the latter) has ruled that to process sensitive personal data without consent is by the very nature of the case an interference with the right to private life under Article 8(1) of the ECHR.[5] Of course, interference with the right

---

[5] See the case of *M.S. v. Sweden* 28 EHRR 313, paragraphs 34–35:

'34. The applicant and the Commission, stressing that information of a private and sensitive nature had been disclosed without her consent to a certain number of people at the Office, maintained that the measure constituted an interference [with her right to private life under Article 8.1]'.

35. The Court notes that the medical records in question contained highly personal and sensitive data about the applicant, including information relating to an abortion. Although the records remained confidential, they had been disclosed to another public authority and therefore to a wider circle of public servants (see paragraphs 12–13 above). Moreover, whilst the information had been collected and stored at the clinic in connection with medical treatment, its subsequent communication had served a different purpose, namely to enable the Office to examine her compensation claim. It did not follow from the fact that she had sought treatment at the clinic that she would consent to the data being disclosed to the Office (see paragraph 10 above). Having regard to these considerations, the Court finds that the

to private life can be justified (as stated in Article 8(2) ECHR) if done in accordance with the law when 'necessary in a democratic society in the interests of national security, public safety or the economic well-being of the country, for the prevention of disorder or crime, for the protection of health or morals, or for the protection of the rights and freedoms of others'.[6] However, this implies that consent must be obtained unless to do so would be impracticable/involve disproportionate effort or be otherwise inappropriate (e.g., because to do so would threaten the overriding rights of others). Consequently, it is at least arguable (and seems to me to be the case) that satisfaction of the conditions laid down by Articles 7 and 8(2) in ways that do not involve the consent of the data subject at least implicitly (as is the case, e.g., with the condition of being for a contract binding on the data subject) requires the obtaining of consent to be impracticable, etc. Only in the case of Article 8(2)(c) does it seem to me that this complex requirement will be satisfied automatically.

Provisions Relating to Journalism, Art and Literary Expression

Article 9 (see also Recital 37) permits exemptions or derogations from the Directive's requirements for processing 'carried out solely for journalistic purposes or the purpose of artistic or literary expression' but only if this is necessary 'to reconcile the right to privacy with the rules governing freedom of expression'. The relevance of this to medical research should be extremely limited.

Duty to Provide Information to the Data Subject

As a means to the protection of data subjects' rights to fundamental rights and freedoms, the Directive grants data subjects specific rights. In my opinion, first and foremost amongst these are the rights to information specified in Articles 10 and 11 (see also Recitals 38–40), which Recital 38 refers to as conditions of fair processing, which links these Articles to the 1st data protection principle. Granted, the Directive does not describe the provisions of Articles 10 and 11 as *rights* of the data subject, but as duties of the data controller. However, because failure to carry out the applicable duty will interfere with the data subjects' specific rights, from a logical point of view these provisions may be characterized as rights, and the main effect of them being characterized as duties of the data controller is to indicate that the data controller's duty does not rest on the data subject making any claim: i.e., the information needs to be provided without the data subject having to make a request for it.

Article 10 (see also Recital 38) covers the case where data are being collected from the data subject, whereas Article 11 covers cases where the data have not

---

disclosure of the data by the clinic to the Office entailed an interference with the applicant's right to respect for private life guaranteed by paragraph 1 of Article 8.'
[6] As, indeed, the European Court of Human Rights found in *M.S. v Sweden.*

been obtained from the data subject. In both cases, the data controller or 'his representative' must provide the data subject with information (except where he already has it) about the identity of the data controller and his representative (if any). In the case of Article 10, the data subject must also be informed about the intended purposes of the processing, whereas in the case of Article 11, the data subject must be informed of the purposes for which data have been or are to be disclosed. In both cases, the data subject must be given any other information required for the processing to be fair. Examples are given. In both cases, the recipients or categories of recipients, and the existence of the right of access to and the right to rectify the data concerning the data subject (granted by Article 12) are mentioned. In the case of Article 11, the requirement to provide this information may be lifted, in particular for statistical purposes or purposes of historical or scientific research, if the provision of information would be impossible or involve disproportionate effort or if recording or disclosure of the data is expressly laid down by law (see also Recital 40), subject to Member States providing adequate safeguards. However, information provision that falls under Article 10 is not explicitly stated to be open to such derogation. While Recitals 38–40 are, at least at first sight, ambiguous as to whether the derogations specified in Recital 40 apply to both the Recital 39 case (obtaining from the data subject) and the Recital 39 case (other cases) or only to the Recital 39 case, the fact that these derogations are only mentioned in connection with Article 11 in the operative part of the Directive indicates strongly that they apply only to the Recital 39/Article 11 case.

It is not at all clear whether Article 10 covers the case of a person who obtained personal data from the data subject and now wishes to use the data for a purpose or to make disclosures that the data subject was not informed about at the time that the data were obtained. The case for saying that it does is that Recital 38 states that purposes must be specified at the time of collection. However, Recital 39 states that exemptions parallel to those provided by Article 11(2) to Article 11(1) apply to disclosures that were not anticipated at the time of the collection. This creates considerable difficulties of interpretation, which I discuss in Chapter 6.

The reason why Articles 10 and 11 are at the core of the protection provided by the Directive is not only that information about the identity of the data controller, etc., is needed for data subjects to be able to exercise the other specific rights that the Directive grants them. If consent of the data subject is, at least as a matter of first presumption, necessary to satisfy the Article 7/8(2) requirement for legitimate processing in connection with sensitive personal data, then, because consent must be informed, information provision is necessary to satisfy the Article 7/8(2) requirement as well.

Power to Exempt from Article 10 and Other Provisions via Article 13(1)

Although there is no derogation from Article 10 explicitly specified within Article 10, it should, however, be noted that Article 13(1) provides for derogation from Articles 6(1), 10, 11(1), 12, and 21 (which imposes a duty on Member States to publicize processing operations) to the extent that this is necessary to safeguard various goals (e.g., national security, defence, the detection and prosecution of crime, taxation policy) that are beyond the remit of EC law (see also Recitals 43 and 44), or (Article 13(1)(g)) to protect the data subject or the rights and freedoms of others (see also Recital 42 in relation to the rights of Articles 10, 11 and 12). (Related to this, Recital 70 states that the Directive allows the principle of public access to official documents [which reflects the ECHR Article 10(1) right to freedom of expression, because this includes the freedom to receive information] to be taken into account when implementing the principles set out in the Directive.)

It is important to note, however, that Article 28(4) requires Member States to provide for each national Supervisory Authority to hear, in particular, 'claims for checks on the lawfulness of data processing lodged by any person when the national provisions pursuant to Article 13' of the Directive apply.

Data Subjects' Right of Access on Request

Article 12 (see also Recital 41) grants a 'right of access', which includes rights to obtain from the data controller

-   confirmation as to whether or not data relating to him or her are being processed and, if so, information at least about the purposes of the processing, the categories of data being processed, and the recipients or categories of recipients to whom the data have been disclosed;
-   intelligible communication of what data are being processed and about the source of this data;
-   knowledge of the logic behind any automated processing at least if covered by Article 15(1);
-   rectification, erasure or blocking of data if its processing does not comply with the Directive (especially on the grounds of inaccuracy or incompleteness);
-   notification to third parties to whom data has been disclosed of the exercise of the last mentioned right (unless this is impossible or would involve disproportionate effort).

In relation to the modification of Article 12 permitted by Article 13(1)(g), Recital 42 specifically indicates that Member States may require the data subject's right of access to medical data to be exercised only through a health professional. Article 12 is also subject to derogation via Article 13(2) 'when data are processed solely for the purposes of scientific research or are kept in personal form for a period that does not exceed the period necessary for the sole purpose of creating statistics', provided that

-   the derogation is by a legislative measure;
-   'there is clearly no risk of breaching the privacy of the data subject'; and

- adequate legal safeguards are provided (in particular that the data are not used to take measures or decisions regarding any particular individual).

Data Subjects' Rights to Object

Article 14(a) grants a right to object to processing on legitimate grounds (as already mentioned in connection with Article 7) and Article 14(b) grants a right to object to processing for the purposes of direct marketing. Whereas the Article 14(a) right may be removed by national legislation, the Article 14(b) may not and data subjects must be informed of this right (the exercise of which must be free of charge and [see Recital 30] does not require reasons to be given) either whenever the data controller envisages the data being processed for direct marketing or before such processing or disclosure to third parties for such processing occurs.

Data Subjects' Right to Object to Decisions Based Solely on Automated Processing

Article 15 (as already alluded to in connection with Article 12) grants data subjects a right not to be subjected to decisions that produce legal effects on them or otherwise significantly affect them, which are based solely on automated processing that is intended to evaluate personal aspects of the data subject (unless certain conditions are satisfied).

Powers to Exempt for Research

The extent to which the Directive permits Member States to exempt medical research from various requirements set by the Directive is (as a category of scientific research/use for statistics) specified at least by Article 13(2), together with Articles 6(1)(b), 6(1)(e), and 8(4) (given that Recital 34 specifies scientific research, amongst other things, is an important public interest). In addition, where processing was already under way before the Directive entered into force (24 October 1998), Article 32(3) permits Member States to provide, on condition that they institute appropriate safeguards, that the processing of data for the sole purpose of 'historical research' (which category is not defined, in particular in relation to research for historical purposes, which is mentioned in Article 6(1)(b)) need not comply with Articles 6, 7 and 8. To this might possibly be added the derogations permitted under Article 8(3) (but only to the extent that medical research may be considered to be a subcategory of preventive medicine, medical diagnosis, the provision of care or treatment, or management of health-care services) and the derogation under Article 13(1)(g) (but only to the extent that medical research is necessary to safeguard the data subject or the rights and freedoms of others). (The power to exempt for research is discussed in Chapter 5.)

Need for Processing to Have the Consent of the Data Controller

According to Article 16, those who are authorized by the data controller to hold or otherwise process data must do so only on the instructions of the data controller unless required to do so by law. (See also Article 17(3), which further specifies that processors who are not themselves the data controllers must be bound by a contract or legal act binding them to the controller. Per Article 17(4), the contract must be in writing or equivalent form.)

Security

Article 17(1) and (2) (see also Recital 46) further requires Member States to provide that the data controller must implement appropriate security measures.

Notification to the Supervisory Authority

Article 18 concerns notification of processing to the Supervisory Authority that must be set up under Article 28 (see also Recitals 48–52). Article 18(1) requires Member States to require the data controller (or his representative) to notify the Supervisory Authority before carrying out any automatic or partly automatic processing. Article 18(5) permits Member States to require notification to the Supervisory Authority of non-automatic processing. Article 18(2) and (3) permits Member States to simplify or exempt from notification (the contents of which are specified by Article 19) under specified conditions, the most important of which where data processed for medical research is concerned is that the data controller, operating in compliance with national law, appoints a personal data protection official who is responsible, in particular, for ensuring in an independent manner the application of national provisions implementing the Directive and for keeping a register of processing operations as required by Article 21(2). Recital 51, importantly, specifies that simplification or exemption from notification does not exempt the data controller from any of the other obligations resulting form the Directive.

In addition to information about the identity of the data controller, the purposes of processing, data subjects, categories of data processed and recipients of data, Article 19(1) requires information about proposed transfers of data to countries outside the European Economic Area (EEA) (which is the EU plus Iceland, Lichtenstein and Norway) and a general description of a preliminary assessment of the security measures required under Article 17.

Requirement for Prior Checking of Processing Presenting Specific Risks to Rights and Freedoms of the Data Subject

Article 20(1) and (2) requires Member States to determine which processing operations are likely to present specific risks to the rights and freedoms of data subjects (about which Recital 53 provides some examples) and to subject these to prior checking by the Supervisory Authority or a Data Protection Official (who must consult the Supervisory Authority if in any doubt), and Article 20(3) permits member States to carry out such checks when preparing legislation that lays down appropriate safeguards for such processing operations. (See also Recital 54.)

Requirement to Publicize Processing Operations

Except in the case of public registers, Article 21 requires Member States to take measures to publicize all processing operations. For processing that requires notification per Article 18, a register must be kept by the Supervisory Authority that contains all the information required per Article 19(1) except that concerning a description of a preliminary assessment. Where notification is not required, Member States must ensure that this same information is available to any person on request.

Requirement to Provide Compensation for Damage Caused by Unlawful Processing

The Directive requires Member States, without prejudice to any administrative remedy, to provide for a judicial remedy for any breach of rights guaranteed by implementing national legislation (Article 22); to provide for compensation from the data controller for damage as a result of unlawful processing operations (except where the controller can prove that he was not responsible for the event causing the damage) (Article 23); and to adopt suitable measures to ensure full implementation of the provisions of the Directive, which must include sanctions for infringing these provisions (Article 24). (See also Recital 55.)

Transfer of Personal Data Outside the EEA

Articles 25 and 26 concern transfer of personal data to 'third countries' (i.e., countries outside the EEA). Personal data may not be transferred to a third country that does not provide for an adequate level of protection (Article 25(1); Recitals 56 and 57) unless with the unambiguous consent of the data subject; or when necessary for the performance of contractual measures between the data controller and the data subject, or at the data subject's request; or in the interest of the data subject in a contract between the controller and a third party; or when necessary or legally required on important public interest grounds or to exercise or defend legal claims; or when necessary in the vital interests of the data subject; or from a public register (Article 26(1); Recital 58). Alternatively, Member States may authorize transfers where the data controller adduces adequate safeguards by e.g., appropriate contracts (Article 26(2); Recital 59), in relation to which the Commission may, in accordance with Article 31(2), decide that certain standard contractual clauses constitute sufficient safeguards, with which Member States must comply (Article 26(4)). Article 25(2) specifies considerations that Member States must take into account in assessing the adequacy of protection in a third country. Member States and the Commission must inform each other of countries they consider do not provide adequate protection (Article 25(3)). If the Commission does not consider protection in a third country to be adequate, Member States must act to prevent transfers of data of the type for which protection is not adequate to that country (Article 25(4)), while the Commission must act to try to remedy this situation (Article 25(5); Recital 59). The Commission may find, in accordance with Article 31(2), that a third country provides adequate protection, and then the Member States must comply with this decision (Article 25(6)). These matters are of special relevance in the case of personal data processed for medical research, because this research is often sponsored by companies based outside of the EEA, and, as Recital 60 indicates, non-compliance with the standards set by Article 8 of the Directive (which deals with sensitive personal data specifically) is of particular concern in relation to third countries. (As regards the powers of the Commission with regard to the transfer of data to third countries, see Recital 66, which makes reference to Council Decision 87/373/EEC.)

Codes of Conduct

Article 27(1) (see also Recital 61) requires Member States and the Commission to encourage the drawing up of codes of conduct to assist with the implementation of the Directive in specific sectors of processing. The Supervisory Authority is required to vet codes drawn up by bodies representing categories of data controllers and to consult with data subjects or their representatives (Article 27.2). Article 27(3) provides a role for the Article 29 Working Party in approving draft Community Codes and amendments to existing Community codes.

Requirement for and Role of a Supervisory Authority

Article 28 requires each Member State to provide for one or more public authorities ('the Supervisory Authority'), which must act in complete independence (see also Recital 62), and which (see also Recitals 63 and 64)

-   is responsible for monitoring compliance with national measures implementing the Directive (Article 28(1));

- must be consulted when administrative and regulatory measures to implement the Directive are drawn up (Article 28(2));
- must be given investigative powers, effective powers of intervention, and the power to engage in legal proceedings regarding violations of the national implementing laws (the exercise of which powers may, however, be appealed through the courts) (Article 28(3));
- must hear claims lodged by any data subject or association representing a data subject, and when Member States are employing their powers under Article 13 must hear claims for checks on lawfulness of processing lodged by *any person* (in relation to which they must at least inform the person that a check has taken place) (Article 28(4));
- must draw up and publish a regular report on its activities (Article 28(5));
- may be asked to exercise its powers by the Authority of another Member State and must co-operate with the Supervisory Authorities in the other Member States insofar as this is necessary for it to carry out its duties (Article 28(6)).

The staff of the Supervisory Authority must be made subject to a duty of professional secrecy with regard to confidential information, which must continue after they have ceased to be employed by the authority (Article 28(7)).

Article 29 Working Party

Article 29 (see also Recital 65) sets up an advisory, independent, Working Party on the Protection of Individuals with respect to the Processing of Personal Data, and specifies the composition and *modus operandi* of the Working Party. The remit of the Working Party is (see Article 30(1); Recital 65) to

- examine any question concerning proper implementation of the Directive in relation to contributing to the Directives aim of ensuring harmonized protection within the EU;
- provide an opinion to the Commission on the level of protection in third countries;
- advise the Commission on any proposed amendments to the Directive or additional proposed Community measures affecting the rights and freedoms of individuals with respect to the processing of personal data; and
- give opinions on codes of conduct drawn up at Community level.

The Working Party's findings on any lack of harmonization must be reported to the Commission (Article 30(2)), and the Working Party may make recommendations on its own initiative (Article 30(3)). The Working Party's opinions and recommendations must be forwarded to the Commission and the Article 31 Committee (Article 30(4)). The Commission must make a report on action it takes on any of these opinions or recommendations to the Working Party, the European Parliament and the Council (Article 30(5)), which must be made public. Finally, the Working Party must make an annual report to the European Parliament and the

Council on the level of protection in Member States and third countries, which must be made public (Article 30(6)).

Article 31 Committee

Article 31 provides that the Commission is to be assisted by a Committee when it proposes to take Community measures. If the Committee agrees (by a majority in accordance with Article 148(2) of the European Treaty) to the measures proposed, they apply immediately. Otherwise, the Commission must submit the measures to the Council (which has 3 months to take a different decision by a qualified majority). It seems from Recital 68 that one of the specific purposes of Article 31 is to enable the Commission to supplement or clarify the principles of the Directive by making specific rules based on those principles for specific sectors. Thus, for example, it is possible, in principle, that the Commission might use Article 31 to implement specific community measures for the use of personal data for medical research.

Deadlines for Implementation and Powers to Make Transitional Exemptions

Article 32(1) requires Member States to have implemented the Directive within 3 years of its adoption (which was on 24 October 1995, hence by 24 October 1998). According to Article 32(2), by 24 October 2001, all processing already underway by 24 October 1998 must comply with the provisions of the Directive, except that Member States may delay conformity with Articles 6, 7 and 8 until 24 October 2007 in the case of processing of data already held in manual filing systems on 24 October 1998. (This implies that data can be subject to processing already underway when it is not already held; but this is not explained. In relation to medical research, one possibility is that data collected from a person after 23 October 1998, thus not held on 24 October 1998, for a project that began processing data on other persons before 24 October 1998, is to be considered being subject to processing already under way by 24 October 1998; but other interpretations may be possible.) This transitional exemption does not, however, extend to the rights under Article 12. (However, according to Recital 69, if data kept in existing manual filing systems is processed during the extended transition period applicable to them, 'those systems must be brought into conformity with these provisions at the time of such processing'.) According to Article 32(3), subject to the provision of suitable safeguards, Member States may permanently exempt data already held in manual filing systems before 24 October 1998 from Articles 6, 7 and 8, where the data are kept for the sole purpose of historical research.

Review of the Directive by the Commission

Article 33 requires the Commission to report to the Council and the European Parliament on the implementation of the Directive at regular intervals, beginning no later than 24 October 2001, and the reports must be made public. It requires the Commission, in particular, to keep under review the application of the Directive to the processing of sound and image data relating to natural persons and to submit any proposals that are rendered necessary by advances in information technology.

Responsibility to Implement the Directive

Article 34 addresses the Directive to the Member States. All EC Directives (as against EC Regulations) require implementation by the Member States and do not generally impose duties directly on private persons or bodies. However, under the doctrine of direct effect developed by the ECJ, once the deadline for implementation has passed, provisions of a Directive that are sufficiently clear and unambiguous to be applied directly by the domestic courts apply directly in the absence of implementing legislation and take precedence over any conflicting legislation.[7] If the domestic courts refuse to apply such provisions directly,[8] then the Member States are liable to penalties.[9]

---

[7] See, e.g., the second *Simmenthal* case, Case 106/77, [1978] E.C.R 629.

[8] That they are required to do so, at least if possible, was established in *Von Colson and Kamann v. Land Nordrhein-Westfalen* (Case 14/83) [1984] E.C.R. 1891.

[9] See *Wagner Miret v. Fondo de Guarantia Salaria* (C-334/92), [1993] E.C.R. I-6911.

Chapter 3

The Concept of Privacy: An Analysis of the EU Directive on the Protection of Personal Data

Mette Hartlev[*]

Introduction

The concept of privacy has been extensively addressed in both legal and philosophical writing. Despite the overwhelming amount of literature, the concept of privacy remains somewhat nebulous. There is no single, unitary perception either of how privacy should be defined, or of how a right to privacy should be justified. Consequently, it is not possible to analyse the concept of privacy in the EU Directive on the basis of a clear and distinct definition. Instead one has to look at the different facets associated with the concept of privacy in order to analyze whether these are reflected in the Directive and—if so—what importance the Directive assigns to these components. In order to encircle the different facets of privacy, I will begin this paper with a brief introduction to the different perceptions of the concept of privacy developed in philosophical and legal literature. Related concepts such as personality, autonomy, integrity and dignity will be touched upon as well.

Different Perceptions of Privacy

There have been many attempts both in philosophical and legal literature to define the concept of privacy. Despite the partly diverging nature of these definitions it is, however, possible to make a rough categorization.

Many scholars characterize privacy in terms of *non-interference*, or as a condition or state in which a person is more or less *inaccessible* to others, on either the spatial, psychological or informational plane.[1] In the same vein, privacy is also

[*] Mette Hartlev, Ph.D., Associate Professor, Faculty of Law, University of Copenhagen, Denmark.
[1] See for example, R. Gavison, 'Privacy and the Limits of Law' (1980) 89 *The Yale Law Journal* 421–471 and W.A. Parent, 'A New Definition of Privacy for the Law' (1983) 2 *Law and Philosophy* 305–338.

defined as *the right to an inviolate personality*, or *the right to be let alone.*[2] According to these conceptions, privacy belongs to or is an inherent part of each individual, and the individual's right to privacy derives from the view that he or she has a justified claim to respect of a private sphere. As I will discuss further later, this conception could be characterized as *integrity oriented*. It is important to notice that within this conception it is necessary to be able to demarcate a private sphere and thus necessary to have an impression of how to distinguish private from public.

Other scholars associate the concept of privacy with a *right or a competence of the individual to determine or control who should have access to the private sphere, including personal information.*[3] This perception could be characterized as *autonomy oriented*. Within this conception the demarcation of a private sphere is not so important as the focus is on the individual's right to self-determination.

Turning to the legal analysis of the right to privacy, one will discover a variety of interests protected by such a legal right. Even the legal terminology varies as the right to privacy in some legal systems is referred to as a right of the personality. In an older comparative study, Stig Strömholm concludes that the right to privacy and the right of the personality are overlapping rights and that these legal entitlements essentially deal with the following phenomena:[4]

(i)   Intrusions, whether committed by means of physical violence or otherwise, into an area, whether in a local or a figurative sense, which a person has an interest in keeping for himself.

(ii) Collecting material, in the broadest possible sense, about a person, either by intrusion or by other methods felt to be unfair.

(iii) Using material about a person, whether lawfully or unlawfully obtained, for publication or for some specific purpose, e.g. as evidence against that person.

According to Stig Strömholm, *intrusions* may occur both as unauthorized entry onto and search of premises or other property, unauthorized searches of the person, medical examination or a blood test, or as intrusions by means of trespass to property or persons. Intrusions may also occur as unauthorized tape recordings, photographing or filming, interception of correspondence, telephone tapping and

---

[2] See for example, S. D. Warren and L. D. Brandeis, 'The Right to Privacy' (1890) 15 *Harvard Law Review* 5: 193–220; R. Pound, 'Interests of Personality' (1915) 28 *Harvard Law Review* 343–365 and 445–457; and J. H. Reiman, 'Privacy, Intimacy and Personhood' (1976) 6 *Philosophy & Public Affairs* 1: 26–44.

[3] See for example A. Westin, *Privacy and Freedom* (New York: Atheneum, 1967), 7; S. Fried, 'Privacy' (1968) 77 *The Yale Law Journal* 475–493; E. L. Beardsley, 'Privacy: Autonomy and selective disclosure' in J. R. Pennock and J. W. Chapman (eds.), *Privacy* (Nomos XIII, New York: Atherton Press, 1971), 56–70; H. Gross, 'Privacy and Autonomy', in J. R. Pennock and J. W. Chapman (eds.), *Privacy* (Nomos XIII, New York: Atherton Press, 1971) 169–181 and R. Wacks, *Personal Information, Privacy and the Law* (Oxford: Clarendon Press, 1989), 19–28.

[4] Stig, Strömholm, *Right of Privacy and Rights of the Personality: A Comparative Survey* (Stockholm: Nordstedt, 1967), 60.

the use of electronic surveillance or other 'bugging' devices. *Infringement in connection with the use of personal information* may happen in different situations, such as disclosure of information given to professional advisers or to public authorities bound to observe secrecy, unwarranted public disclosure of private facts, unauthorized use of a person's name, identity or likeness and misuse of words or other communications from a person. Thus, the rights to privacy and of personality cover a wide range of phenomena and interests. They are fundamentally connected with the individual's interest in being let alone and being protected against unauthorized intrusions whether related to rooms, social relations, activities or personal data. This interest is not solely related to public disclosure or exposure but to physical intrusion as well. Furthermore, the use of another person's name or likeness, and defamation are also covered by this protection. Thus, it is not solely the private sphere that is the object of protection, but also the individual's interest in an inviolate personality as well as the interest in expressing and controlling one's self-identity.

Protection of Personal Data as Part of the Right to Privacy

The object of the EU Directive is the protection of the individual in relation to the *processing* of *personal data*. As illustrated above, the right to privacy is much broader than the individual's right to protection of personal data. Thus, the right to privacy, for example, protects the person's physical integrity and domestic peace, irrespective of whether the purpose of potential intrusions is to obtain private information about the person. The same goes for interception of correspondence, which is an intrusion whether or not the correspondence contains personal information.

Thus, protection of personal data could be described as a particular *part* of the right to privacy. The term *informational privacy* is sometimes used to describe this particular right to privacy.[5]

Privacy and Other Fundamental Values

Privacy is closely related to other fundamental values such as *dignity*, *integrity* and *autonomy*.[6]

The term *dignity* is often used to express the idea that all human beings have an inherent worth based on their humanity.[7] Dignity is closely related to the

---

[5] P. Blume, *Protection of Informational Privacy* (Copenhagen: Djøf Publishing, 2002).

[6] Lee. A. Bygrave, *Data Protection Law: Approaching its Rationale, Logic and Limits* (The Hague: Kluwer Law International, 2002), 134–137.

[7] P. Kemp, 'Four Ethical Principles in Biolaw' in P. Kemp, J. Rendtorff, and N. M. Johansen (eds.), *Bioethics and Biolaw* (Vol. II, Copenhagen: Rhodos, 2000), 13–22. For a comprehensive analysis of the concept of dignity see D. Beyleveld and R. Brownsword *Human Dignity in Bioethics and Biolaw* (Oxford: Oxford University Press, 2001).

concept of *integrity*. Personal integrity can be defined as the inviolability, untouchableness and wholeness of an individual.[8] One may distinguish between physical and mental integrity. The physical integrity of an individual refers to the inviolability of the body, whereas mental integrity is connected with the inviolability of a person's mind. Finally, *autonomy* is often understood as a person's right to self-determination.

These concepts are at the same time both distinct and partially overlapping. The dignity and integrity of an individual have an intrinsic character. Consequently, the dignity and integrity of a person cannot be graded or substituted. Autonomy is different. An individual may be more or less autonomous according to his or her ability to make autonomous decisions. Accordingly, autonomy can be graded, thus proxies may to some extent substitute the autonomy of a person.[9] The individual's right to autonomy could be seen as a *principle of action*.[10] An autonomous person is able to defend his or her right to respect for dignity, but autonomy also allows individuals to give up their privacy and accept invasions of personal integrity.

One could say that privacy contains elements of dignity, integrity and autonomy. However, privacy is still a broader value as it is not only related to a person but also refers to the individual's spatial and social surroundings such as his or her home and family.

Privacy is also closely connected to *confidentiality*. Confidentiality could be seen as a subset of informational privacy, as it prevents the disclosure of information that was originally disclosed within a confidential relationship.[11]

Privacy and Other Interests

The individual's interest in protecting his or her informational privacy must be balanced with the interests of other persons or organizations that need to use information on that individual. This balance of interests is addressed in the Norwegian 'interest theory'.[12] According to this theory a number of interests—both individual and collective—should be considered when processing personal information. In summary, the *individual interests* are usually formulated in terms of confidentiality, insight/access, data quality and protection of private life. The

---

[8] P. Kemp (2000), n. 7 above.

[9] G. Hermerén, 'Informed Consent from an Ethical Point of View' in L. Wästerhäll and C. Phillips (eds.), *Patient's Rights: Informed Consent, Access and Equality* (Stockholm: Nerenius and Santeréus Publishers, 1994), 39–61.

[10] E. Bischofberger, 'Människosyn, integritet och autonomi' in Sven-Olof Andersson (ed.), *Lidandet och makten. Om människovärde och människosyn i hälso- och sjukvå* (Stockholm: Förlagshuset Gothia, 1990) 13–18.

[11] T. L. Beauchamp and J. F. Childress, *Principles of Biomedical Ethics* (5th edn., Oxford: Oxford University Press, 2001), 303–312.

[12] For a more comprehensive description and further elaboration of the interest theory see Lee. A. Bygrave (2002), n. 6 above, 137–143 and D. W. Schartumm, 'Norway' in P. Blume (ed.), *Nordic Data Protection* (Copenhagen: Djøf Publishing, 2001), 79–113.

collective interests are commonly described in terms of citizen friendly administration, the interest in controlling the level of surveillance in society and the interest in a 'robust society'. According to the theory these interests should all be considered and balanced when making decisions regarding the processing of data. In other words, they should be seen as factors that should be taken into account when weighing the pros and cons of a particular phenomenon.

The interest theory indicates that privacy protection must take into account the individual's societal position and role. The right to privacy is not an absolute right but must interact with other rights and values. This is reflected in Article 8 of the European Convention of Human Rights[13] (hereinafter the ECHR) according to which the individual's right to privacy may be constrained if this is necessary in a democratic society in order to protect national security, public order, public health or the rights and freedoms of others.

The Concept of Privacy in the EU Directive

The Interests Protected by the Directive

The title of the Directive is the 'Protection of individuals with regard to the processing of personal data and the free movement of such data in their national laws'. This is interesting as it indicates the scope of interests protected by the Directive. The ambition is to protect the individual and more precisely to protect the fundamental rights and freedoms of the individual in connection with the processing of data. This is expressed in Article 1, according to which the aim is to 'protect the fundamental rights and freedoms of natural persons and in particular the right to privacy with respect to the processing of personal data'.

This is elaborated in more detail in several Recitals to the Directive that contain a number of references to the protection of the individual's 'fundamental rights and freedoms, notably the right to privacy'.[14] In Recital 10 the right to privacy is associated with Article 8 of the ECHR. The scope of Article 8 of the ECHR is very wide.[15] In relation to the processing of data Article 8 covers both the right of access to information and the right not to have private information wrongfully disclosed. As the Directive also protects interests other than privacy, the scope of the Directive is even more extensive. Consequently, the purpose of the Directive is in some respects broader than the protection of privacy as it is also intended to protect other fundamental rights and freedoms in relation to the

---

[13] Convention for the Protection of Human Rights and Fundamental Freedoms as amended by Protocol No. 11, 4 November 1950, Council of Europe.

[14] See, for example, Recitals 1, 2, 7, 8, 9, 10 and 11.

[15] L. Bygrave, 'Data Protection Pursuant to the Right to Privacy in Human Rights Treaties' (1998) 3 *International Journal of Law and Information Technology* 247–284 and B. Kofoed Olsen, *Identifikationsteknologi og individbeskyttelse—en øvelse i juridisk teknologivurdering* (Copenhagen: Djøf Publishing, 1998).

processing of personal data. In other respects, however, the purpose is more constrained, as the Directive is restricted to the processing of personal data.

Integrity Oriented Aspects

In the introduction to my paper, I presented various facets of the concept of privacy outlined in philosophical and legal literature. Some definitions associate the right to privacy with a right to be left alone and a right to an inviolate personality. I have categorized these aspects as *integrity oriented*. Several Articles in the Directive reflect the integrity directed aspects of the right to privacy. I will touch upon some of the most important.

Article 2(a) defines *personal data* as any information relating to an identified or identifiable person. An identifiable person is in turn defined as one who can be identified, directly or indirectly, in particular by reference to an identification number or to one or more factors specific to his physical, physiological, mental, economic, cultural or social identity. This is further elucidated in Recital 26 according to which account should be taken of all the means likely (reasonably) to be used either by the data controller or by any other person to identify the person. This means that, for example, encrypted data are considered to be personal data if someone has access to the encryption key. Using a very wide definition of personal data, it is fair to say that the Directive is focused on the protection of the individual's integrity.

Both international and national data protection laws usually distinguish between *various types of data*. Normally the processing of sensitive data should meet more strict conditions than the processing of data with a lower level of sensitivity. According to Article 8 of the Directive, sensitive data are 'personal data revealing racial or ethnic origin, political opinions, religious or philosophical beliefs, trade union membership or data concerning health or sex life'. This data could—with reference to Recital 33—be characterized as 'data, which are capable by their nature of infringing fundamental freedoms and privacy'. Processing such data is prohibited unless certain conditions are satisfied.[16] Despite the fact that processing is allowed in some situations, it is essential to point out that, in contrast to the conditions relating to ordinary data, these processing conditions are characterized as *exemptions* which require that compliance with them must be particularly ensured. Paying special attention to sensitive data underlines the integrity-oriented aspects of the Directive. However, one could mention that the definition of sensitive data is a bit narrow. Thus, Article 8 does not cover information concerning, for example, criminal records and severe social problems.[17]

The foundations of both international and national data protection laws consist of a number of fundamental principles often referred to as the *principle of legality,* the *collection limitation principle*, the *purpose specification principle*, the *principle*

---

[16] See Articles 8(2)(a)–(e) and 8(3)–8(5) of the Directive.

[17] In the Danish Act on Processing of Personal Data there is a provision (Section 8) specifically dealing with confidential data not covered by Article 8 of the Directive.

of transparency, the *time limitation principle*, the *data quality principle* and the *data security principle*. These principles express the idea of and demand for proportionality also reflected in Article 8(2) of the ECHR. Essentially, the individual's private sphere may not be violated unless this is justified by reference to weighty concerns, and the intrusion should not exceed what is necessary in order to secure these interests. In other words, the violation should be as limited as possible. Article 6 of the Directive, together with Articles 10–12 and Article 17, highlights these principles, thus emphasising the importance attached to the individual's right to be left alone and to an inviolate personality. It is important to notice that it is not possible to derogate from these provisions, even with the consent of the data subject.

The principle of proportionality is also expressed in the demand for *necessity* reflected in several Articles of the Directive.[18] Even though the demand for necessity is vague, it reflects the demand of respect for the individual's personal integrity.

The Directive also deals with the individual's *personality*. The data subject's right of *correction* when data are wrong or misleading protects the data subject against being placed in a false light. The right of access could also be seen as a means of protecting the data subject's personality as access to data may support the individual's right to an identity.

Autonomy Oriented Aspects

Some scholars associate the right to privacy with the individual's right to informational self-determination. This could be categorized as an *autonomy oriented* aspect of the right to privacy. These aspects are also reflected in the Directive.

The data subjects' *consent* is one of the conditions required when processing both ordinary and sensitive data.[19] Consequently, the data subject has some influence on whether data may be processed. It is however still possible to process data without the data subject's consent if other conditions are fulfilled.

The importance attached to the data subject's consent is also expressed in the *definition of a valid consent*. According to Article 2(h), the data subject's consent means any freely given, specific and informed indication of the data subject's wishes. Furthermore, when processing sensitive data the consent shall be explicit— whereas an unambiguous consent suffices when processing ordinary data.

However, it is important to pay attention to the fact that not all data subjects are competent to give a valid consent. Minors and incompetent adults may in both a legal and a factual sense not be able to consent to the processing of data. Furthermore, it may also be difficult for resource-less persons to have a full grasp of the consequences of giving consent, for example many data subjects in certain situations may feel under pressure to give their consent. Consequently, consent requirements may give an amputated protection of the individual's privacy.

---

[18] See, for example, Articles 6–9 of the Directive.

[19] See Article 6(a) and Article 8(2)(a) of the Directive.

Another example of the autonomy-oriented aspects of the Directive is the data subject's right to *object*. According to Article 14 the data subject should be granted a right—at least in cases referred to in Article 7(e) and (f)—to object at any time on compelling legitimate grounds relating to his or her particular situation to the processing of personal data. The right to object provides an opportunity to stop otherwise legitimate processing of data. The data subject also has a right to *object to decisions* which have legal consequences or are of essential importance to him, if the decision is based solely on automated processing (Article 15).

The data controller is responsible for the quality of the data, and is obliged to ensure that data that are inaccurate or incomplete is erased or rectified. However, Article 12(2) also gives the data subject a right of *correction* when data are wrong or misleading, thus supporting the data subject's right to control the processing of information.

The data subject's right *to access and to be informed* are prerequisites both for the data subject to be able to take part in the control of the flow of information, and to know for what purposes information about him/her will be processed.

Both the right to object and the right to correction are important. However, their importance should not be overestimated. The right to object does not give the data subject an ultimate right to stop the processing of data. The objections will only be followed if it is justified to do so, and it is up to the data controller to decide whether this is the case. The right to object may also be set aside in national law.

Balancing of Interests

The integrity and autonomy oriented aspects of the Directive pay attention to the protection of the individual's privacy and other fundamental rights and freedoms. However, the objective of the Directive is not only to protect the rights of the individual. Fundamentally, the purpose of the Directive is to ensure the free flow of information. Consequently, the privacy of the individual should be seen in the context of the societal interest in getting access to and being able to process personal data. Protecting privacy and other fundamental rights is meant to make the free flow of personal information easier. However, in some situations privacy and other rights could be seen as barriers to the processing and free flow of information.

The Directive reflects the fact that in some situations it is necessary to reconcile the right to privacy with other interests. Thus, in a number of situations the processing of data is legitimate provided it is necessary in order to protect vital societal interests or the interests of others.[20] The scope of the purpose-specification principle outlined in Article 1(b) also leaves room for other interests, such as the further use of information for, for example, scientific purposes, which is permitted if appropriate safeguards are provided.

---

[20] See, for example, Articles 6(b)–(f), 7(2)(b)–(e), 7(3)–7(4), 7(6), 9, 11(2) and 13 of the Directive.

Concluding Remarks

It follows from this brief analysis that the Directive reflects both the integrity and the autonomy oriented facets often associated with the concept of privacy. These facets go hand in hand. Together they provide a more comprehensive protection of the individual's rights and freedoms. The integrity oriented aspects are mostly concerned with the protection of the private sphere and the protection of the individual's personality. The autonomy oriented aspects are more focused on the individual's ability to control and determine the use of information relating to him/her whether the information is sensitive or non-sensitive. The weakness of the integrity oriented attitude is the restriction of the focus to private or sensitive information. The integrity oriented attitude also tends to be paternalistic. By contrast, the autonomy oriented attitude has a wider focus and relies on the individual's ability to make autonomous decisions regarding the use of personal data. However, this attitude seems to neglect the factual restraints regarding the individual's ability to act autonomously. If, for example, providing personal data is necessary to get insurance or a job, many individuals will feel inclined or maybe even forced to consent to the dissemination of information. Consequently, focusing both on the data subject's integrity and on his or her autonomy is necessary in order to provide a comprehensive protection of the individual's rights and freedoms.

As indicated above, it is also necessary to balance the interests of the individual against the interests of society and other persons. However, it is worthwhile to take a closer look at how the Directive strikes the balance between these (often) conflicting interests. In relation to medical research the Directive leaves room for exempting the processing from some of the provisions, leaving it up to national laws to provide suitable safeguards. Consequently, the protection of the individual's right to privacy is dependent on the safeguards provided by national laws. It is therefore necessary to analyse the balancing of interests and the safeguards provided in national law to get a comprehensive picture of the importance attached to the protection of individual privacy in relation to biomedical research.

Chapter 4

Anonymization and Pseudonymization: The Legal Framework at a European Level

Carlos María Romeo Casabona[*]

The Problem

The need to use personal data for purposes beyond the initial purpose for which they were collected gives rise to some interesting problems in connection with the juridical aspects of the security of personal data. Some social activities need access to personal data, for example, scientific research and, in particular, research in the field of biomedical science and specifically into genetics.

Genetic research requires in many cases the use of biological samples both from subjects who have taken part in experiments and also those from other people who have not been involved. The results of analyses and other tests can be very useful for the progress of research in certain areas (for example, in pharmacogenetics and in genomics). The advantage of using samples of this nature that were previously stored for other reasons or different purposes, is that it makes research that was previously impossible progressively easier to undertake. However, it can create diverse problems, usually not foreseen by the legislation that regulates research and experimentation on human subjects.

The need to protect biological samples of human origin is related to the information that can be obtained on the individual from whom the samples originate, particularly if such information is predictive or pre-symptomatic. It is associated with the right to protection of genetic data, intimacy and private life and to the prohibition of discriminatory treatment.

It is more and more frequently necessary for the success of biomedical research to have personal data of diverse types, such as those regarding the individual's health or genetic data. Consequently, it is necessary to develop technical processes which will reconcile the important interests of research with the protection of the individuals whose data could be used in such research, in

---

[*] Professor of Criminal Law, Director of the Inter-University Chair BBVA Foundation-Provincial Government of Biscay in Law and the Human Genome, University of Duesto, University of the Basque Country.

order to protect both interests. One such process is the anonymizing of data—which should have the effect of disenabling identification of the individual or of avoiding the linking of such data with the person to whom they belong. On occasions pseudonymization of data has also appeared as an alternative process, although this offers more limited protection to the data subject.

This paper will discuss whether these technical means are sufficiently effective and certain to avoid any process of aggregation of the anonymized or pseudonymized data with identifiable information from the individual to whom they belong—as well as avoiding the person's identification by any other, indirect ways. This issue is of great importance, as it can bring out apparently prejudicial or damaging effects on the rights of protection for the person concerned.

Provisions of Directive 95/46/EC on the Anonymization of Data

In this contribution I will focus my attention on the juridical aspects of the problem outlined above. With such a purpose, I will begin by recalling the text of EC Directive 95/46/EC[1] (from now on 'the Directive'), which is dedicated specifically to the anonymization of data. In relation to this, Recital 26 states the following:

> Whereas the principles of protection must apply to any information concerning an identified or identifiable person; whereas, to determine whether a person is identifiable, account should be taken of all the means likely reasonably to be used either by the controller or by any other person to identify the said person; whereas the principles of protection shall not apply to data rendered anonymous in such a way that the data subject is no longer identifiable; whereas codes of conduct within the meaning of Article 27 may be a useful instrument for providing guidance as to the ways in which data may be rendered anonymous and retained in a form in which identification of the data subject is no longer possible.

The most important fact that we can draw from the text of the Directive is that 'the principles of protection shall not apply to data rendered anonymous in such a way that the data subject is no longer identifiable'. This statement implies that protection will not be given to personal data that have been subjected to an anonymization process. However, what we should understand as 'anonymization' and as 'anonymous data' on the basis of the Directive is not so clear, at least if we only take into account Recital 26.[2]

For these reasons it is very important to clarify these concepts and the juridical reach that they have for the protection of personal data. There is no doubt that if 'anonymized data' is totally anonymous and it is impossible to identify the person concerned, there should be no objection to leaving them out of the protective scope

---

[1] Directive 95/46/EC of the European Parliament and Council, 24 October 1995, on the protection of individuals with regard to the processing of personal data and on the free movement of such data.

[2] D. Beyleveld, D. Townend 'When is Personal Data Rendered Anonymous? Interpreting Recital 26 of Directive 95/46/EC', *World Congress on Medical Law*, 2002.

of the Directive. If, on the contrary, this is not the case, the following could be argued in relation to Recital 26 of the Directive:

a. It could render the person concerned vulnerable to violation of his/her rights.
b. It could infringe some of the principles regarding the collection of data, for example, Art. 6.1(b) of the Directive: 'Personal data must be collected for specified, explicit and legitimate purposes and not further processed in a way incompatible with those purposes'.
c. It could also affect other principles related to the protection of data, such as obtaining the consent of the subject (Art. 7(a) of the Directive), special protection of data relating to the data subject's state of health (Art. 8), as well as the duties of the data controller regarding the information that should be given to the subject (Articles 10 and 11). In particular, Article 11 stipulates that when the data have not been obtained from the data subject, some specific information shall be provided to him at the time of the recording of the data or, if a disclosure to a third party is envisaged, no later than the time when the data are first disclosed.
d. The person concerned would not even have protection in relation to the data because of the specific normative on the matter. Hereinafter we will be able to assess how this happens in relation to the Directive, although it will first be necessary to define its scope.

In summary, anonymization is not a totally innocuous process, because it could generate doubly harmful effects for an affected person: a vulnerability due to deficiency or inefficacy of the technical security measures and a vulnerability due to the lack of juridical protection in certain situations in which this anonymization could be reversible, giving rise to the identification of the interested person.

On the other hand, we should not forget the other interests that can be served by the anonymization and later use of these data, i.e. scientific research. The Directive does not ignore the importance of these interests, providing that further processing of data for historical, statistical or scientific purposes shall not be considered as incompatible as long as Member States provide appropriate safeguards (Art. 6.1(b) of the Directive)[3]. It also establishes that

> where the data have not been obtained from the data subject, Member States shall provide that the controller or his representative must at the time of undertaking the recording of personal data or if a disclosure to a third party is envisaged, no later than the time when the data are first disclosed provide the data subject with at least the following information, except where he already has it (Art. 11.1)

---

[3] Art. 6.1(b): 'Further processing of data for historical, statistical or scientific purposes shall not be considered as incompatible provided that Member States provide appropriate safeguards'.

but:

> paragraph 1 shall not apply where, in particular for processing for statistical purposes or for the purposes of historical or scientific research, the provision of information proves impossible or would involve a disproportionate effort or if recording or disclosure is expressly laid down by law. In these cases Member States shall provide appropriate safeguards (Art. 11.2).

With these preliminary considerations, the magnitude and importance of this question can be understood, as well as its juridical consequences. For these reasons, we will have to clarify in which situations anonymization moves personal data out of the scope of data protection. The interpretation of Recital 26 of the Directive should not be undertaken in isolation, but with reference to the set of Articles and juridical categories that have been established during the last few years. There are diverse approaches to the issue and the differing positions should be explained from the point of view of the different regulations of each Member State, and, from a doctrinal point of view, with attention paid to the debate as to which ones are acceptable and which ones are not.

Before continuing, however, it is necessary to clarify some concepts that are very relevant for the issue, such as: identified or identifiable person, personal data, genetic and health data, and sensitive data, amongst others. This must be followed by clarification of the concepts of anonymization and pseudonymization, as well as the real juridical reach of data protection in the context of anonymization and the applicability of protection principles, for example as relating to the consent of the subject.

Some Previous Approaches

If anonymization is a process that affects personal data, both terms must be defined, as the data are the object of that process. Also, within the category of personal data, there are some data that have special protection: sensitive data. Within this, data concerning health, and genetic data, should be more specifically outlined.

Personal Data and Sensitive Data

The Directive states that *personal data* 'shall mean any information relating to an identified or identifiable natural person', such a person being the 'interested party' (Art. 2(a)).

The definition of personal data allows one to include any information regarding a person, whatever his or her nature or origin, being intimate or not, even if it affects several people at the same time or a family group (in this last case, each one of the individual members of the family).[4] This aspect can be of great importance in relation to data concerning health and genetics.

From this definition it can also be deduced that only a born human being, while alive, can be a data subject ('interested party'). Consequently, the corporate person, the deceased and the unborn are excluded from the scope of protection of the Directive, because they are not 'natural persons' in the juridical sense of the term.[5] With regard to the unborn (embryos and human foetuses), recognition of the quality of personhood will depend on the legal framework of each Member State, although in general such status is acquired with birth. Nevertheless, data concerning a corporate person, the deceased and those still unborn should also have some protection. We should keep in mind that information that can be obtained from them can affect people who are objects of protection in connection with personal data. This is the case for data of biological origin from the deceased and the unborn.

Sensitive data Sensitive data are usually defined as data in connection with which the data subject is more vulnerable when the data is known or used by a third party because of its potential for causing discrimination and other misuse, especially when accessed, used or illicitly disclosed. As a consequence, these data are regarded as needing more intense protection, even without the consent of the data subject if it is necessary in exceptional cases. What is usually regarded as sensitive data are data that reveal racial or ethnic origin, political opinions and religious or philosophical convictions of the data subject, as well as that concerning health and sexuality.[6] The Directive includes this data under the denomination of 'special categories of data'.[7] In this category falls personal data that reveals racial or ethnic origin, as well as data related to health. Although the Directive does not define what should be understood as sensitive data *per se*, it does create a special framework of rules for its protection. This consists of a general prohibition against

---

[4] See further, C. M. Romeo Casabona, *Los genes y sus leyes* (Genes and their law) (Cátedra Inteurniversitaria de dereecho y Genoma Humano y Ed., Bilbao-Granada: Comares, 2002), 63.

[5] British Law on Data Protection of 1998 defines personal data as that of a living person (Section 1).

[6] Consideration of this kind of data as worthy of special protection can already be seen in Convention 108/1981 of the Council of Europe, on the protection of individuals with regard to automatic processing of personal data (Art. 6), although more categories have since been included.

[7] In the Preamble of the Directive the word 'sensitive' is explicitly used: 'Whereas Member States must also be authorized, when justified by grounds of important public interest, to derogate from the prohibition on processing sensitive categories of data where important reasons of public interest so justify in areas such as public health and social protection...' (Recital 34). See also Recital 70: 'Whereas it is not necessary for the data subject to give his consent again so as to allow the controller to continue to process, after the national provisions taken pursuant to this Directive enter into force, any sensitive data necessary for the performance of a contract concluded on the basis of free and informed consent before the entry into force of these provisions'.

processing (in the sense of the definition found in Art. 2(b)), tempered with many recognized exceptions to this rule (Art. 8).

Data Relating to an Identified or Identifiable Person and Anonymous Data

Juridically protected personal data can usually be classified into one of three categories of data, according to the larger or smaller possibility of identification of the person from whom the data are obtained. In the Directive we find similar classification, as outlined below.

Data relating to an identified person Data relating to an identified person is data that appears clearly and directly linked with the person from which it was obtained (data subject).

Data relating to an identifiable person Data relating to an identifiable person is data that seems not to be directly attributable to a certain person, since he or she does not appear to be identified or there is no link between the data and the person. In this category, however, the linking of such data to the person is possible by diverse procedures, which can normally be easily carried out. The connection of the data with the person to whom it belongs can also be obtained by other indirect procedures, such as, for example when the data reveals certain personal or social characteristics that only one person or a very reduced group of people possesses, and those characteristics could be known by others.

The Directive gives a definition of identifiable data, in the following terms: 'An identifiable person is one who can be identified, directly or indirectly, in particular by reference to an identification number or to one or more factors specific to his or her physical, physiological, mental, economic, cultural or social identity' (Art. 2(a)). As it can be noted, this definition does not set any criteria of 'relative' identifiability. But such criteria, however, do appear when the Directive deals with the anonymization of data. This issue is of paramount importance, since the third category of data, that is to say, anonymous data, already sets the limit of non-juridical protection.

On the other hand, the Directive considers a person identifiable in connection with his data if the data are identifiable by means of an identification number. This procedure can be considered as one of the diverse ways to achieve pseudonymization, which means that data subjected to this procedure would be under the scope of protection of the Directive, because it would continue to be personal data.

Anonymous data Anonymous data can be considered as data where the identity of the data subject is not known, and identification is not possible because the data were collected as such, or because although collected with identification, they have later been anonymized. This second type of anonymous data consists in subjecting the identifiable data of a person to a process of dissociation from the data that refers to that person, in such a way that it no longer allows the person's identification. Consequently, it is necessary that such a dissociation process is irreversible, that is to say, that the data cannot return to the form taken previously. As we already know, this procedure is called anonymization.

The Directive does not mention this category of data explicitly, but it is obvious that such data are out of its scope of protection under Recital 26. In this Recital, some apparent discrepancies appear with the Articles of the Directive, specifically with Art. 2(a), since no layers are introduced with regard to the level of difficulty of identification. It only sets down that ' an identifiable person is one who can be identified, directly or indirectly...', without mentioning the level of difficulty of the identification. On the other hand, the Recital seems to contradict, or at least to specify, the reach of the Art. 2(a) since it points out that 'to determine whether a person is identifiable, account should be taken of all the means likely *reasonably* to be used either by controller or by any other person to identify the said person' (emphasis added).

The question that is immediately raised is, what is the juridical value of the Recitals of the Directive in comparison with the Articles? Are they obligatory, or do they only possess an interpretive or explanatory value in relation to the Articles? Undoubtedly, nobody would argue that the preamble lacks juridical value, that it is a merely rhetorical or aesthetic part of the Directive as it does not appear within the preambles of the internal laws.

Even attributing only an interpretive value to the preamble, in relation to the issue in hand, Recital 26 does not seem to contradict Article 2(a) openly, but rather to expand on its contents. But it does have restrictive effects on what should be understood as 'identifiable people's data', because it adds that 'account should be taken of all the means likely reasonably to be used' to identify a person. When those means are not reasonable, the person will no longer be considered legally identifiable and the data will move into the category of anonymous data.

Anonymization

Directive 95/46/EC does not give a definition of what should be understood by anonymization, but as indicated above, it does mention the juridical effects regarding personal data that have been subjected to such a process, i.e. that are anonymous.

Nevertheless, what the Directive understands as anonymization can be deduced. In accordance with the Directive, anonymization refers to any process that makes the identification of the interested person no longer possible (Recital 26). This Recital seems to imply an absolute impossibility of identification due to the anonymization process. Art. 2(a) seems to follow this viewpoint. But, on the other hand, Recital 26 also establishes that 'to determine whether a person is identifiable, account should be taken of all the means *likely reasonably to be used* either by the controller or by any other person to identify the said person' (emphasis added). The word 'reasonably' seems to be opposed to the statement of the Directive previously mentioned: with 'reasonably' the level of *impossibility* of identification is limited to a certain degree (the 'reasonable'), although by extraordinary, complex, expensive and other not-reasonable procedures that person could be identified. Consequently, the concerned person is excluded from the principles of data protection. That is to say, we are assuming that the Directive only requires a relative degree of impossibility of identification.

This definition does not seem completely satisfactory, since it leaves many aspects unresolved.

The German Law on Data Protection[8] may be more satisfactory, since it give a definition of 'depersonalization':

> 'Depersonalization' means the modification of personal data so that the information concerning personal or material circumstances can no longer or only with a *disproportionate* amount of time, expense and labour be attributed to an identified or identifiable individual (emphasis added)(Section 3.6).

Thus, it is proven that the expressions 'identifiable', 'anonymization' and 'depersonalization' do not include the provision of absolute impossibility of the subject's identification, but they rather include only the reasonable procedures, excluding the ones that need a disproportionate amount of time, expense and labour.

The same idea is found in other legal texts, such as the Recommendation of the Council of Europe on the Protection of Medical Data.[9] This text points out that the expression 'personal data' covers:

> any information relating to an identified or identifiable individual. An individual shall not be regarded as 'identifiable' if identification requires an unreasonable amount of time and manpower. In the cases where the individual is not identifiable, data are referred to as anonymous (Principle 1).

In my opinion, the German definition of a disproportionate amount of time, expense and labour includes terms that could be very helpful in interpreting the word 'reasonably' in the Directive. What is reasonable in each situation is however a question to be decided by the controller of the file.

Finally, the reach of the anonymization has a universal scope, that is to say, the impossibility of identification covers both the data controller and any third person ('account should be taken of all the means likely reasonably to be used either by the controller or by any other person to identify the said person', Recital 26).

Medical Data and Genetic Data

The Directive regards data concerning health as data that deserves special protection.

---

[8] Federal Data Protection Act of 20 December 1990 (BGBl. I 1990 S. 2954), as last amended 14 January 2003.
[9] Council of Europe Recommendation R(97)5 of the Committee of Ministers to Member States on the Protection of Medical Data.

The Recommendation of the Council of Europe on the Protection of Medical Data defines what can be understood as medical and genetic data:

> The expression 'medical data' refers to all personal data concerning the health of an individual. It refers also to data which have a clear and close link with health as well as to genetic data (Principle 1).

In fact this definition refers to data concerning health, which is what is relevant to this study, and it also includes data closely linked to health, including genetic data. But genetic data are subject to a specific definition:

> The expression 'genetic data' refers to all data, of whatever type, concerning the hereditary characteristics of an individual or concerning the pattern of inheritance of such characteristics within a related group of individuals. It also refers to all data on the carrying of any genetic information (genes) in an individual or genetic line relating to any aspect of health or disease, whether present as identifiable characteristics or not. The genetic line is the line constituted by genetic similarities resulting from procreation and shared by two or more individuals (Principle 1).[10]

In summary, medical data are data concerning health, in the sense of the definition above. Genetic data are considered to be part of this category.

Data Protection and Scientific Research Related to Health

Again, the Recommendation of the Council of Europe on the Protection of Medical Data gives some extremely relevant conceptual explanations. Indeed, in accordance with Principle 12 ('scientific research'), medical data used for the purpose of scientific investigation will be anonymized:

> Whenever possible, medical data used for scientific research purposes should be anonymous. Professional and scientific organisations as well as public authorities should promote the development of techniques and procedures securing anonymity (Principle 12.1).

As can be deduced from the invitation to promote the development of techniques and procedures that ensure anonymity, it is intended that such anonymity should be tangible. However, the Council of Europe Recommendation assumes the hypothesis that, in some cases, research with non-anonymized personal data is necessary. For that it demands the execution of a group of requirements:

> However, if such anonymisation would make a scientific research project impossible, and the project is to be carried out for legitimate purposes, it could be carried out with personal data on condition that:

---

[10] The Recommendation of the Council of Europe on the Protection of Medical Data, see n. 9 above.

a. the data subject has given his/her informed consent for one or more research purposes; or

b. when the data subject is a legally incapacitated person incapable of free decision, and domestic law does not permit the data subject to act on his/her own behalf, his/her legal representative or an authority, or any person or body provided for by law, has given his/her consent in the framework of a research project related to the medical condition or illness of the data subject; or

c. disclosure of data for the purpose of a defined scientific research project concerning an important public interest has been authorised by the body or bodies designated by domestic law, but only if:

    i. the data subject has not expressly opposed disclosure; and

    ii. despite reasonable efforts, it would be impracticable to contact the data subject to seek his consent; and

    iii. the interests of the research project justify the authorisation; or

d. the scientific research is provided for by law and constitutes a necessary measure for public health reasons (Principle 12.2).

The most prominent thing in these requirements is the requirement of the consent of the individual concerned—or of his or her legal representative, or the intervention of one or several institutions to give their authorization. One of these institutions could be a research ethics committee.

The Application of the Principles of Data Protection in the Context of Anonymization of Data

Legal Effects of Anonymization

The interpretation of anonymization as 'reasonably' irreversible is the one that must prevail, because it is commonly accepted that it is practically impossible to achieve an absolutely irreversible anonymization of data without reducing their content drastically. This would have an undesirable side-effect: the data would have little utility for research or for other legal ends.

Consequently, if personal data has been subjected to anonymization so that the identification of the data subject is not possible by reasonable means, it will be out of the scope of protection of the principles of data protection.

However, if this anonymized data were processed (even in an unreasonable or disproportionate way) and it became possible to identify the data subject again, it would recover the category of personal data and the principles of protection will be applicable to it again.

The Affected Person's Rights: Consent and Information

It has been discussed whether the anonymization process requires the affected person's prior consent or whether it is necessary at least to inform him or her of this process. The second requirement would be demanded for all kinds of personal data, and the first one at least for sensitive data. With regard to this issue we have to consider the requirements of the Directive, in particular the wide definition it gives of 'treatment of personal data', since it includes expressions such as 'modification':

> 'Processing of personal data' ('processing') shall mean any operation or set of operations which is performed upon personal data, whether or not by automatic means, such as collection, recording, organization, storage, adaptation or alteration, retrieval, consultation, use, disclosure by transmission, dissemination or otherwise making available, alignment or combination, blocking, erasure or destruction (Art. 2(b)).

There is no doubt that this paragraph includes the process of anonymization, namely as an act of modification of data (quite apart from later acts of 'disclosure by transmission' and maybe sometimes 'blocking', 'erasure' or 'destruction'), since personal data is subjected to an alteration or mutilation in order to avoid the identification of the person from whom this data originates. The process of anonymization itself is therefore still an act of data processing. This means that, until anonymization is carried out in fact, the data will still be considered as personal data so the principles of data protection will be applicable.[11]

This possibility has been criticized by some authors, because they consider that it would constitute an impossible standard to demand in practice, due to the extraordinary difficulties that it can entail in many cases.[12] Other authors consider that the Directive is incoherent and contradictory on this point, since on the one hand it promotes the protection of privacy and encourages the use of anonymous data, but on the other hand includes the process of anonymization in its definition of 'treatment', prohibiting the anonymization process without the explicit consent of the interested person[13].

However, it has also been argued that anonymization (with or without the aggregation process) does not displace the duty of confidentiality owed to the patients as subjects of the data. This position is based on the risk of identification of the patient despite the anonymization, but also on the fact that the patient would probably not give the information to his or her doctor or pharmacist if he or she knew that it would be transmitted to a company, unless this information were to be used only with his or her consent. In summary, consent continues to be the basic rule when it is sought to use information received in a relationship of trust.[14]

---

[11] See, for example, D. Beyleveld, D. Townend 'When is Personal Data Rendered Anonymous? Interpreting Recital 26 of Directive 95/46/EC', *World Congress on Medical Law*, 2002.

[12] In particular the European Privacy Officers Forum (EPOF), *Comments on Review of the EU Data Protection Directive (Directive 95/46/EC)*, 2002, 4. Available online from: http://europa.eu.int/comm/internal_market/privacy/docs/lawreport/paper/epof_en.pdf (last accessed on 7 June 2004).

[13] Bird & Bird, *Medical Data and Data Protection* (London: Bird & Bird, 2000 and 2001).

[14] For example, as outlined by the UK Competition Commission.

The United Kingdom's Information Commissioner points out some difficulties with anonymous data:[15]

1. Eliminating the name and address is not enough to ensure anonymity. Personal identity can be deduced from non-eliminated data, such as date of birth or postal code.
2. A database controller is not permitted to designate another person to deal with data as his or her representative and to argue that, as this person does not see personal information in itself, he or she is not 'dealing' with data. Such an argument cannot be accepted, because the controller of the data is also responsible for the information used by the data processor.
3. Rare illnesses raise their own problems. It may become impossible for the information to remain anonymous when it concerns a patient with an extremely rare illness.

On the other hand, Recommendation R(97)5 of the Council of Europe considers that every research subject must be informed when research is to be carried out directly by his personal doctor, and that the subject must not have rejected the use of his or her personal data:

> Subject to complementary provisions determined by domestic law, health-care professionals entitled to carry out their own medical research should be able to use the medical data which they hold as long as the data subject has been informed of this possibility and has not objected (Principle 12.3).

As we have seen before, the Directive starts by providing that principles relating to control of data are compatible with its subsequent scientific use, but in Articles 10 and 11, it keeps the obligation of informing the subject. However, it recognizes an exception in the case of data which has not been obtained directly from the data subject: when giving that information is almost impossible or requires a disproportionate effort, this exception is specially applicable to the treatment of personal data with a scientific purpose (Art. 11.2). This means that if giving that information does not require a disproportionate effort, the obligation of giving that information still exists, even if data are to be treated with a scientific purpose. On the other hand, it should be kept in mind that this exception has not been provided when data has been obtained directly from the data subject.

Once data anonymity is totally assured, the obligation of informing the subject and obtaining consent disappears. It is compatible with the principles related to the control of the data that these are used for scientific purposes (Art. 6), but the duty of information to the data subject is retained (Arts. 10 and 11).

An exemption is established: when data have not been obtained directly from the data subject and the provision of such information proves impossible or would

---

[15] See, for example, UK Information Commissioner, *Guidance* (Wilmslow: Information Commissioner, 2001).

involve a disproportionate effort. This exception is especially applicable to the case of processing personal data for scientific purposes (Art. 11.2).

Application to a Real-life Situation: Access to Biological Samples

On this topic we will investigate, on the one hand, the use of samples whose use for such investigation has been foreseen, and on the other hand, the use, with such an end, of samples collected without the initial aim of investigation.[16]

The Use of Samples Whose Use for the Investigation has been Foreseen

In this case, the person's consent is the core point. The consent should refer to both the main act (to take part in a trial, to undergo surgery) and the certain or possible use of the biological sample. For this reason, in the consent forms for an act from which they will obtain samples directly or indirectly (for example a surgical intervention), some possibilities should be contemplated. The consent should cover possibilities such as the following:

1. that they will use the subject's biological samples to carry out genetic analysis for the purposes of an investigation, indicating either which study is contemplated, or that it could happen in the future;
2. that the confidentiality of all the professionals involved in the research will be kept on the results of these analyses and the procedures that have been put in place to ensure that this is the case;
3. that the data or samples will be available for use in other research (indicating which);
4. that the results of the investigation with biological samples from the subject will perhaps give rise to some patentable product or procedure;
5. that the subject rejects any derived economic benefit.

If it is sought to obtain a sample from a person unable to consent or from a deceased person, the general rules on the donation of tissue will be applicable. In the first case the legal representatives will give the consent, as long as such practices are not forbidden in connection with these people. In the second case, the closest relatives of the data subject will give the consent. (For Spain, the Royal Decree 411/1996, of March 1, on the Use and the Banks of Human Tissue with Therapeutic and Scientific Ends—in the case of data obtained from cadavers— although it does not regulate the framework for tissue previously obtained for other ends.)

The requirement of confidentiality is not always a sufficient guarantee of protection for personal data. Because of that, a second approach should be adopted systematically. It consists of establishing procedures to guarantee the

---

[16] See further C. M. Romeo Casabona (2002), n. 4 above, 170.

disassociation of personal data from the biological sample or from any information that could be obtained as a consequence of the analyses that will be carried out. Thus, anonymization of these data would be guaranteed. Although this dissociation procedure should be irreversible, sometimes this kind of anonymization is reversible, for example, when a code or procedure to associate the information with the identity data is included along with the information relating to the sample or the trials (pseudonymization).

Nevertheless, it is not always possible or convenient to have the informed consent of the interested person or to assure the dissociation procedure, as we will confirm next.

Use of Samples Collected Without the Initial Aim of Investigation

With regard to samples already in existence (for example, samples of blood or anatomy, pathological or surgical waste, umbilical cords, etc. stored in a health centre), the problem arises mainly if they are samples from an identified or identifiable subject (reversible anonymization). To have the consent of the relevant subjects is also desirable in these cases. But on many occasions, obtaining consent will not be possible since the subjects have died or their whereabouts are unknown.

Failing the acquisition of this consent, and as an initial measure, it should be attempted to guarantee the dissociation and irreversible anonymization of the personal data. However, this measure may be inconvenient in connection with the methodology of the investigation (e.g. in some epidemic studies). In such a situation the subject's consent extends the scope of use of the personal data, so the consent should be obtained previously. Finally, it can also happen that it is neither possible nor opportune to have the consent of the interested party. In a comparable law (Holland) we do find some concrete rules according to which it can be assessed whether the use of the data is sufficiently justified:[17] that the patient's privacy will not be harmed disproportionately; that the investigation is of general interest; that the investigation is not possible without the nominative personal data; that the affected person has not expressed any objection previously or this objection is not presumable (for example if he or she has already died).

Need for Clarification

The Royal Brompton & Harefield NHS Trust and National Heart & Lung Institute Ethics Committee have issued a clarifying document on the topic: 'Advice to investigators on specific problems in preparing applications for Ethical Review of Research Studies'.[18] There is a Chapter specifically devoted to 'Confidentiality, Pseudonymisation and Anonymisation'. In this Chapter it is stated that:

---

[17]   H. J. J. Leenen, 'Genetics, confidentiality and research' (2000) 7 *European Journal of Health Law*, 365.

[18]   Ethics Committee, The Royal Brompton & Harefield NHS Trust and National Heart & Lung Institute, Royal Brompton Hospital, London.

1. It is most important that subjects who take part in research by donation of specimens should have their confidentiality respected. Immeasurable harm has been done to the confidence of patients and their families in the medical profession by the appearance (whatever the actual state of affairs) of carelessness or inappropriate handling of specimens. This is particularly so where specimens are stored for future use.

2. In some cases, it is clinically necessary or desirable to retain a link between the specimen and the donor, so that for example relevant findings may be reported to the clinician responsible. In such cases, arrangements must be made to ensure strict confidentiality.

The Committee recommends that this be done by coding or the use only of a patient's hospital number, or other equivalent means. This should ideally be done in the clinical context, so that specimens when they reach the laboratory have no identifiers other than the code attached. In this way they are effectively anonymous to the laboratory staff (though not to the clinical team). The Committee characterizes this process as 'pseudonymisation' (or 'staged anonymisation').

It is believed that where relevant clinical information may be derived from specimens, patients will generally appreciate the necessity for the testing and when appropriate, retention of material.

3. In many cases, however, there is no need for the results of laboratory work to be reported to a clinician. There is thus no requirement for personal identifiers of any kind (though clinical characteristics may of course be recorded) and anonymisation in the strict sense presents no disadvantage.

Wherever possible, the Committee recommends that specimens should be labelled in such a way that it is impossible for any person, whether clinician or laboratory worker, ever again to identify any specific individual with the specimen. When all personal links have been permanently broken the specimen can be properly described as 'anonymised'.

Unless there are compelling reasons to the contrary, the Committee expects that *anonymisation* as described in the preceding section will be applied to specimens whether for once only use or for retention in archives or libraries for future use. Only in this way can subjects or their families be assured that no specimen retained is identifiable with them, and confidentiality maintained [emphasis added].

Pseudonymization

Pseudonymization itself does not imply data to be anonymous or to be related to an identifiable person. The answer to the question of to what category of data it belongs should be obtained by consideration of whether it would require unreasonable procedures or disproportionate efforts to achieve the person's identification or not.

However, we should keep in mind that regularly used pseudonymization procedures will result in identifiable data (not anonymous) in most of the cases. Consequently, pseudonymized data will be subject to the principles of protection of personal data.

Pseudonymization could be an adequate means to use in medical or genetic research where it is necessary to have available the identity of the subjects involved in that research, i.e. the anonymization of the data is not recommendable.

In this field, we have to point out the role that can be assumed by ethical committees relating to medical research:

1. They could assume the task of acting as middlemen between investigators and patients in relation to the use of personal data.
2. They could defend and balance the interests of each one of these parties.
3. Members of these committees should accept a legal duty of confidentiality.

Some Provisional Conclusions

General Considerations

As general final considerations it should be kept in mind that medical data and especially genetic data are sensitive personal data, that the principles of protection thereof should be reinforced, including the process of anonymization and of pseudonymization, and that the current European and national authorities and bodies responsible for data protection should be also legally competent for the protection of genetic data as they are for personal data. A specific legal status for biological samples and the genetic testing is thereby needed.

Specific Conclusions Related to Anonymization and Pseudonymization

a. *Anonymization is a relative concept since its irreversibility is not always definite.* It is necessary to assess the difficulty of the process of re-identification. If it is an easy procedure, the protective framework should still be required, since the data would be identifiable. It is irrelevant by whom the re-identification process may be performed.
b. *Personal data which is intended to be subjected to an anonymization process should legally be considered as personal data.* Indeed, when the anonymization has not taken place the data must be considered as personal data in the terms expressed by the Directive. Therefore it is data that should be subjected to all the principles of protection of the Directive. The consent of the interested person should be required in order to subject his or her data to anonymization processes, and he or she should be informed of the use—once the anonymization is made—to which his or her data will later be put. Data could be exempted from this duty of information to the data subject when it is to be used to carry out scientific research (or research with historical or statistical ends) and the execution of the duty is impossible or demands disproportionate effort.
c. *Reversibility of the interested person's identification means reversibility of the legal protection.* Any data that, in principle, does not need to be protected any more under the definition given by the Directive, regains its status as protected from the moment it moves back into the category of personal data again. This

situation exists from the moment when, in spite of having been previously anonymized, the data identifies or allows the identification of a person.

d. *Data which has been pseudonymized is subjected and should continue to be subjected to the system of personal data protection.* Taking into account that pseudonymization is a temporary and reversible system of protection, the data submitted to pseudonymization must be considered data from identifiable persons and must be protected appropriately under the system of protection established for identified persons.

e. *Research ethics committees should have relevant functions* for the protection of the interests of data subjects involved with genetic tests from patients as well as from biological samples, and they:
    -   Could assume the task of acting as middlemen for investigators and patients in relation to the use of personal data.
    -   Could defend and balance the interests of each of these parties.
    -   Members of these committees should be legally bound by a duty of confidentiality.

f. *The need to revise the Directive in relation to the anonymization of data and its legal effects.* In Relation to this issue, three measures would have to be undertaken:
    -   Anonymization and pseudonymization would have to be integrated in the prescriptive part of the Directive.
    -   The legal concept of anonymization would have to be clarified, as well as its legal effects.
    -   The legal status of the process of anonymization should be regulated.

Consideration of Some Cases from the Presented Point of View

1. If A wishes to use data for different purposes than those that were authorized by the data subject after the data has been rendered anonymous: A must comply with the principles of protection with respect to that purpose, including giving information as established in Art. 10.

2. If A discloses information taken from the data to C in a form in which the data subject is not identifiable by C, but A retains the original data in personal form: these data are identifiable data, and consequently the rules for the protection of personal data are in play—A has the duty to provide information to the data subject as well as to obtain his or her consent prior to the transfer of information to C. If C is not aware of the situation he has no duty in relation to the principles of data protection.

3. In case 2 above, if A does not retain the original data in personal form, it is to be considered as anonymized data, but A is affected as described in point one.

Chapter 5

The Scope of Exemptions for Medical Research

Herman Nys

Introduction

In this paper I will assess the scope for exemptions for medical research that Directive 95/46/EC (further called the Privacy Directive or the Directive) allows, highlight any problems of interpretation that the Directive presents, look at the exemptions that the partner countries have made in their laws and present an opinion about whether these are compatible with the aims and objectives of the Directive.

The Directive says nothing on medical research directly.[1] So, it is no surprise that the Directive does not gives a definition of medical research. For this paper the word research should be understood broadly. It means the use of medical (health) data for epidemiology, pharmacovigilance and clinical trials.[2] Research is to be understood as *scientific* research, including both applied scientific research (which means the use of scientific methods without aiming at the creation of new knowledge) and so-called pure scientific research.[3]

Possible Exemptions for Medical Research in the Directive

Article 6(1)(b) (Further Processing for Scientific Purposes)

Article 6 of the Directive contains five principles relating to data quality. According to the second principle (Article 6(1)(b)) Member States shall provide that personal data must be collected for specified, explicit and legitimate purposes and not further processed in a way incompatible with other purposes. *Further processing of data for historical, statistical or scientific purposes shall not be*

---

[1] D. Beyleveld, 'An Overview of Directive 95/46/EC in Relation to Medical Research' in Chapter two of this volume.
[2] S. Callens, 'The Privacy Directive and the Use of Medical Data for Research Purposes' (1995) 2 *European Journal of Health Law* 309.
[3] C. Ploem, *Wetenschapsbeoefening en Belemmerende Privacywetgeving: de Wetgever in Balans?* (Den Haag: Sdu, 2002), 17–18.

considered as incompatible provided that Member States provide appropriate safeguards. These safeguards must in particular rule out the use of the data in support of measures or decisions regarding any particular individual (Recital 29).

Article 6(1)(e) (Storage Longer than Necessary for Scientific Use)

The fifth data quality principle (Article 6(1)(e)) holds that Member States shall provide that personal data must be kept in a form which permits identification of data subjects for no longer than is necessary for the purposes for which the data were collected or for which they are further processed. This requirement is directly in opposition to many research needs for retaining personal data for many years even if later uses cannot be predicted.[4] However, the second sentence of this article states that: *Member States shall lay down appropriate safeguards for personal data stored for longer periods for historical, statistical or scientific use.*

While Article 6(1)(b) uses the term 'scientific purpose', Article 6(1)(e) uses the term 'scientific use'. One may wonder whether this distinction has any importance. The French and the German version of the Directive use in both sub-articles the same notion namely 'fins' (French) and 'Zwecken' (German).

This exemption combined with the previous one is of particular importance for the so-called secondary use of medical data for research purposes. Research on data initially collected for other purposes makes many diverse and important contributions to health. Such research—most of it conducted electronically in databases—includes aspects of epidemiology and public health surveillance, studies of the patterns of occurrence, determinants, and natural history of disease, evaluation of healthcare interventions and services, drug safety surveillance and so on.[5]

Article 8(2)(a) (Processing of Health Data with Explicit Consent)

Article 8 of the Directive holds a number of provisions that could be problematic for health research.[6] Article 8(1) obliges the Member States to prohibit the processing of personal data concerning 'health'. According to Article 8(2)(a) this prohibition does not apply when the data subject has given his or her explicit consent to the processing of such data, except where the laws of the Member State provide that the prohibition may not be lifted by the data subject's giving his or her consent. Article 8(2) offers room for the processing of personal health data for research purposes. Research on health data with the explicit consent of the patient is however considered as very problematic by researchers themselves. For instance, epidemiologists have brought forward a great number of arguments for the benefit

---

[4] W. Lowrance, 'New Laws in Europe' in *Privacy and Health Research* (1997), 2, as available from the webpage: http://aspe.os.dhhs.gov/datacncl/PHR5.htm (last accessed 15 June 2004).

[5] W. Lowrance, *Learning from Experience: Privacy and the Secondary Use of Data in Health Research* (London: The Nuffield Trust, 2002), 1.

[6] W. Lowrance, n. 4 above, 3.

of disregarding the explicit consent rule. It would be impossible, too expensive and too time-consuming to ask for the consent of the patient. Epidemiologists also question whether a patient is really able to consent and if so, if he really is willing to consent. The explicit consent requirement would lead to selective non-response which impairs the value of the research.[7]

Article 8(2)(c) (Processing of Health Data of Persons Incapable of Giving Consent)

Researchers also pointed out that the explicit consent rule would prevent any research with the data of anyone who is unable to give explicit consent, such as children and the mentally disabled. With respect to a data subject who is physically or legally incapable of giving his consent, Article 8(2)(c) provides that the prohibition on processing health data does not apply if it is necessary to protect the vital interests of the data subject or of another person. The scope of this Article is not very clear. Recital 31 adds little to interpret it: 'whereas the processing of personal data must equally be regarded as lawful where it is carried out in order to protect an interest which is essential for the data subject's life'. If research with medical data is 'necessary to protect the vital interests of the data subject or of another person', Article 8(2)(c) allows for the processing of such data. An example could be research on an individual from whom it is not possible to obtain consent and the physical/mental condition that prevents obtaining informed consent is a necessary characteristic of the research population (see Article 26 of the Declaration of Helsinki; according to Article 1 medical research involving human subjects includes research on identifiable data).

Article 8(3) (Processing of Health Data for Health Care Purposes)

According to Article 8(3) the prohibition on processing health data is not applicable where it is required for the purposes of preventive medicine, medical diagnosis, the provision of care or treatment or the management of health care services and where those data are processed by a health professional subject under national law or rules established by national competent bodies, to the obligation of professional secrecy or by another person also subject to an equivalent obligation of secrecy. If medical research may be considered to be a subcategory of preventive medicine, medical diagnosis, the provision of care or treatment or the management of health care services, Article 8(3°) would implicitly contain scope for the exemption of medical research.[8] Lowrance asks 'what kind of health research will be defined as being within the scope of 'preventive medicine, medical diagnosis, the provision of care or treatment or the management of health-care services'? A systematic check should be made against categories of health research as described in Chapter 3 of his 1997 report.[9] Personally I doubt whether Article

---

[7] S. Callens, n. 2 above, 323.

[8] D. Beyleveld, n. 1 above.

[9] W. Lowrance, n. 4 above, 3.

8(3) leaves room for the processing of medical data for health research. Moreover, it is doubtful whether this Article allows for an exemption to the explicit consent rule.

Article 8(4) (Processing of Health Data for Substantial Public Interest)

Subject to the provision of suitable safeguards, Member States may, for reasons of substantial public interest, lay down exemptions in addition to those laid down in Article 8(2) either by national law or by decision of the Supervisory Authority. Recital 34 refers to public health and scientific research as areas where important reasons of public interest may justify derogation from the prohibition of processing of health data. Such derogations have to be notified to the Commission according to Article 8(6). It should be noted that Article 8 of the Directive does not give Member States *carte blanche* in enacting rules to communicate medical data for research purposes without any cooperation of the data subject. According to Callens, such rules would violate Article 8 of the European Convention on Human Rights (ECHR). One can indeed argue that rules allowing the communication of medical data for research purposes without the cooperation of a patient are contrary to the principle of necessity.[10]

Article 11(2) (Exemption from Information to be Given to the Data Subject)

Where data have not been obtained from the data subject (for example, the treating physician communicates medical data to a researcher) Article 11(1) obliges the Member States to provide that the data subject is given the information mentioned in that sub-article. However, according to Article 11(2) this obligation to inform the data subject is not applicable where, in particular for processing for the purpose of scientific research, the provision of such information proves impossible or would involve a disproportionate effort or if recording or disclosure is expressly laid down by law. In these cases Member States shall provide appropriate safeguards.

According to Recital 40, the number of data subjects, the age of the data and any compensatory measures adopted may be taken into consideration in this respect.

Article 13(2) (Exemption from the Data Subject's Right of Access to Data)

Article 12 obliges the Member States to guarantee every data subject the right of access to data relating to him or her. According to Article 13(2) Member States may derogate from Article 12 when data are processed solely for the purposes of scientific research or kept in personal form for a period that does not exceed the period necessary for the sole purpose of creating statistics, provided that the restriction is by a legislative measure, that there is clearly no risk of breaching the

---

[10] S. Callens, n. 2 above, 325.

privacy of the data subject and that adequate legal safeguards are provided (in particular that the data are not used to take measures or decisions regarding any particular individual).

Exemptions for Research in National Laws: Belgium

Further Processing for Scientific Purposes (Directive Art. 6(1)(b))

Article 4 §1,2° of the Belgian law leaves it to the King and states that 'under the terms established by the King after the advice of the Commission for the protection of the privacy, further processing of data for scientific purposes shall not be considered incompatible'. This has been implemented in Chapter 2 of the Royal Decree of 13 February 2001, called: 'further processing of personal data for historical, statistical or scientific purposes'. Neither 'further processing' nor 'scientific purposes' have been defined. However, in the report to the King it is specified that scientific research also means population research with a view to protect and promote public health. Thus, scientific research is understood in a broad sense. Further processing, according to the same report, means that the responsible individual wishes to re-use the data for scientific purposes him or herself or that he or she communicates them to another. The Royal Decree (RD) provides for the following appropriate safeguards:

- *Anonymization.* According to Article 3 the further processing has to be performed in principle on anonymous data that (according to the Report to the King) are by definition not personal data any longer, meaning that their processing does not require any specific guarantees.
- *Coding of data.* If it is not possible to use anonymous data (for example: record linkage or longitudinal research) the researcher has to evaluate whether the research can be done with coded data. In that case Section 2 of Chapter 2 of the RD is applicable. This section provides for the following safeguards. The data are to be coded before further processing for scientific purposes takes place. If the further processing relates to sensitive data (among which are health data), the data subject, before the coding takes place, has to be informed of the scientific purpose of the further processing, the origin of the data, his right to access and correction and his right to oppose the further processing (Art. 14). Article 15 provides for an exemption to this obligation to inform the data subject, based on Article 11(2) of the Directive (see below).
- *Non-coded data.* The further processing of non-coded data is strictly regulated in Section 3 of Chapter 2 of the RD. No distinction is made between health data and other types of sensitive data. According to Article 18, the data subject has to receive precise information on the scientific purposes of the further processing. According to Article 19, he has to give his express consent. Because the Directive does not require written consent but only adequate safeguards, the Government did not follow the suggestion of the Council of State to require a written consent. There was also a practical argument: written

consent would require the individual responsible to write a letter to the data subject who would have to send it back and because he or she has no interest in doing so, he or she would probably not. Article 20 provides for the possibility of an exemption from the obligation to inform the data subject (and implicitly the obligation to obtain consent) based upon Article 11(2) of the Directive (see below).

Storage Longer than Necessary for Scientific Use (Directive Art. 6(1)(e))

Article 4 §1(5°) of the Belgian law provides that, after advice of the Commission for the protection of the privacy, the King has to lay down appropriate safeguards for personal data that are stored for a longer period than necessary for scientific purposes. Chapter 2 of the RD of 13 February, 2001 (containing safeguards in case of further processing for scientific purposes) also implements Article 4 §1(5°) of the Belgian law (Article 2 of the RD).

Processing Health Data with Explicit Consent (Directive Art. 8(2)(a))

Article 7 §1 of the Belgian law prohibits the processing of health-related personal data. According to Art. 7 §2(a) this prohibition is not applicable if the data subject has given his written consent to the processing of these data, on the understanding that the consent may be withdrawn by the data subject at any time. In the case of processing data exclusively on the basis of the written consent of the data subject, the individual responsible for the processing has to previously communicate the reasons for the processing (Article 26 RD). With the requirement of a written consent, the Belgian law is stricter than the Directive that requires explicit consent.[11] This may lead to a different application of the law in the Member States.

The King may lay down in a Decree after advice from the Commission for the Protection of the Privacy in which cases the prohibition of processing health-related data may not be lifted by the written consent of the data subject. Making use of this competence, Article 27 of the RD provides that even with the written consent of the data subject the processing of sensitive data is prohibited when the data subject is in a dependent position towards the individual responsible thus impeding him to give a free consent. This prohibition is lifted when the processing aims to provide an advantage to the data subject.

Processing the Health Data of Persons Incapable of Giving Consent (Directive Article 8(2)(c))

Article 7 §2(f) of the Belgian law provides that the prohibition of processing health data is not applicable if the processing is necessary to protect the vital interests of the data subject or another person, provided that the data subject is physically or legally incapable of giving his or her consent.

---

[11] D. De Bot, Article 7, 5.

Processing Health Data for Health Care Purposes (Directive Art. 8(3))

According to Article 7 §2(j) the prohibition of processing health data is not applicable if processing is necessary for the purposes of preventive medicine or medical diagnosis, the provision of care or treatment to the data subject or to one of his relatives, or the management of health care services operating in the interest of the data subject, and only if those data are processed under the supervision of a health professional.

According to scholars, the explicit consent of the data subject is not required when Article 7 §2(j) is applied.[12] They add that in all these cases the therapeutic relationship between a patient and a health professional is at stake. This is not the case when health data are processed not for the treatment of the data subject himself but for the treatment of one of his relatives. According to the Explanatory Report to the Law, a relative is a genetically related person. This provision is not in accordance with the Directive.[13] It opens the door for non-consensual processing of health data that is not directly in the interest of the data subject such as medical research.

Processing Health Data for Substantial Public Interests (Directive Art. 8(4))

Protection and promotion of public health   According to Article 7 §2(d) the prohibition to process health data is not applicable if processing is necessary for the promotion and protection of public health, including population screening (dépistage in French). This Article can be considered as implementing Article 8(4) of the Directive.[14] In the report to the King preceding the RD of 13 February 2001 it is stated that population screening with a view to protect and promote public health has to be considered as scientific research.[15] If this is the case, one wonders whether Article 7 §2(d) makes much sense. Either public health protection and promotion can be considered as preventive medicine and thus Art. 7 §2(j) applies; or population screening is scientific research and then Art. 7 §4(k) (see below) is applicable.[16] Moreover, no suitable safeguards have been provided by national law up to now.

Scientific research   According to Article 7 §4(k) the prohibition is not applicable if processing is necessary for scientific research and carried out under the conditions established by the King in a Decree agreed upon in the Council of Ministers after advice from the Commission for the Protection of Privacy. This RD is necessary in order to fulfil the requirement of Article 8(4) of the Directive that 'suitable

---

[12] M.-H. Boulanger, S. Callens and S. Brillon 'La Protection des Données à Caractère Personnel....' (2000–2001) *Rev.Dr.Santé*, 334.

[13] M.-H. Boulanger, S. Callens and S. Brillon, n. 12 above.

[14] M.-H. Boulanger, S. Callens and S. Brillon, n. 12 above, 341; they refer (wrongly) to Article 8(3) but they cite Article 8(4).

[15] Report to the King preceding the RD of 13 February 2001, 7846.

[16] M.-H. Boulanger, S. Callens and S. Brillon, n. 12 above, 340.

safeguards' have to be provided for. However, Chapter 2 of the RD of 13 February 2001 only applies to the further processing of health data for scientific purposes. It does not contain any provision regarding the primary processing of health data for scientific purposes.[17] According to Article 8(4) of the Directive, Member States may, either by national law or by a decision of the Supervisory Authority, provide for an exemption. The latter offers no solution in Belgium, because the Belgian Commission for the Protection of Privacy has no decision-making competence. Thus, Article 7 §4(k) remains a dead letter up to now.

Exemptions from Information to be Given to the Data Subject (Directive Art. 11(2))

Further processing of health data for scientific purposes   When health data are further processed in a coded form for scientific purposes, the data subject has to be informed, before the coding takes place, of the scientific purpose and other elements (see above in relation to Article 14 RD 13 February 2001). According to Article 15 this obligation has not to be respected if the provision of such information proves impossible or would involve disproportionate effort and provided the procedure contained in Article 16 has been followed. This Article requires that additional information has to be communicated to the Commission for the Protection of Privacy. This Commission has to make a recommendation on the request not to inform the data subjects within 45 days. This period may be prolonged with another 45 days. If the Commission has not communicated a recommendation after this period has expired, the request is considered to be accepted.

When health data are further processed in a non-coded form, Articles 18 and 19 of the RD of 13 February 2001 require the informed consent of the data subject (see above). According to Article 20 the obligations imposed by Articles 18 and 19 have not to be respected if this proves impossible or would involve disproportionate effort and provided the procedure contained in Article 21 has been followed. This procedure is analogous to Article 16.

Exemption from the Data Subject's Right of Access to Data (Directive Art. 13(2))

According to Article 10 §2 any person has the right to gain knowledge of the personal data that are processed relating to his health either directly or with the assistance of a health professional. If there is apparently no risk of offence against the privacy of the data subject and if the data are not used for taking measures and decisions with regard to an individual data subject, communication may be postponed if the health-related data are processed for purposes of medical scientific research. This is only to the extent that communication would interfere seriously with the research and only postponed until no later than the moment at which the research is terminated. In that case the data subject must have given in advance his

---

[17] D. De Bot, Article 7, 9.

explicit consent to the controller that the personal data may be processed for purposes of medical scientific research and that communication of the personal data relating to him may be postponed for that reason.

According to the Explanatory Report to this Article, this exemption (or better: postponement) from the right of access to data is necessary in order not to make double-blind clinical trials impossible by having to tell a patient to what group he belongs. This Article requires explicit consent but in the light of Article 8(2), this has to be read as a written consent.

Exemptions for Research in National Laws: The Netherlands

Further Processing for Scientific Purposes (Directive Art. 6(1)(b))

Article 9(1) of the Dutch law of 6 July 2000 (the Personal Data Protection Act) provides that personal data shall not be further processed in a way incompatible with the purposes for which they have been obtained. Article 9(2) outlines a series of factors to evaluate whether further processing is 'incompatible'. According to Article 9(3) the further processing of personal data for historical, statistical or scientific purposes shall not be regarded as incompatible where the responsible party has made the necessary arrangements to ensure that the further processing is carried out solely for these purposes. According to the Explanatory Memorandum to the law, necessary arrangements can mean measures of a legal nature such as a code of conduct, a convention, written agreements, but also technical or organizational provisions.[18]

During Parliamentary discussion, Members of the Social Democratic Party have proposed to make a distinction between pure scientific research and commercially financed research (for example, clinical trials). Further processing provided for in Art. 9(3) would only be possible with the former category. The Dutch Government did not accept the proposal because less strict rules should prevail not only for pure scientific research but also for all scientific research. Moreover, as Ploem rightly states, the Directive does not make such a distinction between different categories of research.[19]

Next to this general provision, the Dutch law contains special provisions for the further processing of sensitive data (Art. 23; see below).

Storage Longer than Necessary for Scientific Use (Directive Art. 6(1)(e))

Article 10(2) of the Dutch law provides that personal data may be kept for longer than necessary for achieving the purposes for which they were collected or subsequently processed, where this is for scientific purposes and where the responsible party has made the necessary arrangements to ensure that the data concerned are used solely for these specific purposes.

---

[18] C. Ploem, n. 3 above, 58.
[19] C. Ploem, n. 3 above, 59.

Processing of Health Data with Explicit Consent (Directive Art. 8(2)(a))

Article 16 prohibits the processing of personal data concerning *inter alia* a person's health. According to Article 23(1)(a) the prohibition on processing personal data concerning a person's health does not apply where this is carried out with the explicit consent of the data subject.

Article 23(2) provides for an exemption to the explicit consent rule for the purpose of scientific research (see below).

Even when the data subject has given his explicit consent for the processing of health data (for example, consent for communicating his health data to a researcher) it may be prohibited for the responsible party (the treating physician) to communicate the data. According to Article 9(4) the processing of personal data shall not take place where this is precluded by an obligation of confidentiality by virtue of office, profession or legal provision. According to Hooghiemstra, this disposition means that processing of health data is prohibited when medical professional secrecy so demands. Medical professional secrecy does act as a 'correction' to the general processing rules of the Personal Data Protection Law. In this way, criminal, disciplinary and civil regulations for medical confidentiality are incorporated in general data protection law.[20]

Article 21(4) of the Dutch law contains a very strict provision for the processing of genetic data. It states that 'personal data concerning inherited characteristics may only be processed, where this processing takes place with respect to the data subject from whom the data concerned have been obtained, unless a) a serious medical interest prevails, or b) the processing is necessary for the purpose of scientific research or statistics'. According to Hooghiemstra this provision means that, even with the consent of the data subject, genetic data may not be processed with respect to another person than the data subject him or herself, except in the two cases mentioned in Article 21(4) (a) and (b).[21]

Processing of Health Data of Persons Incapable of Giving Consent (Directive Art. 8(2)(c))

The Dutch law does not contain an explicit provision implementing Article 8(2)(c) of the Directive.

Processing of Health Data for Health Care Purposes (Directive Art. 8(3))

According to Article 21(1)(a) the prohibition on processing personal data concerning a person's health does not apply where the processing is carried out by medical professionals, healthcare institutions of facilities or social services,

---

[20] T. Hooghiemstra, 'The Implementation of Directive 95/46/EC in the Netherlands, with Special Regard to Medical Data' (2002) 9 *European Journal of Health Law*, 225; see also M. C. Ploem, 'Medical Research and Informational Privacy' 17 *Medicine and Law,* 294–295.

[21] T. Hooghiemstra, n. 20 above, 222; see also C. Ploem, n. 20 above, 60; and n. 3 above.

provided that this is necessary for the proper treatment and care of the data subject or for the administration of the institution or professional practice concerned.

In the Dutch literature no indications can be found that this provision also applies to medical research.[22]

Processing of Health Data for Substantial Public Interests (Directive Art. 8(4))

An important public interest According to Article 23(1)(e), the prohibition on processing personal data concerning *inter alia* a person's health does not apply where this is necessary with a view to an important public interest, where appropriate guarantees have been put in place to protect individual privacy and this is provided by law or else the Data Protection Commission has granted an exemption. When granting an exemption, the Commission can impose rules and restrictions. According to Article 23(3) such processing must be notified to the European Commission.

For the purpose of scientific research that serves a public interest According to Article 23(2) the prohibition on the processing of personal data concerning *inter alia* a person's health for the purpose of scientific research does not apply where:

a. the research serves a public interest;
b. the processing is necessary for the research concerned;
c. it appears to be impossible or would involve a disproportionate effort to ask for express consent, and
d. sufficient guarantees are provided to ensure that the processing does not adversely affect the individual privacy of the data subject to a disproportionate extent.

Although this provision may be considered as giving implementation to Article 8(4) of the Directive, notification to the Commission is not mentioned here.

Article 23(2) has a broad field of application. It applies when health data are collected primarily with a scientific purpose but it is also applicable in the case of further processing for scientific purposes of health data originally processed for other purposes and/or stored longer.[23]

With regard to the third condition (exemption from asking express consent), Hooghiemstra states that the patient has influence in relation to the use of medical data for research purposes as far as it would involve a proportionate effort for the researcher to ask for express consent. The general rule in the Data Protection Law

---

[22] See however Canadian Institutes of Health Research, *Selected International Legal Norms on the Protection of Personal Information in Health Research* (December 2001), 45, which states that the Dutch Personal Data Protection Law outlines some non-consensual data processing for health and scientific research and where Article 21(1)a is cited as an example of this—in my opinion, wrongly.

[23] C. Ploem, n. 3 above, 61.

does not even give the patient the right to object.[24] However, in addition to the general rule of Article 23 Data Protection Law, the Netherlands have specific regulations with regard to the communication of health data by the treating physician to researchers (further processing). These are found in Articles 457 and 458 of the Medical Treatment Contracts Act (also called the Patients' Rights Act). According to Article 457, medical data can only be communicated to a researcher with the consent of the patient. Article 458 contains two exceptions to this rule. First, communication of personal data is allowed provided that the research will be carried out without unreasonably violating the patient's right to privacy. Secondly, communication of encoded data is allowed without the patient's consent if asking consent is not possible in view of the nature and the purpose of the research. In both cases, the communication is only allowed if the research project cannot be done with non-identifiable data and if the patient has not objected expressly to the communication. The latter condition implies that the person concerned has to be informed that his data will be communicated for scientific purposes and that he can oppose this communication.[25]

Detailed rules have been laid down by the research community and were published in a Code of Conduct for Health Research. This Code makes a distinction between the use of non-identifiable, identifiable but coded data and other identifiable data. The Code takes into account the rules of both the Patients' Rights Act and the Data Protection Act and has been approved by the Data Protection Authority.[26]

For the purpose of scientific research with genetic data   According to Article 21(4), genetic data (data concerning inherited characteristics) may only be processed where this processing takes place with respect to the data subject from whom the data concerned have been obtained. Even with the explicit consent of the data subject, processing of such data with respect to another person is prohibited unless the processing is necessary for the purpose of scientific research (Article 21(4)(b)). This Article continues, stating that in this case Article 23(1)(a) is applicable which means that the express consent for the processing of genetic data for the purpose of scientific research is required. However, Article 21(4)(b) also refers to Art. 23(2) which means that if all the conditions of this Article are fulfilled an exemption from the explicit consent is possible. According to the Data Protection Act the data subject may not even object. However, also in the case of genetic data the Patients' Rights Act, as *lex specialis*, prevails (see above).

Exemption from Information to be Given to the Data Subject (Directive Art. 11(2))

According to Article 34(4) the obligation contained in Art. 34(1) to give information to the data subject where the data are not obtained from the data subject does not apply if it appears to be impossible or would involve a

---

[24] T. Hooghiemstra, n. 20 above, 224.
[25] C. Ploem, n. 3 above, 66.
[26] T. Hooghiemstra, n. 20 above, 224.

disproportionate effort to provide that information. However, in the case of further processing for scientific purposes, Art. 44(1) is applicable and not Article 34(4).[27] Article 44 provides that where processing is carried out by institutions or services for the purposes of scientific research and the necessary arrangements have been made to ensure that the personal data can only be used for scientific purposes, the responsible party is not required to provide the information referred to in Article 34. The Explanatory Report expressly refers to Article 11(2) of the Directive.[28]

Exemption from the Data Subject's Rights of Access to Data (Directive Art. 13(2))

Article 44 provides that where processing is carried out by institutions or services for the purposes of scientific research and the necessary arrangements have been made to ensure that the personal data can only be used for scientific purposes, the responsible party is not required to comply with a request referred to in Article 35. That Article gives a data subject the right to request the responsible party to inform him or her as to whether personal data relating to him or her are being processed (right to access). The explanatory report expressly refers to Art. 13(2) of the Directive.[29]

Exemptions for Research in National Laws: Norway

Further Processing for Scientific Purposes (Directive Art. 6(1)(b))

Article 11(c) of the Norwegian Act of 14 April 2000 Relating to the Processing of Personal Data (basic requirements for the processing of personal data) provides that the controller shall ensure that personal data which are processed are not used subsequently for purposes that are incompatible with the original purpose of the collection, *without the consent of the data subject.*

According to the last sentence of the same Article, the subsequent processing of personal data for scientific purposes is not deemed to be incompatible with the original purposes of the collection of the data, if the public interest in the processing being carried out clearly exceeds the disadvantages this may entail for natural persons.

Storage Longer than Necessary for Scientific Use (Directive Art. 6(1)(e))

According to Article 28, the controller shall not store personal data longer than is necessary to carry out the purpose of the processing.

---

[27] C. Ploem, n. 3 above, 61, who cites the Explanatory Report.
[28] C. Ploem, n. 3 above, 62. According to Ploem it is not clear whether individual researchers may invoke Article 44. If this would not be the case, the question arises whether they can invoke Article 34(4).
[29] C. Ploem, n. 3 above, 62.

The controller may, notwithstanding the first paragraph, store personal data for scientific purposes if the public interest in the data being stored clearly exceeds the disadvantages this may entail for the person concerned. In this case, the controller shall ensure that the data are not stored in ways which make it possible to identify the data subject for longer than necessary.

Processing of Data with Explicit Consent (Directive Art. 8(2)(a))

Sensitive personal data (defined in Article 2(8)(c) as information relating to health) may according to Article 9 only be processed if the processing satisfies one of the conditions set out in Article 8 (among which is the protection of the vital interests of the data subject and the performance of a task in the public interest) *and* the data subject consents to the processing.

Two remarks: First, consent is required, not explicit or written consent. The definition of consent is in Article 2(7): it is a free, specific and informed declaration by the data subject. Secondly, consent on its own is not a sufficient condition to process health data. Engelschion seems to imply that consent is a sufficient condition: 'health data may, however, only be processed if the processing also satisfies one of the conditions set out in Article 9 in the Personal Data Act. If the processing is based on consent or a statutory authority, the section has no independent position. If the processing is based on the six mentioned exceptions in Article 8, Section 9 sets up *additional requirements*' (my emphasis).[30]

If the data subject gives his or her consent thereto, the principle of confidentiality will cease to apply to the extent of the consent given. Even if the data subject has consented, the controller must decide on the basis of his or her opinion on what is best for the patient and if he or she is in a condition to be able to consent.[31]

In this respect also the Act Relating to the Application of Biotechnology in Medicine applies. This Act prohibits one to request, receive, possess or make use of genetic information resulting from a genetic test on any person. It is also prohibited to ask whether a genetic test has been carried out. This is a prohibition, as in Article 8 Directive, which may not be lifted by the data subject's consent being given.[32]

Processing of Health Data of Persons Incapable of Giving Consent (Directive Art. 8(2)(c))

According to Article 9(c) health data may be processed if one of the conditions set out in Article 8 is satisfied (cf. c) and the processing is necessary to protect the

---

[30] S. Engelschion, 'The Implementation of Directive 95/46 in Norway, Especially with Regard to Medical Data' (2002) 9 *European Journal of Health Law*, 192.
[31] S. Engelschion, n. 30 above, 199.
[32] S. Engelschion, n. 30 above, 196.

vital interest of a person and the data subject is incapable of giving his or her consent.

Processing of Health Data for Health Care Purposes (Directive Art. 8(3))

According to Article 9(g) health data may be processed if one of the conditions set out in Article 8 is satisfied and the processing is necessary for the purposes of preventive medicine, medical diagnosis, the provision of care or treatment or the management of health care services and where the data are processed by health professionals subject to the obligation of professional secrecy.

Processing of Health Data for Substantive Public Interests (Directive Art. 8(4))

For scientific purposes with important public interests According to Article 9(h) health data may be processed if one of the conditions set out in Article 8 is satisfied, the processing is necessary for scientific purposes and the public interest in such processing being carried out clearly exceeds the disadvantages it might entail for the natural person. The requirement of necessity is quite strict and implies that the processing must be necessary without the consent from the individual.[33]

For important public interests According to the last sentence of Article 9, the Data Inspectorate may decide that sensitive personal data may also be processed in other cases if this is warranted by important public interests and steps are taken to protect the interests of the data subject.

Exemption from Information to be Given to the Data Subject (Directive Art. 11(2))

A controller who collects personal data from persons other than the data subject shall, according to Article 20 on his own initiative inform the data subject of which data are being collected. However, the data subject is not entitled to notification if (b) notification is impossible or disproportionately difficult.

Exemption from the Data Subject's Right of Access to Data (Directive Art. 13(2))

The right of access provided for in Article 18 shall not apply if the personal data are being processed exclusively for scientific purposes and the processing will have no direct significance for the data subject (last sentence of Article 18).

Moreover, the right to access pursuant to Article 18 and the obligation to provide information pursuant to Article 19 do not encompass data which must be regarded as inadvisable for the data subject to gain knowledge of, out of consideration for the health of the person concerned or for the relationship to persons close to the person concerned.

---

[33] S. Engelschion, n. 30 above, 193.

Exemptions for Research in National Laws: Denmark

Further Processing for Scientific Purposes (Directive Art. 6(1)(b))

According to Article 5(2) of the Act on Processing of Personal Data, the collection of data shall take place for specified explicit and legitimate purposes and they shall not be further processed in a way incompatible with these purposes. Further processing of data, which takes place exclusively for scientific purposes, shall not be considered incompatible with the purposes for which the data were collected.

Storage Longer than Necessary for Scientific Use (Directive Art. 6(1)(e))

According to Article 5(5) the data collected may not be kept in a form which makes it possible to identify the data subject for a longer period than is necessary for the purposes for which the data are processed.

Processing of Health Data with Explicit Consent (Directive Art. 8(2)(a))

According to Article 7(1) no processing may take place of personal data concerning health. This provision shall not apply where the data subject has given his explicit consent to the processing of such data (Article 7(2)(1)).

According to Article 35(1) a data subject may at any time object in relation to the controller to the processing of data relating to him or her. Where the objection is justified the processing may no longer involve those data.

According to Article 38 the data subject may withdraw his or her consent.

Processing of Health Data of Persons Incapable of Giving Consent (Directive Art. 8(2)(c))

Processing of health data is not prohibited when processing is necessary to protect the vital interests of the data subject or of another person where the person concerned is physically or legally incapable of giving his or her consent (Art. 7(2)(2)).

Processing of Health Data for Health Care Purposes (Directive Art. 8(2)(3))

Processing of health data is not prohibited where processing of the data is required for the purposes of preventive medicine, medical diagnosis, the provision of care or treatment or the management of health care services, and where those data are processed by a health professional subject to a statutory obligation of professional secrecy (Article 7(5)).

Processing of Health Data for Substantial Public Interest (Directive Art. 8(4))

Processing for reasons of substantial public interest According to Article 7(7) exemptions may further be laid down from the prohibition to process health data where the processing of data takes place for reasons of substantial public interests. The Supervisory Authority shall give its authorization in such cases and the processing may be made subject to specific conditions. The Supervisory Authority shall notify the Commission of any derogation.

Processing for scientific studies of significant social importance According to Article 10(1), health data may be processed where the processing is carried out for the sole purpose of carrying out scientific studies of significant social importance and where such processing is necessary in order to carry out these studies. These data may not subsequently be processed for other than statistical or scientific purposes (Article 10(2)). These data may only be disclosed to a third party with the authorization of the Supervisory Authority, which may lay down more detailed conditions concerning the disclosure (Article 10(3)).

Exemption from Information to be Given to the Data Subject (Directive Art. 11(2))

According to Article 29(3) the rules laid down in Article 29(1) (this Article obliges the controller, where the data have not been obtained from the data subject, to provide information to the data subject) shall not apply where the provision of such information to the data subject proves impossible or would involve a disproportionate effort.

Moreover, Article 29(1) shall not apply if the data subject's interest in obtaining this information is found to be overridden by vital private interests, including the interests of the data subject him or herself (Article 30(1)).

Exemption from the Data Subject's Rights of Access to Data (Directive Art. 13(2))

The data subject's right of access to data provided for in Article 31(1) shall not apply where data are processed solely for scientific purposes or kept in personal form for a period which does not exceed the period necessary for the sole purpose of creating statistics.

Two Remarkable Provisions in the Danish Act

Article 2(1) of the Danish Data Protection Act provides that any rules on the processing of personal data in other legislation, which give the data subject a better legal protection, shall take precedence over the rules laid down in this Act. Is the duty to medical professional secrecy a rule on the processing of personal data and does it provide a better legal protection?

According to Article 2(2), the Act shall not apply where this will be in violation of the freedom of information and expression cf. Article 10 of the European Convention for the Protection of Human Rights and Fundamental Freedoms.

Chapter 6

The Duty to Provide Information to the Data Subject: Articles 10 and 11 of Directive 95/46/EC

Deryck Beyleveld*

Introduction

According to Article 10 of Directive 95/46/EC, which applies 'in cases of collection of data from the data subject';

> Member States shall provide that the controller or his representative must provide a data subject from whom data relating to himself are collected with at least the following information, except where he already has it:
>
> (a)   the identity of the controller and of his representative, if any;
> (b)   the purpose of the processing for which the data are intended;
> (c)   any further information such as:
>   -   the recipients or categories of recipients of the data,
>   -   whether replies to the questions are obligatory or voluntary, as well as the possible consequences of failure to reply,
>   -   the existence of the right of access and the right to rectify the data concerning him,
>
> in so far as such further information is necessary, having regard to the specific circumstances in which the data are collected, to guarantee fair processing in respect of the data subject.

According to Article 11(1),

> *Where the data have not been obtained from the data subject* [my emphasis], Member States shall provide that the controller or his representative must at the time of undertaking the recording of personal data or if a disclosure to a third party is envisaged, no later than the time when the data are first disclosed provide the data subject with at least the following information, except when he already has it:

---

* Professor of Jurisprudence, Faculty of Law, University of Sheffield, Director of the Sheffield Institute of Biotechnological Law and Ethics (SIBLE), Co-ordinator of PRIVIREAL.

(a)   the identity of the controller and of his representative, if any;
(b)   the purpose of the processing;
(c)   any further information such as
-   the categories of data concerned,
-   the recipients or categories of recipients,
-   the existence of the right of access and the right to rectify the data concerning him,

in so far as such further information is necessary, having regard to the specific circumstances in which the data are collected, to guarantee fair processing in respect of the data subject.

That the provision of 'further information' referred to in Articles 10 and 11(1) (both specified and unspecified) is for the purpose of fair processing links these provisions to the principle of data protection laid down in Article 6(1)(a), according to which 'Member States shall provide that personal data must be . . . processed fairly and lawfully'.[1]

This linkage is entirely appropriate, because the provision of information to the data subject prescribed by Articles 10 and 11(1) is of central importance to the objective of the Directive, which is to ensure an adequate level of protection of fundamental rights and freedoms (in particular, the right to privacy) of natural persons with respect to the processing of personal data in all Member States. This is in order that Member States should have no legitimate excuse to restrict or prohibit the free flow of personal data between themselves on the grounds that other Member States do not provide adequate protection for fundamental rights and freedoms (see Article 1 and Recitals 1 to 10, especially Recitals 7 to 10).

The right to privacy referred to here is, of course, that provided by Article 8 of the European Convention on Human Rights (ECHR) as a fundamental principle of EC law (see Recital 10). In line with this right, the Directive:

1.   prohibits the processing of sensitive personal data (Article 8(1)), unless certain conditions are satisfied (Articles 8(2)–(7)), which, in principle, reflect (*inter alia*) the need for a justification to be provided for a breach of privacy in the terms of Article 8(2) ECHR.[2] Although the explicit consent of the data subject is only one of the conditions provided by Article 8(2)–(7) of the Directive for the lifting of the prohibition of Article 8(1) of the Directive, it seems to me that this implies (at least in the case of sensitive personal data) that explicit consent must be obtained unless a justification for not doing so exists in the terms of Article 8(2) ECHR;[3]

---

[1] See also Recital 38, which states that the provision of all the Article 10 and 11(1) information is necessary for processing to be fair.

[2] Because the Directive aims to protect fundamental rights and freedoms generally (see Article 1(1)), and not merely privacy, not only Article 8 ECHR is relevant.

[3] This is because the European Court of Human Rights has held in *M.S v. Sweden* [1997] 28 *EHRR* 313, paragraphs 34–35 that to process/disclose sensitive personal data without the subject's consent (even where the information is processed/disclosed to persons acting under

2. provides the data subject with a right:
    -   to find out from the data controller about whether or not personal data relating to him or her is being processed, for which purposes, and to whom it is being disclosed, and about the source of this data (see Article 12(a));
    -   to be told of the logic behind any automatic processing of such data (see Article 12(a));
    -   to secure the rectification, erasure or blocking of processing that does not comply with the provisions of the Directive (see Article 12(b));
    -   to object on compelling legitimate grounds to the processing of personal data relating to the data subject (see Article 14(a));
    -   to object to the use of personal data relating to the data subject being used for purposes of direct marketing (see Article 14(b)); and
    -   not to be subject to any decision that significantly affects the data subject that is based solely on automatic processing of personal data relating to the data subject (see Article 15(1)).

Bearing in mind that Article 2(h) defines 'consent' as 'any freely given specific and informed indication' by which the data subject signifies agreement, possession of the information required to be provided by Articles 10 and 11(1) is clearly necessary for the data subject to give a valid consent. Equally, possession of this information is necessary for the data subject to be able to exercise the rights provided by Articles 12, 14 and 15 of the Directive. Thus, to withhold Articles 10 and 11(1) information from the data subject, is to interfere with the rights of the data subject provided by Articles 12, 14 and 15 and with his or her right to privacy in so far as this requires the data subject to be granted the right to consent to the use of his or her personal data.

In essence, logic and fairness both demand that if a right is granted to someone ('Y') to something ('X') then Y must be granted a right to any necessary means to X as well. For this reason, a right to the provision of the information prescribed or indicated in Articles 10 and 11(1) is implied by Articles 7, 8, 12, 14 and 15. While the Directive does not explicitly present the provision of the Article 10 and Article 11(1) information as a right of the data subject, but as a duty of the data controller, because of the general correlativity of claim rights of a person with duties of others, to present this information provision as a duty of the controller is not incompatible with it being a right of the data subject. However, to present it as a duty of the data controller is appropriate, simply because whether or not the data subject will obtain any knowledge of relevant processing will be very much in the hands of others, especially, the data controller.

---

a duty of confidence) is an interference with the right provided by Article 8(1) ECHR (even though the Court went on to say that in the circumstances of the case the interference was justified under Article 8(2) ECHR). Under Article 8(2) ECHR, a breach of Article 8(1) can only be justified if necessary and proportionate for the legitimate purposes laid down in Article 8(2) and in accordance with the law.

If proper implementation of Articles 10 and 11(1) is crucial to the achievement of the Directive's objectives, then in order to assess the adequacy of national provisions pursuant to the Directive, it is necessary:

1. to determine what powers are granted to Member States to exempt data controllers from the duty to provide Articles 10 and 11(1) information to the data subject; and
2. to assess the adequacy of safeguards put in place to accompany any exemptions from this duty.

In this paper, I argue that (unless Article 13 of the Directive is appealed to), in order to implement Article 10, an unqualified duty must be placed on data controllers. Article 10 does not, however, explicitly differentiate cases where data are currently being obtained from the data subject and cases where data were previously obtained from the data subject and the data controller now wishes to make disclosures or process for purposes that were not envisaged at the time of obtaining.[4] Now, if Article 10 covers *all* cases where data are being, or were, collected from the data subject, this implies that it will be necessary for the data controller to go back to the data subject to provide the data subject with information if processing that was not anticipated at the time of collection is to be permitted (unless an exemption is provided via Article 13). On the other hand, if Article 10 only covers cases where data are being collected from the data subject, then unanticipated future processing by a data controller who obtains personal data from the data subject might seem not to be covered by the Directive (with the implication that Member States may regulate this as they wish). I suggest, however, that the possible 'missing case' is covered by Recitals 39 and 40, which suggests a duty in relation to unanticipated processing where data were obtained from the data subject that is conditional in the same way as cases falling under Article 11(1) (where data were not obtained from the data subject by the data controller). Consequently, I argue while Member States may treat all cases where data are/were collected from the data subject under Article 10, the best interpretation requires 'the missing case' to be dealt with in terms of Recitals 39 and 40. I argue, too, that if Article 13 is appealed to modify this picture then reference to Article 13 (or the conditions it refers to) must be made explicitly in legislation, because Article 28(4) requires Member States to empower anyone to hear claims for checks on the lawfulness of processing that is pursuant to the use of Article 13 to restrict the provisions of Articles 10 and 11(1).

As concerns the issue of adequate safeguards, I argue, principally, that if national implementing measures are to meet the objectives of the Directive, then any processing under legitimate exemptions from the duties prescribed by Articles 10 and 11(1) should be treated as processing likely to pose specific risks to the fundamental rights and freedoms of the data subject, and should, hence, be subjected to prior checking by the Supervisory Authority (or an independent Data

---

[4] While Article 11(1) does cover unanticipated disclosures, it only governs cases where data were not obtained from the data subject.

Protection Official acting under the guidance of the Supervisory Authority), in relation to which I make a few suggestions about the criteria that are relevant in such checks.

Finally, to illustrate my analysis, I examine the UK's implementation of the duty to provide information to the data subject under Articles 10 and 11 of the Directive, and draw attention to what I consider to be its inadequacies. I also examine the effect of this in relation to Section 60 of the Health and Social Care Act 2001 and The Health Service (Control of Patient Information) Regulations 2002 made under Section 60, because these have features that are arguably unlawful in relation to Article 10 of the Directive, in particular, a fact which is obscured by the inadequacies of the UK's implementation.

Powers to Exempt from Article 10 and Article 11(1)

According to Article 11(2),

> Paragraph 1 shall not apply where, in particular for processing for statistical purposes or for the purposes of historical or scientific research, the provision of such information proves impossible or would involve a disproportionate effort or if recording or disclosure is expressly laid down by law. In these cases Member States shall provide appropriate safeguards.

There is no parallel exemption provided from Article 10. However, Article 13(1) provides that

> Member States may adopt legislative measures to restrict the scope of the obligations and rights provided for in Articles 6(1), 10, 11(1), 12 and 21 when such a restriction constitutes a necessary measure to safeguard:
> (a) national security;
> (b) defence;
> (c) public security;
> (d) the prevention, investigation, detection and prosecution of criminal offences, or of breaches of ethics for regulated professions;
> (e) an important economic or financial interest of a Member State or of the European Union, including monetary, budgetary and taxation matters;
> (f) a monitoring, inspection or regulatory function connected, even occasionally, with the exercise of official authority in cases referred to in (c), (d) and (e);
> (g) the protection of the data subject or of the rights and freedoms of others.

This could possibly apply to medical research. For example, there might be cases where medical research to develop biological weapons or, more plausibly, to defend against them, could be necessary for (a)–(c). Provision (d) could be appealed to in relation to the investigation of fraud in medical research. Medical research is also, arguably, an important economic or financial interest of the Member States. In so far as (c)–(e) apply, (f) applies. And, at least in principle, medical research could be argued to be something that individuals have a right to that can be placed in the balance with data protection rights of the data subject.

This said, two things must be borne in mind. First, any restrictions must be necessary to safeguard the interests concerned, and this implies that they will generally have to be applied on a case by case basis, in consequence of which it is arguable that they may not be applied to medical research generically. Secondly, Article 28(4) specifies that

> Each supervisory authority shall, in particular, hear claims for checks on the lawfulness of data processing lodged by any person when the national provisions adopted pursuant to Article 13 of this Directive apply. The person shall at any rate be informed that a check has taken place.

Matters are further complicated by the fact that what situations are covered by Articles 10 and 11(1), respectively, are open to interpretation. Does Article 10 apply to all controllers who have collected personal data from the data subject? Or does Article 10 only apply to controllers at the point at which they are collecting data from the data subject? If the former, then Member States must (unless they restrict Article 10 via appeal to Article 13(1)) provide that a data controller who has collected personal data from the data subject for specified purposes Y without envisaging its use for purposes Z, but subsequently wishes to use the data for Z, must go back to the data subject to inform of this processing, and may not appeal to any disproportionate effort or impossibility in doing so to avoid having to do so, which might seem unreasonable. On the other hand, if the latter, then the case described does not seem to fall under the ambit of either Article 10 or Article 11(1), because everything under Article 11(1) explicitly applies only where the controller did not obtain the data from the data subject.

However, Recitals 38–40 might be of assistance here. Recital 38 states that, in order for processing to be fair,

> the data subject must be in a position to learn of the existence of a processing operation, and, where data are collected from him, must be given accurate and full information, bearing in mind the circumstances of the collection.

Recital 39 then refers to two cases—processing of data that the controller did not collect from the data subject (which is covered by Article 11(1)), and disclosures that were 'not anticipated at the time the data were collected from the data subject' (which is not covered explicitly by either Article 10 or Article 11(1)), and says of both cases that the 'data subject should be informed when the data are recorded or at the latest when the data are first disclosed to a third party'. However, Recital 40 then specifies that it is not necessary for 'this obligation' to be imposed when conditions apply that are essentially those specified in Article 11(2).

What does 'this obligation' refer to? One possibility is that it refers to the cases covered by both Recital 38 and Recital 39. However, if this is so, then Article 10 should have two parts. There should be an Article 10(1), which specifies the obligation, and an Article 10(2), which provides an exemption from Article 10(1) with the same content as Article 11(2). That Article 10 does not have this structure is, I believe, conclusive that Recital 40 refers only to Recital 39 (and not to either Recital 38 or to Article 10). On this basis, Article 10 should be taken to apply only at the point at which data are being collected from the data subject, and the missing case of unanticipated disclosures where the data were collected from the data subject is to be dealt with on Article 11(2) lines by a direct appeal to Recitals 39 and 40 as free-standing provisions. It is quite possible that Article 11(1) was meant to convey this; but its heading unambiguously limits the application of Article 11(1) itself to cases where the information was not collected from the data subject.

To this, it might be objected that Recitals do not *in themselves* have any legally binding force,[5] and that they can only have any force in relation to interpreting Articles in a Directive. Since there is no Article that explicitly covers unanticipated disclosures where data were collected from the data subject, Recitals 39 and 40 cannot be appealed to in order to cover the case of unanticipated disclosures where data were collected from the data subject.

However, in response to this, at least two things can be said. First, even if Recitals have no free-standing legally binding force, this does not prevent them from having a persuasive force, meaning by this that, provided that they do not contradict an Article, they *may*, at least, be appealed to in order to cover cases not covered by the Articles. Secondly, since the main purpose of Recitals is to provide reasons for the Articles, on condition, again, that the Recitals do not contradict the Articles, a teleological approach to the interpretation of a Directive surely permits free-standing use of Recitals to be made where the Articles do not cover important scenarios that are covered by the Recitals.[6]

However, whether or not we can make this response turns on how we choose to interpret Article 10. If we say that Article 10 covers all cases where data were collected from the data subject (thus including data controllers who wish to make disclosures that they did not anticipate or envisage at the time of collection), then Article 10 actually contradicts part of Recital 39 read with Recital 40, and we cannot make this response. On the other hand, if we say that Article 10 only applies at the point of data collection, then there is no contradiction when Recital 39 is read with Recital 40, and we can make this response.

I suggest that the latter is at least a possible reading on purely textual considerations. If so, then I suggest that the use of teleological principles that are well established in EC law[7] also suggests that it is the preferable reading. Consequently, I suggest that using Recital 39 read with Recital 40 to cover

---

[5] See *Gunnar Nilsson, Per Olav Hagelgren, Solweig Arrborn, Agriculture* (Case C–162/97), judgment of 19 November 1998, paragraph 54 of the judgment. However, it is arguable that this is restricted to cases where there is a conflict between a Recital and an Article of a Directive.

[6] For a detailed discussion of the ECJ's treatment of Recitals—see Deryck Beyleveld 'Why Recital 26 of Directive 98/44/EC Should be Implemented in National Law' (2000) 4 *Intellectual Property Quarterly* 1–26.

[7] See L. N. Brown and T. Kennedy, *The Court of Justice of the European Communities* (4th edn., London: Sweet and Maxwell, 1994), 316.

unanticipated disclosures where data were obtained from the data subject is at least permissible, and, indeed, the best reading of the Directive.

Even this, however, does not cover the case of processing for unanticipated purposes when data were collected from the data subject. Nevertheless, if it is permissible to provide an Article 11(2) type exemption for unanticipated disclosures where data were collected from the data subject by appealing to Recital 39 read with Recital 40, then it is surely also permissible to provide such an exemption for processing for unanticipated purposes when data were collected from the data subject.

Finally, it should be noted that both Article 10 and Article 11(1) have an internal restriction to the effect that the additional information referred to in Articles 10(c) and 11(1)(c) need only be provided in so far as necessary to guarantee fair processing. This implies that there might be circumstances in which the provision of such additional information might not be necessary for fairness (and, hence, not obligatory). Consequently, it is open to Member States to make the provision of this additional information in Article 10 subject to proportionality, or practicability, or an equivalent condition. However, it must not be overlooked that this qualification applies only to the additional information of Articles 10(c) (and 11(1)(c)) and not to the information required to be provided by Articles 10(a) and 10(b) (and 11(1)(a) and 11(1)(b)).

The Question of Adequate Safeguards

If there is to be exemption from Article 11(1), then Article 11(2) specifies that Member States must provide appropriate safeguards. The Directive does not, however, specify explicitly or directly what the nature of appropriate safeguards might be. Does this mean that it is entirely at the discretion of the Member States to determine what constitutes appropriate safeguards; or can we infer at least some requirements from the Directive as a whole on the basis of which interpretations of individual Member States could, in principle, be held to be untenable?

The objective of the Directive must constitute the focal point for any specification of appropriate or adequate safeguards. Since the objective of the Directive is to protect fundamental rights and freedoms, in particular privacy, appropriate safeguards must be appropriate measures to protect against breaches of these rights and freedoms. According to standard human rights thinking, in order for there to be a justification for interference with a right, the interference must be necessary for an overriding value, must not be more extensive than necessary, and must be sanctioned by law. In relation to this, appropriate safeguards must be appropriate measures designed to ensure that these conditions are satisfied.

While the Directive does not specify such measures in relation to Article 11(2), it is fairly expansive in relation to exemptions from the duty to notify the Supervisory Authority. When notification is required under Article 18, Article 19(1) requires Member States to provide that the data controller must provide the Supervisory Authority with at least:

(a) the name and address of the controller and of his representative, if any;
(b) the purpose or purposes of the processing;
(c) a description of the category or categories of data subject and of the data or categories of data relating to them;
(d) the recipients or categories of recipient to whom the data might be disclosed;
(e) proposed transfers of data to third countries;
(f) a general description allowing a preliminary assessment to be made of the appropriateness of the measures taken pursuant to Article 17 to ensure security of processing.

This is not dissimilar to the information required to be given to the data subject under Articles 10 and 11(1). Consequently, measures that permit exemption from, or simplification of, notification are, arguably, highly relevant to measures that should accompany exemptions from any duty to inform the data subject.

Unless processing is for the sole purpose of a public register (see Article 18(3)) or for purposes of a political, philosophical, religious or trade union foundation (as specified in Article 8(2)(d)), Article 18(1) requires Member States to provide that wholly or partly automated processing be notified to the Supervisory Authority before it is carried out. Article 18(2) then provides that there may be exemption from, or simplification of, notification

- where, for categories of processing operations which are unlikely, taking account of the data to be processed, to affect adversely the rights and freedoms of data subjects, they [data controllers] specify the purposes of the processing, the data or categories of data undergoing processing, the category or categories of data subject, the recipients or categories of recipient to whom the data are to be disclosed and the length of time the data are to be stored, and/or
- where the controller, in compliance with the national law which governs him, appoints a personal data protection official, responsible in particular:
   - for ensuring in an independent manner the internal application of the national provisions taken pursuant to this Directive,
   - for keeping the register of processing operations carried out by the controller, containing the items of information referred to in Article 21(2),
   thereby ensuring that the rights and freedoms of the data subjects are unlikely to be adversely affected by the processing operations.

I suggest that these provisions should be treated as a model for appropriate safeguards under Article 11(2). Just as Article 18(2) envisages a Personal Data Protection Official standing *in lieu* of the Supervisory Authority to permit exemption from, or simplification of, notification, so the Supervisory Authority (directly) or a Personal Data Protection Official (indirectly) should be viewed as standing *in lieu* of the data subject whenever there is an exemption from the duty to inform the data subject under Article 11(2) (as well as in cases where data were collected from the data subject—to the extent that this is permissible). This is because not to inform the data subject seriously impairs the data subject's ability to exercise the specific rights (to access, objection, etc.) granted by the Directive, which exists to protect fundamental rights and freedoms, and in particular privacy, in consequence of which, not to inform the data subject constitutes a specific risk to these rights and freedoms by the very nature of the case. In effect, the notification provisions should apply *whenever* a Member State avails itself of Article 11(2). There is no difficulty with this; for, although notification is only required for wholly or partly automated processing, Article 18(5) provides that:

> Member States may stipulate that certain or all non-automatic processing operations involving personal data shall be notified, or provide for these processing operations to be subject to simplified notification.

Alternatively, if notification is not to be required then, at the very least, Article 21(3) should be invoked, which requires that Member States must provide that the Article 19(1) notification information (apart from security information of Article 19(1)(f)) must be given to anyone on request for any data not subject to notification).[8]

This suggests a link to the Directive's provision on prior checking. Article 20 requires Members States to ensure that the Supervisory Authority (or an independent Personal Data Protection Official acting in consultation with the Supervisory Authority) conducts a prior check in relation to processing that represents specific risks to the rights and freedoms of data subjects. While it is up to Member States to determine what processing poses these risks, any exemption from the duty to provide information to the data subject surely poses such a risk. Indeed, as I have already suggested, at least in relation to sensitive data, because lack of this information precludes consent, it arguably automatically involves an interference with the right provided by Article 8(1) ECHR, which requires a justification in terms of Article 8(2) ECHR. While disproportionate effort, as referred to in Article 11(2), is relevant to any such justification, it is surely not appropriate for the data controller to make judgements about this in what is the data controller's own cause. Furthermore, I do not consider it adequate to leave it to the Courts to decide the matter when the data subject makes a complaint. Unless there is prior checking, it is possible, indeed likely, that the data subject will not find out. And, even if the data subject finds out, at least in the case of patients and medical research subjects, he or she is in an inherently vulnerable position in relation to those against whom he or she wishes to complain (as well as generally lacking adequate resources to pursue legal actions).

While the judgements made in prior checks need to be made on a case by case basis, it is possible to suggest a number of things about such checks.

First, it is arguable that it is too onerous to require all exemptions from the duty to provide information to the data subject to be subjected to prior checks. However, even if this is so, it does not follow that prior checks should never be required when this exemption applies, and I suggest that they should at least be carried out where the processing touches on matters of religious, moral or general public sensitivity, simply because these are the cases in which persons are likely to have strong and predictable objections.

---

[8] It should be noted, however, that this is subject to restriction via Article 13, which the requirement to notify the Supervisory Authority is not.

Secondly, specific attention must be given to the security arrangements of Article 17 (which are not subject to exemption) when deciding on a justification for exemption from the provision of information.

Thirdly, if processing does not need to be carried out in personal form then any personal data that is to be processed without informing the data subject should be rendered anonymous or at least securely coded. While this, in my opinion, does not preclude a breach of privacy when the data are used for purposes to which the data subject would object,[9] it is nonetheless necessary to limit the breach if it is otherwise held to be justified.

As regards Article 13, Article 28(4) (which requires Member States to provide for the Supervisory Authority to hear claims for checks on the lawfulness of processing whenever exemptions created with reference to Article 13 are applied) provides a safeguard (though not, in my opinion, one that is as adequate as obligatory prior checking would provide). Apart from this, however, the Article 28(4) provision suggests that Article 13 (or the grounds it provides) must be explicitly referred to when Article 13 is used to restrict the application of Articles 10 and 11(1) (or the other Articles it may be used to restrict). This surely suggests that Article 13 should not be something that a Member State can claim in justification when its provisions on Articles 10 and 11(1) are challenged, if this basis has not been claimed in the implementing law. For, unless this basis is claimed it will not be possible for persons to identify what processing they may refer to the Supervisory Authority's attention in relation to Article 28(4).[10]

---

[9] See Deryck Beyleveld and David Townend 'When is Personal Data Rendered Anonymous? Interpreting Recital 26 of Directive 95/46/EC' (2004) 6 *Medical Law International* 2: 73–86.

[10] It should be noted that exempting from the duty to provide information *generally* will, in effect, remove the right to object under Articles 14(a) and 14(b). Since neither Article 13 nor Article 11(2) provides any derogation from Article 14(b), it is probably better for implementing laws to treat the information provision required by the latter separately from that required under Articles 10 and 11(1).

In addition, it should be noted that Article 14(a) specifies that the conditions under Article 7(e) and (f) for removing the prohibition on processing of personal data (processing in the public interest and processing for legitimate purposes of the data controller) may not be deployed without granting the data subject the right to object on compelling legitimate grounds relating to his/her particular situation unless national legislation removes this right. This appears to have the consequence that, whenever there is exemption from Articles 10 or 11(1), the conditions referred to in Articles 7(e) or (f) may not be appealed to in order to legitimate processing, unless the right to object of Article 14(a) is removed for these cases under national legislation. I suggest, further, on the basis of requirements of transparency, that such implementing law under Article 14(a) may not be taken to be implicit in any domestic provisions implementing Article 11(2).

The UK's Implementation of Articles 10 and 11

If the above analysis is correct, then there are essentially three legitimate strategies that Member States can adopt when implementing Articles 10 and 11.

a. They may implement Articles 10 and 11 without any exemptions based on Article 13, or by reference to Recitals 39 and 40. If so, they will require Article 10 information to be given to the data subject whenever a data controller who obtained personal data from the data subject intends to process the data for unanticipated purposes, or to make unanticipated disclosures.

b. They may appeal to Recitals 39 and 40 to create an exemption along the lines of Article 11(2), thereby not requiring a data controller, who obtained personal data from the data subject to provide Article 10 information to the data subject in relation to processing for unanticipated purposes, or the making of unanticipated disclosures if the provision of information would be impossible, involve disproportionate effort, etc.

c. They may create exemptions from the provision of information to the data subject on the grounds provided by Article 13 (whether or not they have appealed to Recitals 39 and 40 to cover the 'missing case' of processing for unanticipated purposes or the making of unanticipated disclosures where the data controller has obtained the personal data from the data subject).

Which of these basic strategies has been adopted by the Member States (and those of the New Member States or NAS that have passed legislation with reference to the Directive) (as well as any other approaches) is beyond the scope of this paper. Here, I will pay detailed attention only to the UK's implementation, the main purpose of which is to illustrate my general analysis of Articles 10 and 11(1).

The UK's Data Protection Act 1998 (DPA) implements Articles 10 and 11 in Schedule 1 paragraphs 2 and 3. There are at least three features of this implementation that merit comment.

First, where data are obtained from the data subject (the Article 10 case), the data controller has a duty to ensure 'so far as practicable that the data subject has, is provided with, or has made readily available to him, the information' (Schedule 1 Part II Paragraph 2(1)(a)). Article 10 does not, however, make this duty subject to practicability, quite probably because it does not recognize the possibility of impracticability in this case. Of course, Article 10 does specify that 'further information' need only be given in so far as this is, taking the specific circumstances into account, necessary for fairness. If 'practicability' refers to this then it is legitimate. However, it must be noted that (in Article 10) this qualification does not apply to the basic information concerning the identity of the controller and the purposes of the processing that are intended, but only to 'further information'. Alternatively, the introduction of a condition of practicability might be interpreted as meaning that information about purposes of processing and disclosures need only be given in so far as these are envisaged or reasonably anticipated. If so, then according to my reading of Recitals 39 and 40, this would be legitimate. It is also legitimate if 'practicability' is intended to qualify the amount and detail of information (about purposes of processing, in particular) that must be provided, rather than as a condition qualifying the duty to provide information at all. However, as the relevant paragraph is worded, it gives no direction about what interpretations are intended[11] (and, see below, it is arguable that an illegitimate interpretation is required to square some provisions of The Health Service (Control of Patient Information) Regulations 2002 with the Directive).

Secondly, the information that must be given is less specific than indicated in the Directive, being information about

(a) the identity of the data controller,
(b) if he has nominated a representative for the purposes of this Act, the identity of that representative,
(c) the purpose or purposes for which the data are intended to be processed, and
(d) any further information which is necessary, having regard to the specific circumstances in which the data are or are to be processed, to enable processing in respect of the data subject to be fair. (Schedule 1 Part II Paragraph 2(3))

While there is nothing improper about this, it is less than helpful not to have included the examples of such further information that the Directive provides.

Thirdly, whereas (where the data were not obtained from the data subject) Article 11(2) of the Directive does not require the information to be provided if this proves impossible, Schedule 1 Part II Paragraph 2(1)(b) states (as Paragraph 2(1)(a) states for the Article 10 case) that the information need only be provided so far as is practicable. Of course, 'impracticable' could be interpreted to mean 'impossible'. It is, however, capable of being given weaker interpretations and quite probably will be.

Part IV of the DPA (Sections 27 to 39) provides general exemptions, some of which are exemptions or powers to exempt from the duty to provide information to the data subject.[12] Many of these exemptions are clearly made, at least implicitly, by reference either to Article 3(2) (which places processing for purely domestic

---

[11] Although the Information Commissioner does not consider this matter explicitly in *Data Protection Act 1998: Legal Guidance* (Version 1, Wilmslow: Information Commissioner, 1998), paragraph 3.1.7.3, 33, the guidance focuses on the quality of the information provided and suggests that the only exemptions from the duty to provide information to the data subject are provided under Part IV of the Act (see below).

[12] Many of the sections give the Secretary of State the power to make regulations. This power has been used in several cases.

In Part IV, the duties implementing Articles 10 and 11 are not identified separately but as part of what is termed 'the subject information provisions' (which also include the subject access provisions of Section 7 that implement part of Article 12), or 'the non-disclosure provisions', which also include the 2nd, 3rd, 4th and 5th data protection principles (cf. Articles 6(1)(b)–(e)), the right to object of Section 10 (cf. Article 14(a)) and the right to rectification, blocking and erasure of Section 14(1)–(c) (cf. part of Article 12) to the extent that these are incompatible with the disclosure in question.

purposes as well as activities beyond the scope of EC law outside of the scope of the Directive) (see Section 36), Article 9 (which permits processing that is solely for journalistic, artistic or literary purposes to be exempted from the data protection principles, though only to the extent that this is necessary to reconcile the right to privacy with the right to freedom of expression) (see Section 32),[13] or Article 13 (which, to an extent, overlaps with Article 3(2)). In relation to Article 13, there are exemptions from the duty to provide information in relation to national security (Section 28), the prevention and detection of crime (Section 29), and various regulatory activities (Section 31). Section 38 empowers the Secretary of State to pass regulations exempting from the duty to provide information in the interests of the data subject, or for protection of the rights and freedoms of others. The basis for some of the other exemptions is less clear: e.g., the powers under Section 30 (to exempt from the subject information provisions in relation to health, education and social work data), Section 34 (in relation to information made public by or under an enactment) and Section 35 (when disclosure is required by law or in connection with legal proceedings). Evaluation of the situation is not helped by the fact that, in Part IV, the provisions implementing Articles 10 and 11 are not identified separately (see footnote 12). This is unfortunate, because some of the exemptions, e.g. that under Section 30, are easier to relate to these conjoined provisions than to those implementing Articles 10 and 11 (and I do not find it surprising that the Regulations that have been made to date under Section 30 concern only Section 7 of the DPA (which concerns subject access) (see Statutory Instruments 413–416, 2000).

Despite what has been said in relation to the DPA's implementation of Articles 10 and 11, it is arguable that the departures from Articles 10 and 11 that the implementation appears to involve are to be justified as use of a Member State's discretion under Article 13. However, no provision is made in the DPA for the Supervisory Authority to hear claims for checks on the lawfulness of provisions pursuant to Article 13 by anyone (as required by Article 28(4)). This is significant enough in relation to the general exemption powers of Part IV of the DPA. However, it might, not unreasonably, be thought that such provision need only be made when these powers are exercised in regulations passed under the relevant Sections. But, at the same time, such a thought reinforces the perception that the provisions of Schedule 1 Part II paragraphs 2 and 3 (which, as they stand, make no reference to Article 13, or any of the justifications for restriction of the Directive provisions that it provides) cannot legitimately rely on Article 13, unless, and until sector-specific regulations are passed under Part IV.

Finally, as regards appropriate safeguards, while the UK does make provision for prior checks of processing likely to present specific risks to fundamental rights and freedoms, it has done so only on condition that the Secretary of State passes regulations specifying 'assessable processing' (see Section 22). However, no such regulations have yet been passed and there is no indication that processing that

---

[13] The exemption of Section 32 is, arguably, too wide in relation to the Directive. However since this exemption has little application in relation to medical research, I will not pursue the matter.

enjoys an exemption from the requirements of Articles 10 and 11(1) will be considered assessable processing.[14] As safeguards, the Secretary of State has specified in the Data Protection (Conditions Under Paragraph 3 of Part II of Schedule 1) Order 2000 (Statutory Instrument No. 185) that, whenever there is exemption from the duty to provide information to the data subject, the data controller must give the information to anyone who requests it, and that data controllers must keep a record of reasons for considering that disproportionate effort would be involved in providing the data subject with the information. This approach is reactive rather than proactive and surely insufficient.

While the Health and Social Care Act 2001 (HSCA) is independent of the DPA, Section 60 of the HSCA raises issues to which the UK's implementation of Articles 10 and 11 of the Directive are relevant.

Section 60 of the HSCA gives the Secretary of State the power to pass regulations (which must be approved by both Houses of Parliament, the so-called 'affirmative procedure') that render it lawful to process personal data without the subject's consent despite any obligation of confidence that is owed to the patient. The following conditions must be satisfied:

a. The regulations must be in the interests of improving patient health care or in the public interest (s. 60(1)).
b. It must not be reasonably practicable to obtain consent, because the regulations:

> may not make provision requiring the processing of confidential patient information for any purpose if it would be reasonably practicable to achieve that purpose otherwise than pursuant to such regulations, having regard to the cost of and the technology available for achieving that purpose (s.60(3)).

Section 60(2)(c) provides that:

> where prescribed patient information is processed by a person in accordance with the regulations, anything done by him/her in so processing the information shall be taken to be lawfully done despite any obligation of confidence owed by him in respect of it.

Section 60(6) then goes on to say,

> Without prejudice to the operation of provisions made under subsection (4)(c),[15] regulations under this Section may not make provision for, or in connection with the processing of prescribed patient information in a manner inconsistent with any provision made by, or under the Data Protection Act 1998 (c. 29).

---

[14] One might, perhaps more accurately, say that the DPA does not provide for prior checking but only provides for provision for prior checking to be made.
[15] Quite clearly subsection (2)(c) is meant. What is subsection (2)(c) in the Act was subsection (4)(c) in earlier drafts. However two subsections (what were subsections 1 and 2) were dropped at the last moment; but hasty editing has not picked up on this. Similarly the Act at various places makes reference to subsection (3) when it means subsection (1).

Section 60(2)(c) is ambiguous. It can be interpreted as stating that regulations passed under Section 60 render processing not unlawful *on account of being a breach of confidence* (but do not necessarily render processing lawful, as there might be reasons other than breach of confidence why processing might be unlawful). Alternatively, it can be interpreted as stating that regulations will render processing of confidential patient information lawful.

The interpretation given is important, because, under the first reading, Section 60(2)(c) says little more than that, once regulations are passed, processing of regulated data will not be a breach of the first data protection principle of the DPA (that data must be processed fairly and lawfully, etc.) *on account of being in breach of confidence*, implying that processing that is contrary to the DPA for any other reason will still be unlawful. However, under the second reading, Section 60(2)(c) appears to claim that processing of regulated data cannot be unlawful on account of breaching any provisions of the DPA.

The second reading is surely not legitimate (though I expect that is the way medical researchers will be tempted to read it). Since the DPA is meant to implement the Data Protection Directive, a claim that the DPA cannot render processing that falls under the regulations unlawful is tantamount to the claim that the Directive cannot render them unlawful, and this is contrary to the doctrine of the supremacy of EC law. However, I imagine that it might be claimed that this is of theoretical significance only, on the grounds that the conditions that must be satisfied for regulations to be passed under Section 60 are sufficient to render processing lawful under the DPA (and, by implication, the Directive).

Let us assess such a claim. To be lawful under the DPA (considering only its first data protection principle), processing of personal data on a person's health must satisfy at least one condition from Schedule 2 of the DPA (cf. Article 7 of the Directive), at least one condition from Schedule 3 (cf. Article 8 of the Directive), conditions of fair processing laid down in Schedule 1 Part II (which include the Act's implementation of Articles 10 and 11), and any other conditions of fair and lawful processing that are applicable under UK law (such as the common law on confidentiality). Because the DPA must, if possible, be interpreted in conformity with the rights of the ECHR recognized by the Human Rights Act 1998 (HRA) (see Section 3 of the HRA), it is arguable (see above) that *at least* Schedule 3 conditions other than consent may not be appealed to unless the obtaining of consent is impracticable.[16] Provision for this is, however, made by Section 60 of

---

[16] This is not the view taken by the UK's Information Commissioner in *Data Protection Act 1998: Legal Guidance* (Version 1, Wilmslow: Information Commissioner, 1998) paragraph 3.15, 30, where it is stated that: 'All the conditions provide an equally valid basis for processing. Merely because consent is the first condition to appear in both Schedules 2 and 3, does not mean that data controllers should consider consent first'.

However, at least where the data controller is carrying out public functions (which doctors in the NHS do), the Commissioner appreciates that the HRA applies and that it would be unlawful to use private sensitive data without consent unless there is an overriding justification for doing so (see paragraph 3.14, 30). This does not sit easily with the view given at 3.15. Perhaps, the Commissioner takes the view that the other conditions provide

the HSCA. Equally, Section 60 is in line with the requirements of justifying a breach of the right to privacy of Article 8(1) ECHR under Article 8(2) ECHR when it specifies that the regulations must be made in the interests of healthcare, or the public interest. Then, as far as fair processing is concerned, Section 60 arguably satisfies Schedule 1 Part II paragraph 2 of the DPA (cf. Articles 10 and 11(1) of the Directive), because this does not require information to be given to the data subject in so far as it is not practicable to do so (and it is arguable that if consent is not practicable then provision of information to the data subject is also not practicable).

However, this latter point raises the question of the adequacy of the UK's implementation of Article 10 of the Directive, in particular; for (as I have already pointed out), Article 10 does not make provision of information to the data subject conditional on 'practicability', and while Article 13 gives Member States the power to restrict Article 10 in such a way, the UK has not explicitly appealed to Article 13 for this purpose, and an explicit appeal seems to be necessary if Article 28(4) is to be satisfied.

Furthermore, it must not be forgotten that Article 14(a) specifically does not permit public interest aims to render processing legitimate unless the data subject is given the opportunity to object, unless this right is removed by legislation. The DPA has not done so explicitly. Indeed, in removing the right to object in relation to a number of other conditions of Article 7, but not in relation to the claim to the public interest (see Section 10 of the DPA), the UK would seem to have retained the right to object in relation to public interest justifications for processing without consent.

Then, if Section 60 of the HSCA itself can be questioned, so too can The Health Service (Control of Patient Information) Regulations 2002,[17] that has been passed with reference to the HSCA. While there are numerous difficulties with interpretation of these provisions, and the provisions are important for the second phase of the PRIVIREAL project in relation to the statutory role they create for research ethics committees, I shall not consider these here, as this would take us too far from issues specific to Articles 10 and 11 of the Directive. However, in relation to the latter, it should be noted that Regulation 2, *inter alia,* permits personal data on cancer patients to be recorded on cancer registries without the consent of the patients. By implication, this permits the data to be recorded without even informing the patients, because in order to satisfy Section 60 of the HSCA it must be reasonably impracticable to obtain consent for the regulation to be valid, and it is surely impracticable to obtain consent only if it is impracticable to inform the patient. However, the Regulations do not discriminate between the clear Article 10 case where data are being obtained from the data subject, the less clear Article 10 case (where data were obtained from the data subject but the controller now

---

justifications in these terms. I disagree, because for an Article 8(2) ECHR justification to apply it must be necessary to interfere with the right provided by Article 8(1), and it will not be necessary if consent can be obtained (and will not in itself threaten more important rights).

[17] Statutory Instrument 2002, No. 1438.

wishes to use it for an unanticipated purpose, which I have argued is covered by Recitals 39 and 40) and those cases that fall under Article 11. Thus, the Regulations can only be acceptable under the HSCA (let alone the Directive) if it is true that it is impracticable to get patients' consent for their data to be entered on cancer registries when the doctor is in the process of getting this data from the patient.

Related to this, it should be noted that Section 60 of the HSCA is supposed to be an interim measure until means of respecting confidentiality consistent with the public interest/interests of health care can be developed (which is reflected in Section 60(4), which provides that the Secretary of State must review the provisions annually). However, if it is considered impracticable to get consent from patients who are in front of the doctor, then it is exceedingly difficult to see what measures could possibly be produced to render regulations unnecessary.

In order to put all of this in proper perspective, it is necessary to appreciate that Section 60 of the HSCA is the result of a concerted campaign by epidemiologists, who have pressed for all medical research to be exempted altogether from the DPA.[18] The thrust of the arguments presented, which focused on cancer research, was that it is impracticable to get consent from patients for the entry of their personal data on cancer registries and for the use of this in medical research and because the patients' clinicians would not always co-operate, resulting in less than 100 per cent of cases being entered on cancer registries, which would seriously compromise the value of the data. The fact that such arguments were accepted by Parliament, is, in my opinion, nothing short of scandalous. In approving Regulation 2 of The Control of Patient Information Regulations, Parliament either accepted the ridiculous view that doctor's reluctance to ask their patients for consent (or to give them the opportunity to object, which is more directly relevant to the issues raised by Articles 10 and 11 of the Directive) renders the getting of consent impracticable, or the view that it is in the public interest not to obtain consent (or to give the opportunity to object) because the fact that some patients might not consent (or might object) would seriously compromise the quality of data on cancer registries. However, in relation to the second possibility there is no reason to believe that more than a small percentage would refuse to give consent or object, there is no reason to assume that consent is related to the clinical condition in question, and a 100 per cent sample is, in any event, impossible as, for cancer generally, 100 per cent must mean 100 per cent of the human race.

Concluding Remarks

In this paper I have presented a very personal view, which many will no doubt find controversial. What centrally guides my analysis is the conviction that the

---

[18] See 'Cancer experts call for action on GMC's confidentiality rules' (2 November 2000) *Health Service Journal*, 4.

Directive must be interpreted and applied by attention to its objectives, remembering that according to Article 249 EC (ex Article 189), Directives are binding on Member States in relation to the 'result to be achieved'. Since, in this case, the result to be achieved includes the protection of fundamental rights and freedoms (albeit, because of the competence of the EC to legislate, only as means to the free-flow of personal data between the Member Sates) my analysis is guided by considerations of principle that are always implicated whenever attention to fundamental rights and freedoms is central. While others may have different views on what the implications of protection of fundamental rights and freedoms are, it is not debatable that such a focus must be central. It should also be obvious that the duty to provide information to the data subject of Articles 10 and 11(1) is vital if data subjects are to be able to exercise their fundamental rights and freedoms. Indeed, I do not believe it to be a distortion to say that these two Articles are the lynchpin of the whole Directive, in that any failure to implement these provisions adequately will fundamentally undermine the objectives of the Directive. Whether or not the partners in the PRIVIREAL Project are capable of reaching a consensus about the issues raised in this paper, the issues raised in it are, consequently of the first importance in relation to any assessment of whether the Member States have adequately implemented the Directive (and *a fortiori,* will be of equal importance later in the PRIVIREAL Project in relation to any recommendations that the Project will wish to make to the European Commission).

Chapter 7

Overriding Data Subjects' Rights in the Public Interest

David Townend[*]

Directive 95/46/EC on data protection (hereinafter the Directive) does not confer absolute rights upon individuals. This is for a number of reasons: the relative nature of the human rights from which the Directive stems and which it seeks to construct in the heart of European law, the purposes of the European Union, and the construction of the Directive. Therefore, the rights conferred upon individuals are in balance with other rights—rights of other citizens either individually or collectively as the State. This chapter addresses the origin and nature of the balance in relation to the appeal to override data subjects' fundamental rights and freedoms in the 'public interest', it shows how this has been accepted in Member States' laws, and then it discusses the difficulties in making the appeal to override the data protection rights of individual data subjects in the public interest, especially in relation to medical research. It concludes that the difficulties in making the appeal can be overcome by basing it within the framework of rights arising from the necessary requirements of human rights themselves rather than by making an appeal outside the framework of human rights.

Relative Rights and the General Nature of Human Rights

There are very few rights that are absolute. The 'just war' arguably shows that there is no absolute right to life,[1] and it is perhaps only the ban on torture and inhumane or degrading treatment, the right against slavery, and the right not to be punished without a law that are truly absolute human rights.[2] The fundamental rights and freedoms that are the concern of the Directive are found in the European Convention on Human Rights and it must concern all these rights. However, there

[*] In preparing this paper, I had the enormous benefit of discussions with Professor Stefano Rodota. I am grateful to Professor Rodota for his most helpful observations and comments on the ideas underpinning this work. I am also grateful to Professor Deryck Beyleveld and to Ms Jessica Wright for their help. The mistakes are mine alone.
[1] European Convention on Human Rights and Fundamental Freedoms (ECHR), Article 2.
[2] Articles 3, 4 and 7, ECHR, given the effect of Article 15.

are a number of rights and freedoms that are perhaps of immediate concern in data protection, namely the rights that everyone has 'to respect for his private and family life, his home and correspondence',[3] to freedom of religion, conscience and thought,[4] and the prohibition against discrimination in enjoying these rights.[5] However, these rights are very much held in competition with other rights and are held in balance with other rights-holders' claims. Within the Convention, there are two balances to consider in assessing the nature of the rights: the relationship of the rights within themselves and the relationship of competing rights-holding individuals.

The primary Convention right which the Directive seeks to protect is Article 8. The first part of Article 8(1) creates rights for everyone 'in respect for his private and family life, his home and his correspondence', commonly thought of as a right to privacy. Article 8(2) immediately places constraints upon the right, constraints that indicate that the rights are held balanced against public interest considerations, because

> [t]here shall be no interference by a public authority with the exercise of this right except such as is in accordance with the law and is necessary in a democratic society in the interests of national security, public safety or economic well being of the country, for the prevention of disorder or crime, for the protection of health or morals, or for the protection of rights and freedoms of others.[6]

The Convention is not of the European Union,[7] and elements of 8(2) are not matters over which the Union has competence.[8] However, the remainder of 8(2) does give situations within which an appeal to override the rights of the individual can be made generally, and in particular to appeals to public interest that could be made in relation to medical research. Article 9(1) gives everyone 'the right to freedom of thought, conscience and religion; this right includes freedom to change his religion, belief and freedom, either alone or in community with others and in public or private, to manifest his religion or belief, in worship, teaching, practice and observance'. Again, the right is constrained in Article 9(2) 'only to such limitations as are prescribed by law and are necessary in a democratic society in the interests of public safety, for the protection of public order, health or morals, or for the protection of the rights and freedoms of others'.

Two fundamental elements of interest are visible in the constraints upon these rights: the public interest in the protection of health and morals, and the protection of other rights holders. Undoubtedly, there will be a general attempt by the state to move towards the appeal to the protection of public order, crime prevention and national security in response to increased terrorism, but more subtle appeals, for

---

[3] Article 8, ECHR.
[4] Article 9, ECHR.
[5] Article 14, ECHR.
[6] Article 8(2), ECHR.
[7] Although the move towards the new Constitution of the Union clarifies the relationship of human rights to the Union.
[8] National security, crime and punishment.

example in medical research, can also be accommodated with appeals to the two fundamental elements. The protection of health, while not making explicit the need for health research to protect the public, is arguably within the range of possible arguments for overriding the interests of the data subject in the public interest. That the opportunity to raise the appeal to public interest must be lawful and promulgated is included in the constraint, but can be accommodated by a reference in domestic law to such an opportunity. The crucial factor is that the rights are internally balanced against the rights of others. How that balance should be operated will be discussed later: at present it is sufficient to note that there is an internal balance within the fundamental rights and freedoms that forms a wide public interest.

The internal constraints within the individual Articles place a first balance upon the fundamental rights and freedoms. Second, within the Convention, Article 10(1) presents a direct opposition to the right to privacy in the right of everyone to 'freedom of expression ...[including] freedom to hold opinions and to receive and impart information and ideas without interference by public authority and regardless of frontiers'. Article 10(2) constrains the right in a similar way to the previous rights:

> The exercise of these freedoms, since it carries with it duties and responsibilities, may be subject to such formalities, conditions, restrictions or penalties as are prescribed by law and are necessary in a democratic society, in the interests of national security, territorial integrity or public safety, for the prevention of disorder or crime, for the protection of health or morals, for the protection of the reputation or rights of others, for preventing the disclosure of information received in confidence, or for maintaining the authority and impartiality of the judiciary.

This then creates a limited right to privacy in confidential information, but because the state 'may' regulate there is no guarantee, and the balance is one of determining the public interest in the competing elements.

Clearly then at the heart of the European Convention on Human Rights is a balance between the private rights of the individual and the public interests of other individuals either alone or collectively, and the public interest in maintaining the private rights. They are well accepted in this form. For example, the Council of Europe Committee of Ministers Recommendation to Member States on the Protection of Medical Data[9] indicated that the Committee was 'aware of increasing use of automatic processing of medical data by information systems, not only for medical care, medical research, hospital management and public health but also outside the health-care sector' and 'aware that progress in medical science is dependent to a great extent on the availability of medical data on individuals', but equally was 'convinced of the importance of the quality, integrity and availability of medical data for the health of the data subject and his family' and convinced of the desirability to regulate the collection and processing of medical data, to safeguard the confidentiality and security of personal data regarding health, and to

---

[9] R (97)5, adopted by the Committee of Ministers on 13 February 1997.

ensure that they are used subject to the rights and fundamental freedoms of the individual, and in particular the right to privacy'. Thus the appeal to Member States to produce appropriate data protection is framed firmly in the concepts of the European Convention on Human Rights and has the balance of rights at its heart. How then do these find protection in the European Union?

Fundamental Rights and Freedoms in the European Union

The individual Member States are bound as signatories to give adequate protection of Convention rights for their citizens. As members of the European Union, they seek to achieve this protection collectively, in respect of personal data through the Data Protection Directive as the detailed working of the new general right to Data Protection. The rights and freedoms of citizens to data protection have grown since the first concerns about the power of computer processing of data in the early 1980s to an unprecedented prominence for data protection under the European Union Charter of Fundamental Rights, Article 8. This is a separate right from the right to respect for private and family life.[10] Article 8 has three parts that encapsulate the rights expressed through the Directive:

1. Everyone has the right to the protection of personal data concerning him or her.
2. Such data must be processed fairly for specified purposes and on the basis of the consent of the person concerned or some other legitimate basis laid down by law. Everyone has the right of access to data which has been collected concerning him or her, and the right to have it rectified.
3. Compliance with these rules shall be subject to control by an independent authority.

It is particularly interesting that the structure of the Charter is different from the Convention, in that there is not the immediate qualification of the rights. Thus, data protection in the Directive, with its protection of fundamental rights and freedoms, especially privacy, is concerned with the same rights concerning Dignity, Freedoms, Equality, Solidarity, Citizens' Rights, and Justice that are common between the Charter and the Convention or developed in the Charter. Thus, the balancing between rights must remain, but the internal balancing with the public interest is not explicit. As the rights are held by all individuals, the balance is implicit as it is necessary to judge competing rights where they are in conflict. However, the right to override the interests of the data subject in a more general public interest is not clear. This is, arguably, a matter of how the public interest is understood.[11] The Charter and the Directive must first be considered in the light of general competence of the European Union.

---

[10] Article 7, Charter of Fundamental Rights.
[11] See discussion below.

Directive 95/46/EC is concerned, as is all the work of the European Union, primarily in creating a single economic market across Europe.[12] The Directive facilitates this through creating conditions of protection of the fundamental rights and freedoms of individuals and especially the right to privacy,[13] thus enabling the free transfer and use of personal data between Member States within an environment of assured minimum acceptable protection. The minimum protections answer, in relation to data protection, the individual Member States' obligations to protect the Convention rights of their citizens in respect of the treatment of their personal data through the creation of the baseline rights, thus producing a stable and guaranteed protective environment within which the individual can be assured of the fair and lawful processing of their personal data. The minimum protections therefore extend as far as the competence of the European Union extends. Thus, there are boundaries to the protection of the rights reflecting the boundaries of the competence of the European Union, for example in relation to matters of national security, of crime and punishment and the like. These are matters of the public interest, but the data subjects' rights may be overridden by Member States in respect of appeals to these forms of the public interest because the European Union, and therefore the Directive, does not have the authority to create and require a framework which dictates how the balance of rights should be conducted in respect of public interest issues of, for example, national security or crime detection. A Member State may respect the data protection rights of individuals in the face of national security interests, but this is not a matter for the Directive. Clearly then, data protection rights are fragile in the face of appeals to these forms of the public interest.

There are many tensions in the interpretation of when data protection rights can be overridden. Most obviously in these days of increased threats to the individual through terrorism, and increasingly intrusive reactions by states to the perceived threats, there are many calls for the subjugation of the rights of the individual citizen to the extension of the rights of the state to ensure the public interest in 'national security'. However, the future development of the Union may take the Union beyond the single market and bring competence in this area of the public interest. Indeed, it is a tension that lies at the heart of the third pillar of the Treaty and the new direction of the Union away from simple commerce to commerce within a shared European social culture.

The Appeal to the Public Interest in Directive 95/46/EC and in Domestic Legislation

Directive 95/46/EC gives distinct rights to data subjects in respect of personal data relating to that identified or identifiable individual,[14] namely the right to access

---

[12] See Recitals 1 to 10, Directive 95/46/EC.
[13] Article 1, Directive 95/46/EC.
[14] Article 1, Directive 95/46/EC.

personal data and to require information to be erased or corrected,[15] the right to object to processing,[16] and rights in respect of certain automated decisions.[17] Further, the data subject will have rights to information about the data controller and the processing of the data when the data are collected directly from the data subject, and may have further information rights where the data are passed to third parties or where the data controller wishes to process the data for unforeseen purposes.[18] Article 13(1)(g) of the Directive provides general exemptions from the data protection principles,[19] the information provisions,[20] the rights to access, correct and erase data,[21] and the publicizing of processing operations.[22] These are provided for 'the protection of the data subject or of the rights and freedoms of others'. Article 13 can only be exercised, within the Directive, where such an exemption is provided for in 'national legislation' and where the exemption is 'necessary' in a democratic society as mentioned in Article 8(2) of the European Convention on Human Rights. Thus the Member State must chose to provide for the exemption in its domestic law. Further, where such exemptions are claimed, Article 28(4) indicates that the Member State's Supervisory Authority must safeguard the rights of the data subject whose rights are overridden, by testing the validity of the claim when requested so to do. The Articles are supported by Recitals 42 to 44. Recital 42 indicates that access to medical information may be restricted so that it is only available through a health professional. Recital 43 indicates the right of the Member State to restrict access to information

> in so far as they are necessary to safeguard, for example, national security, defence, public safety, or important economic or financial interests of a Member State or the Union as well as criminal investigations and prosecutions and action in respect of breaches of ethics in the regulated professions.[23]

This underlines the limits of the competence of the European Union. Note, however, the qualifiers used here, 'in so far as they are necessary' and 'important', and that there is no blanket appeal to a 'public interest' exemption.

---

[15] Article 12, Directive 95/46/EC.

[16] Article 14, Directive 95/46/EC.

[17] Article 15, Directive 95/46/EC.

[18] Articles 10 and 11, Directive 95/46/EC; see D. Beyleveld, 'The Duty to Provide Information to the Data Subject: Articles 10 and 11 of Directive 95/46/EC', chapter 6 above.

[19] Article 6(1), Directive 95/46/EC.

[20] Articles 10 and 11(1), Directive 95/46/EC.

[21] Article 12, Directive 95/46/EC.

[22] Article 21, Directive 95/46/EC.

[23] Similarly, Article 26(d) allows for the transfer of data outside the European Union and European Economic Area to other 'third party' countries on 'important public interest grounds': Recital 50 illustrates the meaning of 'important public interest grounds' as 'for example in cases of international transfers of data between tax and customs administrations or between services competent for social security matters'.

The 2003 Report of the European Commission on the Directive[24] indicates some instances where the requirement to provide for Article 13 has been introduced into Member States' laws. They point to the UK (where provisions allow for the Courts to determine the public interest on a 'case by case basis'), Greece (where the exemption applies only for national security or in the investigation of 'particularly serious crimes' and then only with special permission from the Supervisory Authority), Finland (where the full scope of the Directive exemption is not invoked, requiring access 'regardless of secrecy provisions' and a certificate from the data controller indicating that the exemption has been used and why it has been used), and Luxembourg (which has similar provisions to Finland and requires an additional notification to the Supervisory Authority giving the reasons for the exemption).[25] Further, the report then shows that the safeguards for the data subject to implement Article 13(1)(g) are equally varied within the jurisdictions. Some have general provisions, others have very specific appeals, for example in Denmark, to an 'overriding private interest', or in the UK to specific circumstances (e.g. confidential job references) where disclosure '"would be likely to prejudice" the interests of the data controller'.[26]

Thus, the relative nature of the rights is itself balanced by safeguards: the appeal to override the interests of the individual citizen is here in the specific case and the protection is therefore at the Member State level through vetting by the relevant Supervisory Authority. In the same way, rights in sensitive personal data may be overridden but at a Member State level of policy and with more extensive safeguards. Article 8(1) provides for a general ban on the processing of sensitive personal data. Article 8(4) provides an exemption from this ban, providing for Member States to allow the processing of personal data when it is in the 'substantial' public interest. Article 8(6) provides and requires the safeguard: the European Commission must be notified of the exercise of the 8(4) exemption. There are two issues here. First, the meaning of the 'substantial public interest' and second the effectiveness of the safeguard.

Recital 34 illustrates the meaning of 'substantial public interest', suggesting that the following are within the term: 'public health and social protection, especially in order to ensure the quality and cost-effectiveness of the procedures used for settling claims for benefits and services in the health insurance system, scientific research and government statistics'. While medical research is not specifically included, it could clearly be argued to be within the ambit of these definitions and, in terms of the public interest, to be as weighty a matter as issues of accounting in healthcare. The issue is, however, a political decision. Member States are charged, and arguably through Article 8(6) the Commission should

---

[24] 'Technical Analysis of the Transposition in the Member States', part of the Commission's First report on the implementation of the Data Protection Directive (95/46/EC), available online at http://europa.eu.int/comm/internal_market/privacy/lawreport_en.htm (last accessed on 5 March 2004), 23–24.

[25] N. 24 above, 23.

[26] N. 24 above, 24.

ensure, through Recital 34, 'to provide specific and suitable safeguards so as to protect the fundamental rights and the privacy of individuals'.

It is difficult to see the exact effectiveness of the provisions for reporting to the European Commission, however, in 2003 the Commission's own report on the impact of the implementation of the Directive indicated that 'provisions adopted on the basis of Article 8(4) are only very rarely notified to the Commission by Member States'.[27] They indicate that by 2003 only the UK and Finland had made notifications under the requirements, but also that certain countries (France, the UK, Belgium, Luxembourg, Sweden, Denmark and Finland) have particular exemptions for the processing of sensitive personal data for research which is in the substantial public interest (and in France that has specifically related to medical research). They conclude that because other Member States do not have specific laws, they cannot suggest that they have not used the exemption, referring in particular to Germany, Portugal, Spain and Sweden where they have used 'other laws' to allow the processing. Of greatest concern in terms of the effectiveness of the Article 8(6) safeguard, the Report further states that 'in some of these, there is no formal guarantee that such processing will be subject to the "suitable safeguards" demanded by the Directive, but in some, in particular in Sweden, the authorities are reviewing such laws to ensure that they conform to the Directive'.[28]

In regard to both Articles 8 and 13 the Commission's report of 2003 does not inspire confidence in a satisfactory regime of safeguards across the Member States. Likewise, the PRIVIREAL questionnaire produced interesting answers to the questions concerning the exemptions allowed under Articles 8 and 13. First, in relation to exercising the exemption available under Article 8, all the EU countries and Norway indicate that the right has been exercised in their jurisdiction. Some States[29] give a general provision, while the others make specific provisions, in which a small number include medical or research processing. In the New (2004) Member States and NAS, for example, in the Czech Republic an Article 8-type exemption exists to eliminate an immediate danger to the data subject's property, in Estonia medical and genetic information can be processed in circumstances provided for in the law, in Poland the law follows the provisions of the Directive, and in Malta the Minister can prescribe the relevant provisions.

In the Article 13 position, a number of PRIVIREAL participants suggest that, within their jurisdictions, 'the fundamental rights and freedoms of others' could be capable of including medical research,[30] whereas others indicated that Article 13(1)(g) has not been used in this way. In New (2004) Member States and NAS, for example, Estonia permits Article 13-type processing to protect the life, health or freedom of the data subject and third parties, Latvia gives exemptions to the

---

[27] N. 24 above, 14–15.

[28] N. 24 above, 14–15.

[29] Denmark, France, Germany, and Luxembourg.

[30] Some give examples, for example in Sweden where the processing of sensitive personal data is allowed for medical research (subject to REC approval) and in the UK Health and Social Care Act 2001 and Regulations 2 and 5 of the subsequent regulations, Statutory Instrument 1438.

information obligations to protect the rights of others, and Poland allows the use of sensitive personal data without consent for the vital interests of third persons.

Through the PRIVIREAL responses, it can be seen that the majority of States allow for exemptions in the public interest. The examples of specific exemptions in the public interest (beyond simple appeals to 'the public interest') include issues of national security, social security, criminal data, crisis management and humanitarian measures, pension management, damage to property, and the operation of the insurance industry. The place of medical research as a specific example of exemption in the public interest is not uniform. Only two of the countries (Sweden and the UK) are reported by participants to provide for exemption specifically for 'medical research', although from the Commission report, the French also have a law that predates the Directive to allow for such processing.[31] Of the remaining states, only Latvia does not provide exemptions at all, and in Slovakia there is no law on the matter. In the remainder, the public interest is defined to include scientific, statistical or historical research, and in some countries matters of public health or other health-related emergencies are included. As is suggested elsewhere in relation to the interpretation of 'scientific, statistical or historical research', this can very easily and naturally include medical research. Further, some States refer generally to the 'public interest', the 'substantial public interest', or the 'important public interest' alongside specific examples, without more specific definitions of how to interpret the same.

Participants indicate that States employ a variety of safeguards when the exemption is used and the processing of sensitive personal data is allowed. These range from strict rules or anonymization of data to approval by a specific authority. In some States, the scope of research must be defined either, as in the Netherlands, within the legislative framework, or, as in the UK and in Belgium, by the Executive; in Lithuania the research must be approved by the Government or other delegated authority. The majority (but notably not all) of EU States, Norway, and Cyprus, Estonia and Malta all require the approval of the Supervisory Authority. In Sweden, the vetting of the decision is placed with the Research Ethics Committee, and in Italy the approval of both the Garanta and the Superior Health Council is required for the overriding of rights in the public interest.

It is clear that the provisions within the Directive that allow the fundamental rights and freedoms of individuals to be subjugated to the rights of others in the public interest (beyond those areas where the European Union has no competence) are used by States. Further, it is clear that medical research is within the scope of the exemption employed in some States, and could be in many others. The requirements for safeguards to protect the data subject in the situation of the overriding of their rights is piecemeal, with some States providing a very high level of protection to both the identity and dignity of the data subject whereas in others the data subject is afforded limited protection despite the Directive. However, the definition of 'public interest' is very unclear and yet this is the heart of the overriding of the individual's rights. The crucial element to take from the

---

[31] N. 24 above, 14–15.

provisions outlined is that decisions about the scope of 'public interest' and where it will override the rights of individual data subjects can be taken by three distinct authorities; Government and ministers, Supervisory Authorities, and the Courts. How, then, should those groups decide what is in the 'public interest'?

How Should we Perceive the Public Interest and How Should we Apply it?

The public interest is used throughout the law to override individual's legal rights and the only common feature is that it is used in very different ways and largely on a case-by-case basis. For example, in France, *ordre public* is well established. One cannot use a copyright in English law to prevent the publication of material that is in the public interest by a claim that the publication infringes the copyright.[32] Likewise, confidentiality cannot be maintained in the face of the greater public interest.[33] Patents cannot be granted against the public interest.[34] In administrative law, the concept of a public interest defence is well established in many countries' jurisprudence.[35] It is a concept that also finds interesting relatives in the law. It is common in jurisprudence to find examples where land and personal property can be requisitioned by the state.[36] This is a further example of the public interest. One could argue that issues of crime, punishment and the deprivation of individuals' liberty are equally shoots from the root of public interest. It is a wide and well established principle throughout law. However, it is not a well defined principle or concept. What is in the public interest?

In recent UK copyright and privacy cases that have turned on the public interest defence, the Courts have had to examine the right of the public to access materials, overriding the rights and freedoms of others (particularly privacy). The key to the approach taken is found in English law in *Francome*.[37] Sir John Donaldson MR considered the meaning of the phrase and made the important distinction that 'public interest' should be that which is in the interests of the public and not merely that in which the public is interested or by which it is titillated.[38] So gossip about celebrities is the latter, whereas information about Government ministers that goes to their competence to discharge their office could be a matter of public interest. Information about celebrities' ability to perform their social function and the freedom of the press to report it, however, is not as clearly

---

[32] See for example in the UK, the Copyright, Designs, and Patents Act 1988, s. 171(3) and *Lion Laboratories v. Evans* [1985] QB 526, but see *Hyde Park v. Yelland* [2000] EMLR 363.

[33] See for example the discussion in *Campbell (Appellant) v. MGN Limited (Respondents)* [2002] EWCA Civ 1373 (Court of Appeal), (see also the first instance judgement in the case [2002] EWHC 499 (QB) and also the recent House of Lords decision [2004] UKHL 22.

[34] In the UK, The Patents Act 1977.

[35] See for example the 'Spycatcher' case: *A-G v. Guardian Newspapers (No. 2)* [1998] 3 All ER 545.

[36] For example in the UK see the Planning and Compulsory Purchase Act 2004.

[37] *Francome v. Mirror Group Newspapers Ltd* [1984] 1 WLR 892.

[38] N. 37 above at 898.

defined, and the *Francome* definition does not produce clarity for individual cases. The difficulty is a conceptual one that goes to the heart of the nature of the rights involved.

The public interest can be defined through a number of different theoretical models. The way in which the public interest is argued to override the individual's rights generally suggests, perhaps, that there is a collective right of a group of rights-holders, society at large or the mass, against which the individual's right is balanced. A number of Member States weigh the damage to the individual with the collective benefits of the processing of the data. It is an appeal to a measurement of the weight of benefits and damages, a quantitative assessment that points to the benefits or utility offered to the masses by the damage to the individuals. This links the public interest firmly in a 'utilitarian' balancing of benefits. This is a very attractive method of framing the public interest, used in many Courts.

The first danger with this conception of rights and the public interest is that, because the equation is not firmly centred in individual rights, such an interpretation allows a variety of interests to be weighed against the fundamental rights and freedoms of individuals. The issues of concern that are argued as significant elements in the balance are very broad and the appeal to the 'public interest' can easily become an appeal to political judgements. While this is perhaps acceptable where the public interest is decided by elected representatives within parliamentary safeguards, it is not acceptable for unelected decision-makers (for example Supervisory Authorities or judges) to make political decisions with unfettered discretion.

Second, if one operates with the balance of the individual against the mass, the inevitable imbalance in favour of the majority can immediately be understood: a substantial damage to the particular individual is soon outweighed by the sum of the individually negligible benefits to the other individuals within the collective.

Further, such a utilitarian balancing of rights is in danger of missing that, in the European Union, the purposes of the Union are themselves matters of the public interest and not matters of private interests against public interests. It is in the public interest to create a single market and to ensure that individual rights and freedoms flourish through its ever more effective operation. Therefore, there is a strong argument, made by a number of PRIVIREAL participants, that one of the chief reasons for granting rights in data protection and confidentiality are to assist in the public interest of creating a single market through building confidence in individuals to participate and to release their data in an environment in which they trust that their rights are respected adequately. This is particularly true in relation to medical care and research. It is not only in the interests of the individual citizens but in the wider public interest that individuals trust their medical practitioners and researchers sufficiently to go to their doctors and disclose their conditions fully and truthfully. It is in the public interest that early diagnosis reduces risks of infection, it reduces costs, it develops a healthy work force: when people do not trust their doctors it is not in the public interest. The danger of employing the utilitarian calculation of the public interest is that the individual feels threatened in the face of the majority, and that threat translates to a reluctance to participate which is of itself a danger to the public interest.

This is a purely pragmatic argument, outside any moral or equitable considerations about the operation of the utilitarian scheme. However, there are strong deontological concerns about the operation of the Utilitarian approach, particularly that the individual is considered as a means to the ends of the majority. Public interest can, and I would argue must, be conceived as a part of the protection of fundamental rights and freedoms, and very much as an essential part of that regime of protection, rather than a necessary departure from it. Indeed, this is in line with the tenor of Article 8(2) of the European Convention on Human Rights when it talks of the 'protection of rights and freedoms of others'. Because the rights held by the individual through the Convention and the Directive are not absolute rights, they are held in balance with the rights of other individuals. Therefore, the public interest must be balanced by considering the situation as balances between individuals, not between the individual and a sum of the community of other individuals. Thus, the rights of single individuals must stand against other single individuals in the balance if individuals are not to be used instrumentally.

In the practice of the Supervisory Authorities, Courts, and Governments, the public interest balance should be considered to be between the actual individual and a potential individual, thus: where it is reasonably foreseeable that the fundamental rights or freedoms of a potential individual would be jeopardized by upholding the rights and freedoms of another actual individual causing greater damage to the potential individual than would be suffered by the actual individual whose rights would be overridden, then overriding those rights would be justifiable in the public interest.

Here then the public interest becomes grounded in the same rights and freedoms that the Directive (or indeed any other rights-giving instruments with a public interest defence position) seeks to defend. In order to breach the fundamental rights and freedoms of the actual individual, the balance must be struck with a reasonably foreseeable potential individual, that is not a specific actual individual, but a person who is imaginable in the community. The danger must then be understood in the following terms: that enforcing the right of the actual individual against the potential would cause greater damage by denying his or her rights. It is not that those rights are potential (for example different from the rights of the actual right-holder); they are the fundamental rights and freedoms of an unknown but not unforeseeable individual from within the community.[39]

For example then, if a State proposed to use, without the safeguards of consent, any data gathered from routine gynaecological examinations in hospitals as a data set for a large research programme to develop a more effective chemical contraception, then this could constitute a denial of the rights of privacy and dignity of those who disagree with the use of chemical contraception. The appeal of the State would be to the public interest in undertaking the research on the grounds of greater utility for those who would derive a benefit from the more effective contraception. That would be to appeal to different criteria from those

---

[39] I am grateful to Professor Beyleveld for his insight on this point.

that sought to protect the rights and freedoms of the individual: collective rights against individual rights, not the same equation. By introducing the potential individual who could be averted from greater jeopardy than that suffered by the objecting actual rights-holder, the calculus is placed on a fair and equitable footing. A reasonably foreseeable potential individual in such a situation would be, perhaps, the teenager who would not become pregnant, or perhaps the woman whose physical pain is greatly relieved by taking the drug: the actual rights-holder suffers the damage of being complicit against his or her will and beliefs in the production of the drug. The calculus, however, does not give an automatic answer to whose rights should prevail in the particular case; it is simply a more equitable method of framing the decision-making process.

Conclusion

The current climate is one where many appeals are made to override individuals' fundamental rights and freedoms. They are applied to questions of national security and the like. If we all carry biometric data on identity cards and all surrender something of our privacy, so the argument runs, the opportunities for terrorism or fraud are reduced. If we allow free access to our medical data, medical science will advance more quickly and more effectively and we will not stand in the way of the healing process for others. It is part of a social contract that we participate in this as citizens. The arguments are freely made, often without showing a proof against their internal flaws. It is the external challenge, however, that has the most impact upon the arguments, and one that goes to the heart of the public interest as indicated above. It is worth considering the position by way of conclusion.

If one compels the individual to participate in the face of their personal beliefs and sensibilities, especially in relation to medical research, then their only option to avoid being made complicit in an action against their beliefs is to withdraw from the process completely. This could have catastrophic effects not only for the individual, but for the whole of society. If trust in the treatment of personal data is to be maintained, then individuals must feel that their rights are treated with respect. Treating individuals with respect by showing that their rights are balanced against the suffering of other single individuals will maintain and strengthen that trust.

Chapter 8

Genetic Information and the Data Protection Directive of the European Union

Lasse A. Lehtonen[*]

Introduction

The Directive on the Protection of Personal Data (95/46/EC) establishes a set of data protection principles that should be implemented in the legislation of the Member States. These principles apply to all kinds of data and all kinds of activities where personal data are processed. The Directive also includes several exemptions where Member States have the power to derogate from the protection of the privacy of the data subject for another compelling social interest. In health care, for example, a lot of sensitive data are traditionally processed with or without the explicit consent of the data subject.[1] The prohibition of the processing of sensitive data is not applied to medical data in health care on the basis of an exemption in Article 8 of the Directive.

Medical research, however, is not health care within the meaning of this exemption, since it does not directly benefit an individual patient, but is carried out for the more general benefit of society. It is therefore left to the Member States to decide how they will weigh the interests of society in medical knowledge against the interests of the individual with regard to privacy, and how extensive the exemptions for research that they make in their legislation will be.[2] They must, however, always arrange adequate safeguards for the privacy of the data subject. Furthermore, the Data Protection Directive is not the only European regulation on the use of personal data in medical research. The data protection principles should be viewed together with the principles of medical research as they are formulated,

[*] Department of Public Law and Department of Clinical Pharmacology, Helsinki University Central Hospital, PO Box 720, 00029 HUS, Helsinki, Finland (email: lasse.lehtonen@hus.fi).
[1] L. Lehtonen, *Potilaan yksityisyyden suoja* (A-sarja No: 230, Vammala: Suomalainen Lakimiesyhdistys, 2001), 332–339 (the patient's right to privacy, in Finnish with an English summary).
[2] S. Callens, 'The privacy directive and the use of medical data for research purposes' (1995) *European Journal of Health Law* 309–340.

for example, in the Bioethics Convention[3] of the Council of Europe.[4] These principles state that the interests and welfare of the human being shall prevail over the sole interest of society or science.[5] Therefore, medical research should be taken as an area where the interests of the society are restricted both by the data protection principles and by the requirements in the 1947 Nüremberg Code for informed consent for human subject research.[6]

The use of genetic data in medical research is one of the areas where the interests of society and the interests of the individual may conflict.[7] Genetic data are linked not only with a particular individual, but with his or her relatives as well, making consenting for genetic research more complicated than for some other types of research.[8] Furthermore, applications for the use of genetic data are rapidly increasing, creating a lot of uncertainties for the person who initially consents to release some sensitive genetic information for research.[9] At present, there are no finalized regulations or guidelines specifically on the use of genetic data in medical research in the European Union.[10]

Types of Genetic Information

Genetic information is conceptually the *order of the base pairs* in DNA strands. This order as such is mostly nonsense, since only part of the base pairs form functional genes that partly or totally determine a property of an individual. Only some two per cent of the human genome codes are for proteins, while over 50 per cent represent base pair sequences whose function is less well understood.[11] The

---

[3] Bioethics Convention of the Council of Europe, European Treaty Series No. 164. Full title: Convention for the Protection of Human Rights and Dignity of the Human Being with regard to the Application of Biology and Medicine.
[4] Medical Research Council; Personal Information in Medical Research (2000), as available from the webpage: http://www.mrc.ac.uk/pdf-pimr.pdf (last accessed on 29 June 2004).
[5] H. Goodare and R. Smith, 'The rights of patients in research' (1995) *British Medical Journal* 1277–1278.
[6] S. Lötjönen, 'Ihmiseen kohdistuva lääketieteellinen tutkimustoiminta ja siihen soveltuvat oikeussäännöt' (1997) *Lakimies* 856–879 (human subject research and its legal regulation, in Finnish).
[7] G. J. Annas, 'Rules for research on human genetic variation—lessons from Iceland' (2002) *New England Journal of Medicine* 1830–1833.
[8] J. R. Gulcher and K. Stefansson, 'The Icelandic healthcare database and informed consent' (2000) *New England Journal of Medicine* 1827–1830.
[9] N. Meincke, 'Geenit kertovat. Geenitestit lääkintä- ja bio-oikeuden näkökulmasta' (1999) *Lakimies* 1202–1221 (genetic testing from the standpoint of medical law, in Finnish) and P. R. Reilly, 'Efforts to regulate the collection and use of genetic information' (1999) *Archives of Pathology and Laboratory Medicine* 1066–1070.
[10] S. Engelschion, 'The implementation of Directive 95/46/EC in Norway especially with regard to medical data' (2002) *European Journal of Health Law* 189–200.
[11] A. E. Guttmacher and F. S. Collins 'Genomic medicine—a primer' (2002) *New England Journal of Medicine* 1512–1520.

stretches of repetitive sequences are sometimes known as 'junk DNA', even though they constitute an informative historical record of evolutionary biology and provide a rich source of information for population genetics.

In lay language, however, genetic information is *the presence or absence of a functional gene*. Thus genetic information can be seen as a categorical variable that an individual either has or does not have. Part of this categorical genetic information is transcribed to proteins that give an individual a property (height, skin colour or even a hereditary metabolic disease). Some of this information is latent (recessive) and can either make one susceptible to a disease or be transferred to one's offspring. Current data indicates that the human genome includes approximately 30 000 to 35 000 genes. This number is substantially smaller than was previously thought. Only about half these genes have recognizable motifs, or DNA-sequence patterns, that suggest their possible functions. Whereas it was once dogma that one gene makes one protein, it now appears that more than 100 000 proteins can be derived from these 30 000 to 35 000 genes.[12]

Table 8.1 Types of Genetic Data

Data type	Genotype information	Phenotype information
Order of base pairs	Similarity or dissimilarity	Relative or non-relative
Categorical data	Presence of absence of a gene	Presence or absence of a property (in an individual/tissue sample)*
Probability data	Presence or absence of a gene or a combination of genes	Presence or absence of a risk for a disorder or a probability of response to therapy

Note: * Mutations that are known to cause a disease have been identified thus far in only some 1000 genes. However, it is likely that nearly all human genes are capable of causing disease, if they are altered.

While 'genetics' is the study of single genes and their effects, 'genomics' is the study of the functions and interactions of all the genes in the genome. Genomics has a broader scope than genetics. The science of genomics relies on direct experimental access to the entire genome and applies it to common disease conditions. Most disorders are due to the interactions of multiple genes and environmental factors. Genetic composition may have either protective or pathological role variations in these diseases. In such a multifactorial disease the presence or absence of a certain gene or genes does not indicate that a person will have the disease. However, their presence will predict that the person in question

---

[12] N. 11 above.

has a certain probability of developing this disorder. The different types of genetic data and its implications are presented in Table 8.1, above.

One characteristic of the human genome that has medical and social relevance is that, on average, two unrelated persons share over 99.9 per cent of their DNA sequences.[13] However, given that more than three billion base pairs constitute the human genome, this also means that the DNA sequences of two unrelated humans vary at millions of bases. Many efforts are currently under way to catalogue these variants, commonly referred to as 'single-nucleotide polymorphisms' (SNPs), and to correlate these specific genotypic variations with specific phenotypic variations relevant to health. Some SNP–phenotype correlations occur as a direct result of the influence of the SNP on health. More commonly, however, the SNP is merely a marker of biological diversity that happens to correlate with health because of its proximity to the genetic factor that is actually the cause. The term 'proximity' is only a rough measure of physical closeness; since it actually connotes that a recombination between the SNP and the actual genetic factor has occurred only rarely, when the genetic material has passed through 5000 generations of our common ancestral pool.

It should be noted that the knowledge of genetics has had an increasingly important role in medicine already for over a century.[14] Genetics and genomics are not even now likely to become an information-based science enabling every person to know from birth the ailments he or she will have and the perfect way to treat them. However, medical genetics, which once was used to diagnose a handful of relatively rare diseases inherited in a simple mendelian fashion, has expanded into new territories. It can help in the prediction of a healthy person's risks of some common diseases such as cancer and cardiovascular disease. It can be used in the analysis of patterns of gene expression as an adjunct to conventional diagnostic methods (histopathology, evaluation of multigenic diseases and responses to environmental agents and drugs). The pace of this expansion will be limited not only by the pace of discovery, but also by the need to educate practising physicians, their co-workers, and their patients about the uses and shortcomings of genetic information. Furthermore, the expansion in the utility of genetic data has long-reaching impacts on the way we see an individual. Therefore, many legal and ethical issues have to be widely discussed and taken into consideration when genetic data are utilised.

Genetic Information as Sensitive, Health-related Data

In the Recommendation of the Committee of Ministers of the Council of Europe R(97)5 on the Protection of Medical Data, it is stated that '*medical data*' refers to all personal data concerning the health of an individual. It refers also to data that

---

[13] N. 11 above.

[14] T. Hooghiemstra, 'Introduction to special privacy issues' (2002) *European Journal of Health Law* 181–188.

has a clear and close link with health as well as to genetic data. The expression *'genetic data'* refers to all data, of whatever type, concerning the hereditary characteristics of an individual or concerning the pattern of inheritance of such characteristics within a related group of individuals.

As indicated above, much of an individual's genetic information is directly linked to that individual's health. It is not only linked to one's health but it is collected and used in the health care system by health care professionals. Article 8 of Directive 95/46/EC[15] prohibits the processing of data concerning health. At first glance, one could think that this automatically restricts all uses of genetic data.

Even though genetic data are most often used in the health care context, all individual physical properties (skin colour, hair, height etc.) are more or less determined by genetic factors. Much of this information is disclosed to anybody meeting the person in question without anybody thinking that one actually sees the expression of the genetic data of that particular individual. Furthermore, it should be remembered that some of the data processed within the health care system is not considered sensitive at all.[16] For example, the age and domicile of a person often impact profoundly on where and by whom the patient will be treated. This information is not considered to be data concerning health even when it is processed by health care personnel. Furthermore, disclosure of common information is not restricted by medical confidentiality.

It is clear that some genetic data are more sensitive than other genetic data. It is also clear that the mere fact that the information is processed by health care personnel does not make the information sensitive. However, at the moment there are no explicit criteria to determine whether genetic data are actually sensitive or not. Basically, four distinctions could be made:

1. *Genetic data collected by health care personnel*
   a.   for health care purposes
   b.   for other purposes
2. *Genetic data collected by lay persons*
   a.   for health care purposes
   b.   for other purposes

For category 1(a) both the legal and ethical requirements on medical confidentiality and the data protection requirements of sensitive health data apply. For category 1(b) at least the requirements on medical confidentiality apply, but the applicability of the restrictions for the processing of sensitive data are less clear. For example, paternity tests are carried out by health care professionals, but since this information is not collected for health care purposes, the resulting information on paternity can be processed by various public authorities.

For category 2(a), the restrictions on data processing clearly apply, but the persons processing the data are not bound by the specific medical confidentiality

---

[15] Directive 95/46/EC on the Protection of Individuals with Regard to the Processing of Personal Data and on the Free Movement of Such Data.
[16] N. 11 above.

requirements of health care personnel (these could be persons reimbursing health care costs etc.). Often other confidentiality requirements are set for these persons by law, but the extent of confidentiality varies. Category 2(b) is the most problematic, since the persons processing the data are not bound by medical confidentiality requirements and it is even questionable to what extent the prohibition on the processing sensitive health data applies, since one can always make the argument that genetic data are not actually sensitive health data, even though many authors claim that this is always the case. An example of this type of data are the DNA banks of the immigration officials, which are used to assess whether or not persons applying for asylum belong to the same family. These data are, and will be, used by different EU Member States for various police purposes.

In section 4.8 of the Recommendation of the Committee of Ministers of the Council of Europe R(97)5 it is stated that the processing of genetic data for the purpose of a judicial procedure or a criminal investigation should, however, be the subject of a specific law offering appropriate safeguards. The data should only be used to establish whether there is a genetic link in the framework of adducing evidence, to prevent a real danger or to suppress a specific criminal offence. In no case should it be used to determine other characteristics that may be genetically linked.

For other purposes the collection and processing of genetic data should, in principle, only be permitted for health reasons and in particular to avoid any serious prejudice to the health of the data subject or third parties.[17] However, the collection *and processing of genetic data in order to predict illness may be allowed for in cases of overriding interest and subject to appropriate safeguards defined by law.* A typical example of overriding interests could be the protection of workers from the risks related to exposure to carcinogens at work (Directive 90/394/EEC), since it is actually mandatory for employees to process personal health data for this purpose (Articles 14–15 of Directive 90/394/EEC).

Exemptions from the Prohibition of Processing of Health Data

Despite the basic prohibition on the processing of health-related data, there are several exceptions to this rule.[18] The allowed exemptions are listed in paragraphs 2–5 of Article 8 of Directive 95/46/EC. Paragraph 3 explicitly states that paragraph 1 (the prohibition) shall not apply where processing of the data is required for the purposes of preventive medicine, medical diagnosis, the provision of care or treatment or the management of *health care services,* and where those data are processed by a health professional, subject under national law or rules established by national competent bodies to the obligation of professional secrecy, *or by*

---

[17] N. Meincke, *Geenitestit—Oikeudellisia kysymyksiä* (Saarijärv: Lakimiesliiton kustannus, 2001), 60–80 (genetic testing—legal issues, in Finnish).
[18] L. Lehtonen, 'Henkilötietolaki ja lääketieteellinen tutkimus' (2000) *Suomen Lääkärilehti* 3015–3019 (data protection legislation and medical reserach, in Finnish).

another person also subject to an equivalent obligation of secrecy. Thus for category 2(b) relating to processing genetic data presented above, similar confidentiality requirements should be in place as are required for health care personnel.

One important issue here is the definition of health care. In a modern complex society, many functions of society are associated with the social services and health care is part of the social services. Especially in a welfare society of Scandinavian type, where health care is managed by public authorities, one could easily extend the management of health care services to include almost all financial decision-making in the public sector.[19] However, when one thinks about health care services and the intention of the exemption, the processing of sensitive health data should be allowed only for the management of a particular health care unit and only when there is a direct link between the individual person (the patient) and that unit.

The Research Exemption

Scientific research is not listed in Article 8 as an exemption from the prohibition of the processing of sensitive health data. On the basis of the introduction to Directive 95/46/EC (Recital 34) Member States are, however, authorized to derogate from the prohibition on processing sensitive categories of data for scientific research.[20] This is permitted, when important reasons of public interest so justify, and if specific and suitable safeguards of privacy are provided for the processing. The wording of this introduction is also specified in Article 8.4, where it is stated that additional exemptions for the processing of sensitive data may be laid down by national law or by a decision of the Supervisory Authority in the substantial public interest, but the European Commission must be notified of these exemptions.

Public interest is a very general concept that may include many aspects that are thought to be important in the continuing development of society. Public interest may require that scientific research, as such, be carried out to improve the health of the population, despite some infringement of the rights of the individual. Since these infringements are clearly possible, national legislation should provide the legal safeguards that are necessary to prohibit and revise all unjustified infringements of privacy. Even though the Directive does not explicitly define the safeguards, they may not fall below the adequate safeguards defined in Article 8 of the Council of Europe's Convention for the Protection of Individuals with regard to Automatic Processing of Personal Data.[21] This Convention also requires that every person must have the right:

---

[19] N. 1 above, 373–397.

[20] N. 18 above.

[21] Convention for the Protection of Individuals with regard to the Automatic Processing of Personal Data of the Council of Europe (ETS No. 108).

- to establish the existence of an automated personal data file and its main purposes, as well as the identity and habitual residence or principal place of business of the controller of the file;
- to obtain at reasonable intervals and without excessive delay or expense confirmation of whether personal data relating to him is stored in the automated data file as well as communication to him of such data in an intelligible form;
- to obtain, as the case may be, rectification or erasure of such data if this has been processed contrary to the provisions of domestic law;
- to have a remedy if a request for confirmation or, as the case may be, communication, rectification or erasure is not complied with.

At the end of the day, anybody should have access to a legal remedy for unauthorized data processing, even when it is carried out in the name of scientific research and there are exemptions on the obligation to actively inform the registered person of the processing of his or her personal data.

The Use of Genetic Data in Scientific Research

Directive 95/46/EC does not contain any specific regulations on the use of genetic data in scientific research, but this type of research is covered by the general research exemptions.[22] In section 4.7 of the Recommendation of the Committee of Ministers of the Council of Europe on the Protection of Medical Data R(97)5 it is stated that genetic data collected and processed for scientific research should only be used for these purposes or that the data subject must be allowed to take a free and informed decision on these matters.

The concept of 'scientific research' is not defined in the Directive or in the Recommendation. It has, however, some typical features. It aims to increase knowledge, the message is aimed for the scientific community (i.e. the results of the research are public), and it is more or less non-profitable. Thus, for example, pharmaceutical research that aims to develop new drugs for commercial purposes falls outside the strict concept of scientific research.

There are several designs for scientific research that utilize genetic data:

1. prospective protocols, where new samples are taken for defined purposes,
2. retrospective protocols, where existing samples are analyzed for new purposes,
3. retrospective protocols, where no new analyses are performed, but existing data on previous samples is used for new purposes.

---

[22] Tietosuojavaltuutetun toimiston; Tietosuoja ja tieteellinen tutkimus henkilötietolain kannalta (published December 1999) (data protection and scientific research, in Finnish), as available from the webpage: http://www.tietosuoja.fi/3147.htm (last accessed 29 June 2004).

It should be noted that patient's rights extend both to the use of samples and to the use of data derived from the samples. Directive 95/46/EC applies only to the processing of the data. Therefore, samples can be transferred to countries that are not considered 'safe' for data protection and analyzed there for their genetic content without any restrictions by the Data Protection Authorities.

When samples are taken for prospective protocols, the use of the samples and the data derived from them is based on the informed consent of the patient.[23] Since processing done with the explicit consent of the data subject is, according to Article 8.2 of the Directive, one exemption from the prohibition on processing sensitive data, there are no major issues involved with the processing of this data. It should be noted that explicit consent means that the data subject has knowledge of what type of genetic data will be processed in association with the protocol.

When existing samples are analyzed for a new purpose and the data are processed, the Directive presumes that either the consent is explicit enough to cover the data processing or that a new consent has been requested. In addition to the requirements of the Directive, one should also remember the requirements of the Convention of the Council of Europe for the Protection of Human Rights and Dignity of the Human Being with Regard to the Application of Biology and Medicine (Bioethics Convention), Article 22 of which states that tissues samples may be used for a purpose other than that for which they were removed only if this is done in conformity with appropriate information and consent procedures.

Retrospective protocols using existing data from different sources are typically epidemiological study protocols. The data protection principles and the use of epidemiological data (including genetic data) were widely discussed when the Directive was formulated. Since there are no specific restrictions on the utilization of genetic data in epidemiological research, it can be used as any other medical data, that is, the Member State can derogate from the prohibition on processing sensitive data for an important public interest when adequate safeguards for the privacy of the data subject are guaranteed (including the appropriate notification of the Data Protection Authority on the study).

Data Protection and Ethics Committees

Ethics committees have been part of medical research for years, but their legal status has been unclear.[24] However, after the implementation of Directive 2001/20/EC on the Approximation of the Laws, Regulations and Administrative Provisions of the Member States relating to the Implementation of Good Clinical

---

[23] M. Nenonen and H. Sorvari, 'Arkaluonteisten henkilötietojen käyttö kliinisessä tutkimuksessa' in L. -M. Voipio-Pulkki *et al*, *Kliinisen tutkijan opas* (Jyväskylä: Duodecim, 2000), 99–110 (the use of sensitive personal data in clinical research, in Finnish).

[24] L. Lehtonen, 'Sairaanhoitopiirin eettinen toimikunta ja sen oikeudellinen asema' (1999) *Suomen Lääkärilehti* 4421–4426 (the legal standing of the health care district ethics committees, in Finnish).

Practice in the Conduct of Clinical Trials on Medicinal Products for Human Use, the status of ethics committees in the Member States will be standardized.

Article 6 of Directive 2001/20/EC states that Member States shall take the measures necessary for the establishment and operation of ethics committees and lists the issues that the ethics committee has to consider when giving its opinion. Furthermore, Article 3 of Directive 2001/20/EC mandates among other things that clinical trials may be carried out only if the rights of the subject to physical and mental integrity, privacy and to the protection of the data concerning him in accordance with Directive 95/46/EC, are safeguarded.

Many clinical trials nowadays collect blood samples for genetic tests to identify new drug targets etc. Pharmaceutical authorities are currently preparing detailed guidance for ethics committee applications and the procedure to be used in clinical drug research. This development will in the future standardize the good practices that should be used for the processing of genetic data in association with pharmaceutical research, and might influence the practices of ethics committees with regard to other types of research as well.

Conclusions

Data Protection Authorities and ethics committees reviewing medical research frequently encounter questions relating to the use of genetic data in medical research. Despite the recommendation that anonymous data should be used whenever possible, personal genetic data are and will be used to analyze the associations of genes with disease and to identify new targets for therapy. When genetic data are collected and they are identifiable with a person or persons, they should be considered to be like any other personal data. Therefore, the data protection principles should be followed in its usage. Furthermore, genetic data at present are considered to be sensitive medical data, the processing of which for research requires either the explicit consent of the data subject or authorization by the Supervisory Authority in cases where the compelling interests of the society override the right of an individual to privacy. Furthermore, the question of whether or not the benefits of gathering genetic information without the consent of the data subject justify this intrusion, should be the subject of consideration by an independent ethics committee as required by the Bioethics Convention of the Council of Europe. The Supervisory Authority evaluating the necessity of processing identifiable data will not, however, receive this ethical evaluation. The ethics committees, on the other hand, are currently poorly equipped to evaluate whether or not the data protection principles are followed in genetic research. One solution for this problem could be that an authorization from the Data Protection Authority should always be obtained for genetic research and that for this authorization an independent ethics evaluation should be made. In any case, the processing of genetic data for research should never be carried out on the basis of consideration by the investigator alone or by a sponsor company financing the research.

PART II
REPORT FRAMEWORK AND
COMPARATIVE STUDIES

Chapter 9

EU, Norway and NAS Law
Report Framework

Deryck Beyleveld and David Townend

These questions were given to the PRIVIREAL Members in February 2002 in order to guide the first part of the project. Hereafter can be found the questions asked to the EU countries, Norway and the (at that time) NAS countries. Some of the questions were adapted to the NAS countries and are specially mentioned. The domestic reports published in the companion volume[1] to this book from the PRIVIREAL series often use these questions as a framework for their reports.

In general, when answering questions 1–19 below, members were also asked to comment on any special provisions or features of the law in relation to genetic research involving humans.

Question 1

The Directive (see Article 1(a)) aims to protect fundamental rights and freedoms, in particular privacy, in relation to the processing of personal data. Personal data are defined in Article 2(a) as data relating to an identified or identifiable natural person (referred to as 'data subject'), and an identifiable person is 'one who can be identified directly or indirectly' from the data.

-   In your implementing law, does it matter who can identify the data subject in relation to the data being personal data?
-   Does your law extend data protection to the dead, or does it only apply to the living?

Question 2

Recital 26 says that 'the principles of protection must apply to any information concerning an identified or identifiable person', but 'shall not apply to data

---

[1] D. Beyleveld, D. Townend, S. Rouillé-Mirza, J. Wright (eds), *Implementation of the Data Protection Directive in Relation to Medical Research in Europe* (Aldershot: Ashgate Publishing Ltd, 2004).

rendered anonymous in such a way that the data subject is no longer identifiable'. Article 2(b) defines processing of personal data as 'any operation or set of operations which is performed on personal data'. Suppose, then, that person A obtains personal data from person B for purposes X (which are notified to B as Article 10 requires).

a.   If A wishes to use this data for purposes Y, but will only do so after the data have been rendered anonymous, does A have to comply with the principles of protection with respect to purposes Y (and, in particular, with Article 10)?

Suppose A discloses information taken from the data to C in a form in which the data subject is not identifiable by C, but (i) A retains the original data in personal form; or (ii) A does not retain the original data in personal form.

b.   How does this affect the need of (a) A or (b) C to comply with the principles of protection with respect to processing for purposes Y?

Question 3 (EU and EEA Countries)

The Directive provides that Member States may exempt processing of data for historical, statistical or scientific purposes from some of the rules on the lawfulness of the processing of personal data. More specifically,

i.   Provided that Member States provide appropriate safeguards, further processing for these purposes 'shall not be considered as incompatible' with the 'specified, explicit and legitimate purposes' for which the data were collected (Article 6.1(b)); data may be kept in personal form for longer than necessary for the purposes for which the data were collected (Article 6.1(e)); and the provision of information under Article 11.1 is not necessary if it 'proves impossible or would involve a disproportionate effort or disclosure is expressly laid down by law'.

ii. The prohibition on the processing of the special categories of data of Article 8.1 is lifted where one of the conditions listed in Article 8.2 apply. But, apart from where the explicit consent of the data subject is given (Article 8.2(a)), these do not have any clear application to medical research. However, Article 8.3 lifts the Article 8.1 prohibition for purposes of preventive medicine or medical diagnosis where the processing is by a health professional subject to national laws or rules of national competent bodies creating an obligation of professional 'secrecy' (or by another person subject to equivalent rules). And (subject to the provision of suitable safeguards) Member States may lay down exemptions from Article 8.1 additional to those of Article 8.2 by national law or decision of the Supervisory Authority in the substantial public interest (see Article 8.4) (which must be notified to the Commission per Article 8.6).

iii. Subject to adequate legal safeguards, and there being clearly no risk of breaching the privacy of the data subject, Member States may by legislative measures restrict the rights of Article 12 if (a) the data are processed purely for purposes of scientific research or (b) 'are kept in personal form for a period which does not exceed the period necessary for the sole purpose of creating statistics' (Article 13.2).

iv. Most generally, given that medical research might be held to protect the rights of others, Member States may adopt legislative measures to restrict the obligations and rights provided for in Articles 6.1, 10, 11.1, 12 and 21 for the protection of the rights of others (Article 13.1.(g)). In this case, however, the Supervisory Authority must hear claims for checks on the lawfulness of processing lodged by any person (Article 28.4).

Questions:

a. How does your law interpret 'compatible' and 'incompatible processing'?
b. What are considered to be appropriate/adequate/suitable safeguards?
c. Does preventive medicine and medical diagnosis cover medical research?
d. Under what circumstances/conditions is it considered that there is clearly no risk of breaching privacy?
e. Have any exemptions from Article 11 information provision been provided by law?
f. What discretion has been exercised in relation to further substantial public interest based exemptions to Article 8.1?
g. To what extent, if any, and to what effect, has Article 13 been used to exempt medical research (and what provision for checks has been made)?

Question 3 (Newly Associated States)

The Directive provides that Member States may exempt processing of data for historical, statistical or scientific purposes from some of the rules on the lawfulness of the processing of personal data. Specifically, provisions are seen directly above number (i) to (iv), Question 3 (EU and EEA countries). How does your law stand in relation to these provisions?

Question 4 (EU and EEA Countries)

Are the conditions laid down in Articles 7 and 8 for legitimate processing treated as partially lexically ordered or as open alternatives? In particular, is it necessary to get consent/explicit consent unless this would be impracticable or inappropriate? Or is it acceptable to rely on non-consent alternatives even if consent would be practicable and not inappropriate?

Question 4 (Newly Associated States)

How does your law stand in relation to the conditions laid down in Articles 7 and 8 for legitimate processing? Insofar as your law allows, at least in principle, for processing under conditions other than consent of the data subject, is it necessary to get consent unless this would be impracticable or inappropriate? Or is it acceptable to rely on non-consent alternatives even if consent would be practicable and not inappropriate?

Question 5

What provisions (if any) have been made for the processing of a national identification number or other general identifier (per Article 8.7)? (Article 8.7 gives Member States the power to determine the conditions under which a national identification number or any other general identifier may be processed. If this power is unlimited, then Article 8.7 creates scope for exemptions for medical research using such identifiers that are without limit. We would, therefore, appreciate partners' thoughts on the interpretation of Article 8.7, independently of their Reports.)

Question 6

a.   Is there provision (see Article 14(a)) for the right to object on compelling legitimate grounds (at least where this is to be justified in part via Article 7(e) or (f)); or has this right been removed by national legislation?
b.   How is 'compelling legitimate grounds' interpreted?

Question 7 (EU and EEA Countries)

Article 10 covers the case of collection of data from the data subject. Article 11.1 deals with the case where data have not been collected from the data subject. The case of information provision where the data have been collected from the data subject and the data controller now wishes to process for a purpose not originally notified to the data subject when the data were obtained is not covered explicitly by Articles 10 and 11.1. However, it is arguable that the situation where obtaining persons wish to use the data for what were at the time of the obtaining not anticipated purposes is covered by Recital 39, and that read with Recital 40 this imposes obligations in this situation equivalent to those operating under Article 11.1.

-   In, any event, in relation to this (Articles 10 and 11.1; and Recitals 39–40), how has the requirement for information provision to the data subject been implemented?

Question 7 (Newly Associated States)

Article 10 covers the case of collection of data from the data subject. Article 11.1 deals with the case where data have not been collected from the data subject. The case of information provision where the data have been collected from the data subject and the data controller now wishes to process for a purpose not originally notified to the data subject when the data were obtained is not covered explicitly by Articles 10 and 11.1. However, it is arguable that the situation where obtaining persons wish to use the data for what were at the time of the obtaining not anticipated purposes is covered by Recital 39, and that read with Recital 40 this imposes obligations in this situation equivalent to those operating under Article 11.1.

- In any event, how does your law stand in relation to these rights of information?

Question 8 (EU and EEA Countries)

In relation to Article 18(2).

- Have any simplifications of or exemptions from notification to the Supervisory Authority (as required by Article 18.1) been provided that cover medical research? (And if so, what?)

Question 8 (Newly Associated States)

In relation to Article 18(2).

- Is notification to a supervisory body required? If so, when? If so, how does your law stand in relation to Article 18.1 in relation to medical research?

Question 9

In relation to Article 20 (and see also Article 28.3).

- Have any provisions for prior checking of processing operations been made that cover processing for medical research? (And, if so, what?)

Question 10

In relation to Article 21.

- What provisions have been made for publicising processing operations? In particular are there any provisions for publicising the medical research operations and the keeping and operation of various registers (DNA databases, cancer registers, etc.)?

Question 11 (EU and EEA Countries)

Who has standing to bring possible breaches of the principles of protection to the attention of the Supervisory Authority or the Courts? (See, in part, Article 28.4; Article 28.6). In particular, what is the position of independent ethics committees reviewing research in relation to their bringing suspected breaches of the principles of protection to the attention of the Supervisory Authority?

Question 11 (Newly Associated States)

Who has *locus standi* to make official complaints or bring legal actions for breaches of your law? (See, in part, Article 28.4; Article 28.6). In particular, what is the position of independent ethics committees reviewing research in relation to their bringing suspected breaches of the principles of protection to the attention of any Supervisory Authority?

Question 12 (EU and EEA Countries)

Article 26.2 (unlike Article 26.1, which provides for compulsory derogation) provides for optional derogation from Article 25 (which specifically prohibits transfer of personal data to countries outside the EEA that do not provide adequate data protection) when the data controller adduces adequate safeguards.

- What provisions have been made in relation to Article 26.2?

Question 12 (Newly Associated States)

Article 26.2 (unlike Article 26.1, which provides for compulsory derogation) provides for optional derogation from Article 25 (which specifically prohibits transfer of personal data to countries outside the EEA that do not provide adequate data protection) when the data controller adduces adequate safeguards.

- What restrictions on transfer of personal data to other countries are there in your law, and how do they match the Directive?

Question 13

Article 28 regards the requirement to set up a Supervisory Authority or authorities.[2]

a. Is medical research or the use of medical data more generally treated as a special sector with its own Supervisory Authority?
b. What powers are given to the Supervisory Authority or authorities?

Question 14 (EU and EEA Countries)

Article 24 requires Member States to lay down sanctions for infringement of the provisions implementing the Directive.

- What are the penalties for breaches of the principles of protection?

Question 14 (Newly Associated States)

Article 24 requires Member States to lay down sanctions for infringement of the provisions implementing the Directive.

- What are the penalties for breaches of your law?

Question 15

Article 23.2 permits Member States to exempt data controllers from liability where they can prove that they are not responsible for the event giving rise to damage.

- Are controllers exempted from liability if they prove that they are not responsible for the events giving rise to damage (or are offences treated as strict liability offences)?

Question 16 (EU and EEA Countries)

Consent is defined in Article 2(h). However, 'explicit consent' is not defined.

- What is required to turn into explicit consent (see Article 8.2(a)) a freely given informed indication by which the data subject unambiguously (see Article 7(a)

---

[2] Question 13 for NAS countries also asks if a Supervisory Authority has been established.

and Article 26.1(a)) signifies his agreement to the processing of personal data relating to him?

Question 16 (Newly Associated States)

Consent is defined in Article 2(h) (and see Article 7(a)). However, 'explicit consent' (see Article 8.2(a)) is not defined.

-   Are such distinctions made in your law? If so, how are they defined?

Question 17 (EU and EEA Countries)

Article 32.2 permits Member States to provide an exemption until October 24 2007 from Article 6, 7 and 8 (but not from Article 12) for the processing of personal data already held in manual filing systems on 24 October 1998.

-   Has advantage been taken of the derogation permitted under this Article; and if so what?

Question 17 (Newly Associated States)

Article 32.2 permits Member States to provide an exemption until October 24 2007 from Article 6, 7 and 8 (but not from Article 12) for the processing of personal data already held in manual filing systems on 24 October 1998.

-   What implementation period and transitional periods, if applicable, has your country been granted to comply with the Directive?

Question 18 (EU and EEA Countries)

Article 32.3 permits Member States, subject to suitable safeguards, to exempt data kept for the sole purpose of historical research from Articles 6, 7 and 8.

a.   How is 'historical research' interpreted?
b.   Has the exemption referred to been made?
c.   If so, what are considered to be suitable safeguards?

Question 18 (Newly Associated States)

Article 32.3 permits Member States, subject to suitable safeguards, to exempt data kept for the sole purpose of historical research from Articles 6, 7 and 8. Does your law have such an exemption? If so:

a.   How is 'historical research' interpreted?
b.   What are considered to be suitable safeguards?

Question 19

The PRIVIREAL project must pay special attention to the use of data in genetic research. In relation to this:

-   Are DNA samples (or human biological material) treated as personal data (and, if so, under what conditions)?

Chapter 10

Comparative Study on the Implementation and Effect of Directive 95/46/EC on Data Protection[1] in Europe: General Standards

Ségolène Rouillé-Mirza and Jessica Wright[*†]

Contents

---

[1] Directive 95/46/EC of the European Parliament and of the Council of 24 October 1995 on the protection of individuals with regard to the processing of personal data and on the free movement of such data (referred thereafter as 'Directive 95/46/EC') *Official Journal L 281 23/11/1995*, 31–50.

[*] Co-ordinating Co-workers, PRIVIREAL, University of Sheffield, UK.

[†] Many thanks to David Townend, PRIVIREAL co-ordinator, for his input and advice while writing this report.

Introduction

Medical research is not subject to a separate data protection regime at the European Union level, but is governed by both general and particular provisions within the Directive. Chapters 10 and 11 of this volume draw on the reports prepared by the partners of the PRIVIREAL project to give a comparative analysis of the implementation of the 95/46/EC Directive on Data Protection in Member States of the EU[2] and the EEA, and to assess the law on data protection in the Newly Associated States (NAS)[3] and its relationship to the requirements of the Directive. Chapter 10 first deals with the general law and then Chapter 11 specifically with law relating to medical research.

The country reports were based on a framework of questions focusing on particular issues of data protection law, which can be found earlier in this volume,[4] some of the questions were slightly different for the then NAS than for the EC countries. All of the country reports are published in the companion volume.[5]

---

[2] Austria, Belgium, Denmark, Finland, France, Germany, Greece, Ireland, Italy, Luxembourg, Netherlands, Portugal, Spain, Sweden and the UK.

[3] Bulgaria, Cyprus, Czech Republic, Estonia, Hungary, Latvia, Lithuania, Malta, Poland, Romania, Slovakia and Slovenia. All have recently become EU members except Bulgaria and Romania, but as duties in relation to implementation of the Directive are different, they may on occasion be considered separately from the other pre-2004 EU members. Reports were received for each of these countries, with the exceptions of Cyprus and Slovakia.

[4] D. Beyleveld and D. Townend 'EU, Norway and NAS Law Report Framework', Chapter 9 of this volume.

[5] D. Beyleveld, D. Townend, S. Rouillé-Mirza, J. Wright (ed.), *Implementation of the Data Protection Directive in Relation to Medical Research in Europe* (Aldershot: Ashgate Publishing Ltd, 2004).

In certain states[6] of the current EU and EEA, legislation on data protection can be seen from the 1970s. The central focus of this early legislation and the Council of Europe protection for data from 1981 was automated data processing.[7] Directive 95/46/EC[8] is of enormous importance because it is a completely new regime in human rights protection, covering all systematic processing of data. It is expressly designed to '...respect the fundamental rights and freedoms, notably the right to privacy',[9] within the wider purposes and competence of the European Union. Its language may resonate with the earlier legislation, but its concepts are in a different league. It has been implemented throughout the EU, with the exception of Ireland.[10]

As Europe grows, the Newly Associated States will become bound to adopt the new data protection regime of the Directive. For some,[11] this human rights protection was a fundamental mark of independence and statehood in the 1990s. For others, the concepts and protections for personal data are only now being developed in line with future compliance requirements.

It must be noted that while the Directive requires a robust regime of protection for personal data, it does not preclude Member States from developing protection beyond the scope of the Directive. A simple example of this is where the European Commission has no legal competence to legislate, for example in relation to Member States' national security. A first key principle to recognize is that the Directive provides a universal standard of protection for certain fundamental rights and freedoms of the citizens across the EU (both old and new countries) and across the EEA. This standard is a bedrock assurance that data will be treated equally, fairly and lawfully, and thereby the Directive ensures that no barriers can be erected by Member States to prevent the free movement of data within the EU and EEA on the grounds of potential harm to individuals' rights in relation to their personal data. Further, within this spirit, the universal bedrock can be built upon by Member States, allowing them to produce greater protections for their citizens within their own implementation of the Directive.

Having looked at different sources[12] we conclude that three main changes

---

[6] For example, Sweden, Germany, Austria, France, Norway and Luxembourg.

[7] The Convention for the Protection of Individuals with Regard to the Automatic Processing of Personal Data was adopted by the Council of Europe in 1981. This Convention greatly influenced the wording of the following data protection laws, as well as the laws adopted in the 1970s, since the Committee of Ministers of the Council of Europe had adopted two resolutions in 1973 and 1974 in order to prepare the 1981 Convention.

[8] Implemented on 24 October 1998.

[9] Recital 2, Directive 95/46/EC.

[10] In both countries, the implementation is at the time of writing going through Parliament and the draft legislation has been used in this analysis.

[11] For example in Slovenia, the Czech Republic, Hungary and Slovakia.

[12] Domestic law reports of the PRIVIREAL Members, see n. 5 above, and 'Privacy and Human Rights 2002: An International Survey of Privacy Laws and Developments' Electronic Privacy Information Centre (Washington DC, USA) and Privacy International (London, UK), 2002. Available online at http://www.privacyinternational.org/survey/phr 2002/ (last accessed on 5 March 2004).

result from the adoption of the new data protection laws implementing the Directive. The first of these is the extension of the types of processing regulated by the laws. The new data protection laws apply to the processing of automatic and manual files and to processing operations where the controller is either a private or a public body. This extension has been realised in the majority of the European Countries. The second main change is the creation of a Supervisory Authority or the attribution of more powers to it. In the majority of the (pre-2004) NAS, their latest law has required the creation of a Supervisory Authority. Before, there was generally no such public authority in these countries. In the EU and EEA countries, such an Authority had already been created in the first laws except for in Austria, Greece and Italy who created it when enacting the most recent laws. However, some of the EU and EEA countries used the opportunity of creating a new law to increase the powers of their Supervisory Authority.[13] The third main change brought by the new laws was the provision of more rights to the data subjects. Thus, the laws establish a new right of access and a right to object for the data subjects. The laws also attach more importance to the data subjects' consent in relation to the lawfulness of a processing operation. Finally, some of the new laws in these countries generally increase the duties of the controllers.

Other changes less common than those mentioned above can also be pointed out. For instance, some domestic laws have created distinct provisions for the processing of sensitive data and the processing of personal data for the purpose of scientific research, which was not the case in previous laws. Finally, the creation of special provisions for the transfer of personal data to third countries (outside of the EU/EEA) and for the processing of personal data when using video-surveillance can be noted.

In all these cases we can see an effort made by the countries to adopt the provisions of the Directive by extending the scope of their law, by giving more rights to the data subjects or by creating a Supervisory Authority.

Further general observations can be made in relation to the position of the (pre-2004) NAS and implementation of the Directive. The first is in relation to the accession criteria that the potential European Union members (NAS) must meet to be accepted for accession. The accession criteria required that potential members must adopt the common rules, standards and policies that make up the EU law, and in Chapter 24[14] the ratification of the European Convention for the Protection of Individuals with Regard to the Automatic Processing of Data[15] was required as a key human rights instrument. All countries have ratified this Convention. The accession criteria also contain as a 'goal' the implementation of the Data Protection Directive as well as other requirements in relation to the protection of personal

---

[13] See section below on both the creation and powers of Supervisory Authorities, 174–178.

[14] In Chapter 24 of the regular reports relating to the accession criteria and the ability to assume the obligations of membership, available on the European Commission web page on enlargement 'EU Enlargement–A Historical Opportunity: from cooperation to accession' available on: http://europa.eu.int/comm/enlargement/intro/criteria.htm#Accession%20 criteria (last accessed on 15 October 2003).

[15] See n. 7 above.

data. The country reports assess whether the countries meet these requirements and goals, and indicate that, by 2002, many countries had not completely met the goals of the accession criteria relating to data protection. The most commonly reported difficulty concerns the functions and capabilities of the Supervisory Authority, especially in relation to the adequate provision of staff and equipment.

In writing this comparative study, alongside the country reports, we have referred to the Commission's report of 2003 on the transposition of Directive 95/46/EC[16] for the NAS.

This chapter focuses on general provisions of data protection law in Europe that do not apply specifically to medical research but this is not to say it could not concern it in certain circumstances. The scope of data protection in Europe will be studied before analysing some of the rights granted to data subjects and duties imposed on controllers. The consent requirement, conditions for processing sensitive data and the rights to information and to object will be focused on. Finally, the safeguards and the other means of protecting the standards of the Directive will be analysed and compared through Europe.

The Scope of Data Protection in Europe

The scope of data protection is limited in the Directive with regard to the type of data which is processed, the data subjects and the types of processing involved. Three questions relate to this: the definitions given in the countries surveyed to 'personal data', 'natural persons' and even 'legal persons'; the interpretation of an 'identifiable person' and the effect of anonymization; and, the transitional provisions which make certain manual processing exempt from data protection provisions.

Natural Persons and Legal Persons: Is there Consistency Across Countries in Relation to Who the Data Subject Can Be?

The Directive states in Article 2(a) that 'personal data' shall mean any information relating to an identified or identifiable natural person ('data subject'). This definition opens two interesting questions: is the Directive making a distinction between legal and natural persons, and then between the living and the dead?

Natural and legal persons The Directive itself does not refer to legal persons in Article 2, but it does refer to them in Recital 24:

---

[16] The Commission's report includes a technical analysis and impact study, consultation with Data Protection Authorities, position papers from interested parties, an online consultation and the 'First report on the implementation of the Data Protection Directive (95/46/EC)'. These are all available online at http://europa.eu.int/comm/internal_market /privacy/lawreport_en.htm (last accessed on 5 March 2004).

... the legislation concerning the protection of legal persons with regard to the processing of data which concerns them is not affected by this Directive.

In a small number of countries, namely Austria, Italy and Luxembourg and Denmark (only part of the legislation), states have chosen to implement parallel data protection to legal persons alongside the protections afforded to natural persons by the Directive. This means that, in those countries, the data subject can also be a legal person such as a company, corporation or other entities with a legal personality.

This situation is discussed by Korff[17] in his study on legal persons in relation to the processing of data relating to such persons. Korff argues that many of the rights the Data Protection Directive was drafted to cover[18] can also apply to legal persons.[19] However, there is little enthusiasm from industry for such an inclusion. Confindustria, an organization representing the manufacturing and service industries in Italy, opined[20] that the protection of legal persons by the Personal Data Act[21] (and other aspects of it) is cumbersome and overprotective. Further, the 2002 consultation on the implementation of the Directive[22] by the EC included many statements on the inclusion of legal persons within the scope of the Directive, including one from the Confederation of British Industry (CBI) stating:

As Recital 24 makes clear, legal persons should not be dealt with under data protection legislation, and a consistent approach on this should be taken to ensure a truly single market.[23]

There is therefore a need for balance to be struck, and preferably consistency, in relation to the protection of legal persons under data protection legislations across the EC, EEA and NAS countries.

---

[17] D. Korff, 'Study on the Protection of the Rights and Interests of Legal Persons with regard to the Processing of Personal Data Relating to Such Persons', for the Commission of the European Communities, (2000).

[18] For example, from the European Convention on Human Rights: Respect for Private Life (Article 8), Freedom of Expression (Article 10), Non-discrimination (Article 14), Right to Fair (and informed) Trial (Article 6), Freedom of Association (Article 11), and Freedom of thought, conscience and religion (Article 9) (Korff 2000, n. 17 above, 3–12).

[19] N. 17 above, 15.

[20] Confindustria 'Implementation of Directive 95/46/EC in Italy' 2002, 1. Available online: http://europa.eu.int/comm/internal_market/privacy/docs/lawreport/paper/confindustria_en.p df (last accessed 9 September 2003).

[21] Protection of Individuals and Other Subjects with Regard to the Processing of Personal Data. Act No. 675 of 31.12.1996, Italy.

[22] The position papers are available online at: (last accessed 9 September 2003) http://europa.eu.int/comm/internal_market/privacy/lawreport/paper_en.htm.

[23] The Confederation of British Industry 'Comments on Directive 95/46/EC re Data Protection' 2002, 5. Available online from: http://europa.eu.int/comm/internal_market/ privacy/docs/lawreport/paper/cbi_en.pdf (last accessed 9 September 2003).

Natural person: living or dead? The majority of countries have interpreted the Directive as referring only to living people, either by direct law or in practice. A minority of countries also impart some sort of data protection to deceased persons, which indicates either that they interpret the word 'natural' to also refer to the deceased, or that they chose to extend their law to also cover deceased individuals.

As the Directive is silent on the point, consideration of the European Convention on Human Rights,[24] as one of the main foundations of the Directive, offers some assistance. The Convention applies to 'everyone' (Article 1). This has been interpreted to apply to legal persons in some cases,[25] as outlined by Korff.[26] However, the Convention case law is inconclusive on the point, although the significance of the extent of the right is seen in *Velikova v Bulgaria* (2000):

> In the light of the importance of the protection afforded by Article 2, the Court must subject to the most careful scrutiny complaints about deprivation of life…(at 68)

The main reasons that it is difficult to afford the dead 'rights' under the Directive are:

1. Much of the Directive appears to contain 'active' rights, for example the right to information, and other rights that individuals cannot directly enjoy when dead.
2. Who is responsible for enforcing these 'active' rights if they do apply?

The interpretation of this depends very much upon the nature of the rights that they might enjoy. This presents conceptual difficulties in some jurisdictions where the dead have no rights,[27] however three possible conceptualisations could be given to rights of the dead:

1. the dead may enjoy rights for themselves;
2. the dead may enjoy rights through their remaining personal representatives; and,
3. the dead do not enjoy rights for themselves, but interested parties enjoy rights that relate to the dead person.

Clearly the first position is the most difficult to hold when one considers enforcement of the right by the dead person, and if that were the only way of understanding the first position it would be ridiculous. The only way that such rights could be enforceable is for them to be considered as part of the estate of the

---

[24] The Convention for the Protection of Human Rights and Fundamental Freedoms. The Council of Europe, ETS No. 005, 1950.

[25] The European Commission for Human Rights has accepted cases relating to legal persons including *Air Canada v UK* (1993), *Observer and Guardian v UK* (1991) and *Holy Monasteries v Greece* (1994) (Korff 2000, n. 17 above, 16–17).

[26] N. 17 above.

[27] For example, in France.

dead person and enforceable by the legal representative of the dead person. This is the protection afforded by the second conceptualisation. However, the first conceptualisation can be useful if it concerns the *inter vivos* expectations and actions of the living person before death. If one acts in reliance of a respect that is offered by society for the dignity of a dead person, for example by taking part in a particular piece of medical research with promises about the use of one's personal data, then one has a legitimate expectation that the state will respect and maintain one's rights after one's death. Thus, protection in such an example could be afforded passively to the dead by a requirement on researchers to register their work and purposes, and any changes to the processing of the data, with a Data Protection Authority. The final conceptualisation offers protection for the living and makes the dead the objects rather than the subjects of the rights, and therefore removes the enforceability problem.

It is important, in trying to interpret the meaning of 'natural person' in this context, to ask what rights the Directive envisages and how they might be enjoyed. In other words to make a judgement of the proper baseline interpretation of the Directive. The 'active' rights which dead people themselves could not enjoy with respect to their personal data are: the right to access, to object, to be informed and to complain (to a Supervisory Authority or Court). The data controller's duty to obtain informed consent in certain cases, could also not be enacted. Those provisions which are relatively independent of whether the data subject is alive or dead include: the main data protection principles (except to the degree that fairly and lawfully (Article 6(1)(a)) applies to all the 'active' rights in the Directive), the processing conditions (except consent), implementing appropriate security measures, notifying the commission, and the requirements surrounding third country transfer (except consent). It can be seen here that it is therefore difficult for the dead, in themselves, to have all the rights under the Directive. There is a solution, however, that 'someone' can enact these 'active' rights on behalf of the dead person. This would perhaps traditionally be a close relative, spouse or legal representative. Indeed, in most countries in the case of medical information relating to the death of the data subject, the aforementioned people can have access to this data, but it is unclear whether this is under conceptualisation two or three.

Therefore, five levels of protection that are possible to afford to the dead under the Directive can be seen:

A. No protection at all.
B. Sector-specific protection (for example, for medical records only).
C. Protection only for those rights independent of whether the data subject is alive or dead.
D. Protection only for certain parts of the Act, including some active rights, enforced by another.
E. Full protection, and the active rights are enforced by another.

The enforcement by another could be for the dead person's protection or for the benefit of another *living* person, and could be by a legal representative, the interested party or on his or her behalf, or by a Supervisory Authority.

The way in which each jurisdiction has chosen to interpret 'natural person', as in all matters of implementation, can be in either evident in the legislation that implements (transposition of the Directive) or dependent on the interpretation of the legislation by Courts or a Supervisory Authority, for example.

Transposition: definitions of the data subject in domestic law   Different jurisdictions have chosen to interpret the scope of the Directive in the following ways:[28]

1. *Natural person* Belgium, Czech Republic, Denmark, Estonia, Greece, Italy, Latvia, Lithuania, Malta, Netherlands, Norway, Poland, Romania, Slovakia, Slovenia, Spain.
2. *Physical persons* Bulgaria, Denmark,[29] France.
3. *Natural or legal persons* Austria, Italy, Luxembourg.
4. *An individual* Germany.
5. *Singular individual* Portugal.[30]
6. *A private individual* Finland.
7. *Natural person who is alive* Sweden.
8. *Living individual* Ireland, UK.

The first definition, that of 'natural persons' is the same as the Directive, and will receive consideration later in the chapter, as will that of physical persons, singular individuals and individuals. These will mainly be analysed by looking at what happens in practice. That of 'natural or legal persons' has already been partly examined in relation to legal persons.

The definitions of German and Finnish law do not refer to natural, physical or legal persons, and as such their meanings cannot be immediately understood. However, as noted by the EuroITCounsel in its report *Data Protection Law in Europe*[31] for the 2002 Consultation on the Directive, later reference to him/her in the Finnish definition leads one to conclude it is only about humans. Whereas in the available English translation Germany uses the term 'individual', the EuroITCounsel Report states that Germany defines the data subject as a natural person.[32]

---

[28] Hungary shall be discussed below in the section on 'extending protection to deceased persons in practice'.

[29] In the English translation of the Danish Act on Processing Personal Data, it states 'natural person', but in the Danish translation it states 'fysisk person', or physical person.

[30] In the English translation of the Portuguese Act on the Protection of Personal Data, Article 3a it states 'natural person', however, after correspondence with Helena Moniz, our Portuguese member, she says the expression in the law is 'singular individuals' meaning any of us, and excludes 'juridical persons' such as societies, foundations or companies.

[31] EuroITCounsel 'Data Protection Law in Europe', 2002. Available online at: http://europa.eu.int/comm/internal_market/privacy/lawreport/paper_en.htm (last accessed on 7 September 2003), 32.

[32] N. 31 above, 47.

The most interesting interpretations of this part of the definition of data subject, are the last two types of definitions above; that of a 'natural person who is alive' and a 'living individual'. This shows that these countries (Sweden, Ireland, UK) directly interpreted the Directive as only applying to living persons. Sweden's definition, although perhaps not in-line with the Directive, emphasizes the fact that the Act only applies to a natural person who is alive, which suggests that generally, a natural person can be seen to be a person either living or dead. It is also interesting to note that the UK's definition was questioned, although not changed, in the post-implementation appraisal of its Data Protection Act 1998[33] where;

> [t]here was a suggestion that personal data protected during a person's life should not lose that protection immediately upon the person's death.[34]

Transposition: direct mention of deceased persons in the law   The 1996 Italian Personal Data Act[35] is the only active data protection Act surveyed to include a specific clause on deceased persons, separate from the definition of the data subject. It states as below:

> The rights as per paragraph 1, where relating to the personal data of a deceased, may be exercised by anyone who is interested in them (Section 13(3)).

The rights referred to, in Section 13 paragraph 1, include the right to be informed, the right to access, rectification, erasure, blocking, anonymization, updating, and the right to object. The Italian report[36] states that the rest of the Personal Data Act only applies to living data subjects, therefore, those rights independent of whether the data subject is living or dead, only apply to living persons (a category D, above, level of protection).

Estonia's legislation, the Personal Data Protection Act,[37] does contains direct provisions relating to deceased persons. Article 12(3) states that the consent of an individual is effective for 30 years after death, and Article 13(1) states that where there is no consent, relatives can consent in written form.[38] The relatives included

---

[33] Data Protection Act 1998, Chapter 29, UK.

[34] Lord Chancellor's Department, *Data Protection Act 1998: Post-Implementation Appraisal, Summary of Responses to September 2000 Consultation,* Section A, 2001, UK.

[35] Protection of Individuals and Other Subjects with Regard to the Processing of Personal Data Act No. 675 of 31.12.1996, Italy.

[36] Dr. Roberto Lattanzi 'Processing of Personal Data and Medical/Scientific Research within the Framework of Italy's Legal System' in D. Beyleveld, D. Townend, S. Rouillé-Mirza, J. Wright (ed.), *Implementation of the Data Protection Directive in Relation to Medical Research in Europe* (Aldershot: Ashgate Publishing Ltd, 2004), 193–208.

[37] Personal Data Protection Act passed 12 February 2003 (RT[1] I 2003, 26, 158), entered into force 1 October 2003.

[38] Ants Nõmper 'Personal Data Protection Regulation in Estonia and Directive 95/46/EC' in D. Beyleveld, D. Townend, S. Rouillé-Mirza, J. Wright (ed.), *Implementation of the Data Protection Directive in Relation to Medical Research in Europe* (Aldershot: Ashgate Publishing Ltd, 2004), 73–85.

are the spouse, parent, grandparent, child, grandchild, brother or sister. There is therefore, potentially, full protection for the deceased person's rights for 30 years (an E level of protection), which can be enacted by the relative, or the individual's consent. There are exceptions for data that includes only the name, sex, date of birth and death, and the cause of death and also for data from a subject who died over 30 years ago.[39]

Extending protection to deceased persons in practice The countries where data protection extends someway to the dead (other than relating to the cause of death) in practice are; the Czech Republic, Denmark, France, Hungary, Latvia, Lithuania, Malta, and Portugal.

Czech Republic The Data Protection Office issued a statement (no. 7/2002) that after the death of a data subject, the provisions in which the data subject has 'civil' rights are not valid.[40] However, when processing personal data, those provisions of the Act on Protection of Personal Data[41] which are independent of the fact the data subject is alive or dead remain in force.[42] The Czech Republic therefore falls into category C above, that it offers protection only for those provisions independent of whether the data subject is alive or dead.

Denmark The position here is much like the Czech Republic, in that there is protection under the Act on the Processing of Personal Data[43] where the provisions are independent of the fact the data subject is alive or dead, but only where there is a need for protection. Time-limits are also imposed, and these are based on individual cases.[44] Denmark falls here under category C. In Denmark, there is also the Act on Patient's Rights,[45] Section 28 which allows family members to obtain certain information on a deceased person.[46] This is sector-specific, B, level of protection.

---

[39] Ants Nõmper, n 38 above.
[40] Martina Kocourkova and Lukas Prudil 'Implementation of Directive 95/46/EC in the Domestic Law of the Czech Republic' in D. Beyleveld, D. Townend, S. Rouillé-Mirza, J. Wright (ed.), *Implementation of the Data Protection Directive in Relation to Medical Research in Europe* (Aldershot: Ashgate Publishing Ltd, 2004), 47–55.
[41] 101 Act of 4 April 2000 on Protection of Personal Data and on Amendments to some Related Acts, Czech Republic.
[42] Martina Kocourkova and Lukas Prudil, n. 40 above.
[43] Act No. 429 of the 31 May 2000 on Processing of Personal Data, Denmark.
[44] Professor Mette Hartlev 'The Implementation of Data Protection Directive 95/46/EC In Denmark' in D. Beyleveld, D. Townend, S. Rouillé-Mirza, J. Wright (ed.), *Implementation of the Data Protection Directive in Relation to Medical Research in Europe* (Aldershot: Ashgate Publishing Ltd, 2004), 57–71.
[45] Act No. 482 of 1 July 1998, Denmark.
[46] After communication with Professor Mette Hartlev, author of n. 44 above.

France The position here is that, in principle, both the future law and current Act only applies to living individuals.[47] However, there are a few cases where limited protection is extended to the dead. Within the Bill of Law,[48] Article 56, information concerning deceased persons can be processed in any case, unless the data subject expressly refused this while he/she was alive. In Article 40(6) and (7), the heirs can request that information being processed on a deceased person be updated to reflect this, and when enacting this, they can also ask for confirmation of such processing. This means there is some protection, but only where the data subject has refused in writing when alive. The heirs can also be seen to be enacting a right on behalf of the data subject. In specific relation to medical information on the deceased individual, Article L. 1110-4 of the Public Health Code states that '… medical secrecy does not prevent information concerning a deceased person to be disclosed to his/her legitimate representatives, if they need to know the cause of the death, to defend the memory of the deceased person or to exercise their rights, unless the data subject expressed his/her opposition to this before his/her death'.[49] These types of action can only occur if the data subject has not written an objection before his or her death to remove the rights of relatives, and the relatives have satisfactorily explained their reasons.[50] Thus, the French protection falls under two levels, B (sector-specific) and D (protection for certain parts of the Act, including some active rights).

Hungary In Hungarian law, based on the structure of the Civil Code, two types of persons are differentiated: human beings (natural persons) and legal persons. In Title one of the Civil Code human beings have legal capacity from birth until the last moment of death. However, both in the Health Care Act, as well the Processing and Protecting Health and Connected Personal Data Act[51] (HDP Act), data of a deceased person remains personal data, and only in certain cases may close relatives ask for the disclosure of such data (for instance when relatives need these data for the purposes of their own health care). Even data on the circumstances and cause of death are considered as health data within the protection of the HDP Act, but these can be accessed by his or her legal representative, immediate relative and/or descendant after a written request.[52] This

---

[47] Isabelle de Lamberterie 'Protection of the Private Life in Relation to Medical Research in French Law' in D. Beyleveld, D. Townend, S. Rouillé-Mirza, J. Wright (ed.), *Implementation of the Data Protection Directive in Relation to Medical Research in Europe* (Aldershot: Ashgate Publishing Ltd, 2004), 97–119.

[48] Bill of Law voted by the Senate on the 1 April 2003, on protection of individuals with regard to processing of personal data and modifying Law no. 78–17 of the 6 January 1978, France.

[49] It is interesting that the Public Health Code uses the terms rights in relation to deceased persons.

[50] Isabelle de Lamberterie, see n. 47 above.

[51] Act no. XLVII of 1997, Hungary.

[52] This position was elucidated after correspondence with Professor Judit Sándor, author of 'Protection of Health Care Data in the Hungarian Law' in D. Beyleveld, D. Townend, S. Rouillé-Mirza, J. Wright (ed.), *Implementation of the Data Protection Directive in Relation*

appears to fall under a level B (sector-specific) type of protection, as this focuses on health care data.

Latvia   The Personal Data Protection Law[53] only extends protection to the deceased in certain cases—for example, genetic research or operations with health records.[54] There is no general rule to apply to the data protection law, therefore the level of protection can be said to be B, sector-specific.

Lithuania   As seen in relation to Latvia, the interpretation of the amended Lithuanian law on the Legal Protection of Personal Data[55] suggests a sectoral protection by different legal instruments. Information can be published with the consent of the data subject's spouse, parents or children.[56] However, information on a person's health remains confidential after death.[57] This protection can be seen to be sector-specific, B.

Malta   No distinction is drawn between living and dead persons in the Maltese Data Protection Act[58] and therefore it applies equally to both.[59] There is, however, no provision for the enactment of 'active' rights under the Directive nor under the Maltese Law, and as such, the law can only be seen to apply to those provisions which are independent of whether the data subject is alive or dead (level C).[60]

[to] *Medical Research in Europe* (Aldershot: Ashgate Publishing Ltd, 2004), 157–174.

[53] Personal Data Protection Act adopted by the Saeima on the 23rd March 2000, Latvia.

[54] Professor Judit Sándor 'Protection of Health Care Data in the Hungarian Law' in D. Beyleveld, D. Townend, S. Rouillé-Mirza, J. Wright (ed.), *Implementation of the Data Protection Directive in Relation to Medical Research in Europe* (Aldershot: Ashgate Publishing Ltd, 2004), 157–174.

[55] Law Amending the Law on Legal Protection of Personal Data of the 11th June 1996, No. I-1374 Vilnius (As amended on the 21 January, 2003 No. IX-1296), Lithuania.

[56] Lithuanian Civil Code, Article 2.2.3 (paragraph 1); Asta Cekanauskaite and Professor Eugenijus Gefenas 'The Implementation of Directive 95/46/EC in Relation to Medical Research in Lithuania' in D. Beyleveld, D. Townend, S. Rouillé-Mirza, J. Wright (ed.), *Implementation of the Data Protection Directive in Relation to Medical Research in Europe* (Aldershot: Ashgate Publishing Ltd, 2004), 219–228.

[57] Ministry of Health Decree on Confidentiality 1999/12/16 No. 552, paragraph 7, Lithuania; Asta Cekanauskaite and Professor Eugenijus Gefenas, see n. 56 above.

[58] Data Protection Act of the 22 March 2002 to make provision for the protection of individuals against the violation of their privacy by the processing of personal data and for matters connected therewith or ancillary thereto. ACT XXVI of 2001, as amended by Act XXXI of 2002, Malta.

[59] Dr. Pierre Mallia, Prof. Ian Refalo, Prof. Maurice Cauchi and Mr. Etienne Calleja 'The Implementation of the Data Protection Directive 1995/46/EC in Malta' in D. Beyleveld, D. Townend, S. Rouillé-Mirza, J. Wright (ed.), *Implementation of the Data Protection Directive in Relation to Medical Research in Europe* (Aldershot: Ashgate Publishing Ltd, 2004), 255–271.

[60] Dr. Pierre Mallia, Prof. Ian Refalo, Prof. Maurice Cauchi and Mr. Etienne Calleja, see n. 59 above.

Portugal   In theory, the Portuguese Act on the Protection of Personal Data[61] applies to both living and deceased persons. In practice the situation as regards more active rights is a little different.[62] The Data Protection Authority has only recognized that, aside from having access to data relating to the deceased data subject's cause of death, other information can be obtained on the subject only under certain conditions. For example, access can be gained if it is required for legal action, or, in relation to medical data, if the information may be relevant to a relative's current symptoms.[63] It would therefore, in both of the outlined cases, be of interest to the relative (not specifically the deceased data subject) to obtain the information, and cannot be said to afford direct protection to the deceased. The Portuguese law can therefore be said to fall under level B.

Conclusions: deceased and natural persons   In many cases it is difficult to distinguish whether the 'rights' given to dead persons are really their rights, or those of the 'interested party' who enacts them; between conceptualisations two and three. In some countries, such as Italy, it suggests this directly: 'The rights as per paragraph 1, where relating to the personal data of a deceased, may be exercised by anyone who is interested in them'.[64]

The customary contrast to 'natural person' is 'legal person' and not deceased person. This is reflected by Recital 24 of the Directive which states that the processing of personal data related to legal persons is not affected by the Directive, suggesting that a natural person is therefore a person who is not a legal person.[65] This would indicate that those countries who have interpreted this differently are incorrect in doing so. The countries in question may also have interpreted this wording in-line with customary practice in the national law. This would however indicate the need for clarification on the meaning of 'natural persons'. Without such, the law cannot be said to be consistent across Europe.

The Definition of an Identifiable Person

Introduction   According to the Directive;

> 'personal data' shall mean any information relating to an identified or identifiable natural person ('data subject'); an identifiable person is one who can be identified, directly or indirectly, in particular by reference to an identification number or to one or

---

[61] Act no. 67/98 of the 26 October 1998 on the Protection of Personal Data, Portugal.

[62] Helena Moniz and Catarina Sarmento e Castro 'Report on the Implementation of Directive 95/46/EC in Relation to Medical Research in Portugal' in D. Beyleveld, D. Townend, S. Rouillé-Mirza, J. Wright (ed.), *Implementation of the Data Protection Directive in Relation to Medical Research in Europe* (Aldershot: Ashgate Publishing Ltd, 2004), 319–340.

[63] Helena Moniz and Catarina Sarmento, see n. 62 above

[64] Section 13(3), Personal Data Act.

[65] D. Beyleveld, 'An Overview of Directive 95/46/EC in Relation to Medical Research', Chapter 2 of this volume, 6.

more factors specific to his physical, physiological, mental, economic, cultural or social identity (Article 2a).

This definition is important, because it outlines when and why data can become personal, thereby falling under the scope of the Directive and its principles. The statement 'an identified or identifiable person' raises the question of how a person becomes identified or identifiable and by whom they can be identified. The second part of the definition attempts to shed some light on how a person can be identifiable by stating that this can be either 'directly or indirectly'. In relation to this, Recital 26 also outlines that:

> ...to determine whether a person is identifiable [directly or indirectly], account should be taken of all the means likely reasonably to be used either by the controller or by any other person to identify the said person...

Recital 26 also seems to answer the question of who—either the controller *or* any other person.

This section will look at the interpretation of the countries of this provision relating to *who* can identify the data subject.

Who can identify the data subject, and how   Often the domestic laws of the EU, EEA and NAS make no specific comments as to *who* can identify the data subject. In most cases the answer to this question cannot be certain by reference to the law, and very often it is interpreted in practice to mean that as there is no mention of *who* (as in the main body of the Directive), it refers to *anyone*. For further investigation of this situation, it is useful to break down the methods of identification into two categories—direct and indirect identification. In relation to direct identification making the data personal, the interpretation is generally that it is anyone who can make this type of identification. The main question relating to identification falls under the second category—who can indirectly identify the data subject. There are strong implications if it is agreed that anyone can indirectly identify the data subject. A main example here is coded or pseudonymized information passed to an individual, B, who does not hold the 'key' to the code. Is this coded information personal data to that individual and does he or she have to obey the principles of protection?

There are two reasons this information could be indirectly identifiable:

1. Controller A still holds the personal information—meaning the data B holds is potentially indirectly identifiable *by A*.
2. Controller A holds the 'key' to the coded information, which could come into possession of B or any future processors of the data to enable him to identify the people concerned, making it indirectly identifiable *by B* or another processor.

This may have effects on controllers who routinely (and often because the Data Protection Acts themselves require it) code data in order to process it for research or other reasons. This would mean that any coded or pseudonymized information is not truly anonymous and that the principles of data protection must always be respected for coded or pseudonymized data.

Other issues arise if the Directive is interpreted to mean that data are personal if they can be indirectly identified by *anyone*—as for data ever to be fully anonymous, there can be no instance *anywhere in the country*, or perhaps, the world, where information exists which can possibly be used to link 'anonymized' data to the individual. This would apply not just to information coming into the possession of the data controller to make identification possible, but also if the 'anonymized' data could fall into the hands of someone who, using their own information, can identify the data subject. An example is that as identification can also be by factors specific to the physiological identity (Article 2a), data concerning occurrences of very rare diseases could be identified by individuals or a society who know a data subject with this disease. Another aspect to consider is that, with the expansion and growth of new computer technologies, it is becoming easier and faster to store and search very large amounts of information. These technologies have also created new forms of potential personal data, like the IP number, and new ways of storing sensitive personal information such as preferences and linking them all together to create detailed information about an identifiable individual. There are specific laws governing information created by these new technologies, such as the 2002 Directive on Privacy and Electronic Communications.[66] The fact remains that the internet or computers could be used as a means to identify data previously not seen as personal.

It is difficult to know what direct and indirect means in the context of the Directive. A lack of clarification means it is difficult to interpret who can undertake these types of identification. This lack of definition also makes it unclear as to when data can ever be considered as anonymous. Recital 26 states that both types of identification are only considered possible when reasonable means are used, thus perhaps solving the problem outlined above in relation to indirect identification. If there can be a 'cap' placed on the means needed to identify an individual this would define the limits of indirect identification. The analysis below includes consideration of how countries have interpreted both who can identify the data subject, and what 'reasonable means' are.

The domestic laws The implementing laws differ in a few key ways in relation to the above points of who can identify the data subject and reasonable means, either:

A.   They have used the same or similar wording to the main body of the Directive, with no reference to Recital 26 provisions.
B.   They have used the same or similar wording to the Directive, and *added* some qualifying statements related to Recital 26 and reasonable means.

---

[66] Directive 2002/58/EC of the European Parliament and of the Council of 12 July 2002 concerning the processing of personal data and the protection of privacy in the electronic communications sector (Directive on privacy and electronic communications) *Official Journal L 201*, 31/07/2002, 37–47.

C. They have used different wording to the Directive and have their own interpretation of both Article 2a and Recital 26.

These different ways of interpretation are examined individually below.

A: Same or similar wording to the Directive, with no reference to Recital 26 provisions In this case it is difficult to determine who can identify the data subject, and therefore what is classed as identification. As IMS Health[67] note in their review of the Directive[68] for the recent consultation:

> Where this definition is transposed unqualified into a Member State's national law, there is a possibility that the concept will be strictly interpreted by the regulator or the courts, in such a way that data will remain 'personal' and subject to the law if individuals remain *in any way* identifiable.

This highlights the problems which can be faced where there is no qualification for the Directive's definition in the national law. In these cases it is interesting to examine what happens in practice. Often they include reference to the Recital 26 provisions in legal guidance but not in the actual law. Also, as Recital 26 states, codes of conduct may be a useful instrument for providing guidance on the ways in which data may be rendered anonymous and retained in a form in which identification of the data subject is no longer possible. Countries to fall under this category are: Belgium, Cyprus, Estonia (some laws, for example the 2000 Human Gene Research Act, outline when data are considered anonymous[69]), Greece, Italy, Lithuania, Luxembourg, Malta, Portugal, Romania and Sweden. These issues have been discussed in Parliament in Sweden with the conclusion that any person can identify the data subject directly or indirectly, no matter if this process takes a large amount of time, money or other resources.[70] In general, as these countries do not extend the definition in the main body of the Directive, the reports seem to concur that provisions relating to direct or indirect identification mean that *anyone* can identify someone, and as there is no mention or interpretation of 'reasonable means', there is no limit on the possibilities of indirect identification.

B: Same or similar wording to the Directive, and added some qualifying statements related to Recital 26 and reasonable means In these countries, interpretation of who can identify the individual are the same as the Directive—seemingly meaning

---

[67] A company which collects data from hospitals, general practice and pharmacies across the European Community.

[68] IMS Health *European Commission Review of the EU Data Protection Directive (Directive 95/46/EC)*, 2002, 2. Available online from: http://europa.eu.int/comm/internal_market/privacy/docs/lawreport/paper/imshealth_en.pdf (last accessed 9 September 2003).

[69] Ants Nõmper, n. 38 above.

[70] Professor Elisabeth Rynning 'Processing of Personal Data in Swedish Health Care and Biomedical Research' in D. Beyleveld, D. Townend, S. Rouillé-Mirza, J. Wright (ed.), *Implementation of the Data Protection Directive in Relation to Medical Research in Europe* (Aldershot: Ashgate Publishing Ltd, 2004), 381–402.

anyone can identify the person. The countries mentioned individually below have however placed a 'cap' on indirect identification as outlined by Recital 26.

Czech Republic Under the Czech Act on the Protection of Personal Data,[71] data are not considered as identifiable where 'inadequate quantity of time, effort or material resources are required to determine the identity of the data subject (Article 4a)'.

Denmark The Danish law contains a very simple definition, simply that personal data are any 'information relating to an identified or identifiable natural person…(Section 3(1)1)', there is no mention of direct or indirect identification. However, in the travaux préperatoire Article 2(a) of the Directive is cited, as is a reference to Recital 26. In Denmark the travaux préperatoire are also considered to be binding.

Germany The German Federal Data Protection Act[72] includes a definition of 'depersonalisation' which means '… the modification of personal data so that the information concerning personal or material circumstance can no longer or only with a disproportionate amount of time, expense and labour be attributed to an identified or identifiable individual (Section 3(6))'.

Poland The Polish Act on the Protection of Personal Data[73] states that data are not identifiable when identification requires an 'unreasonable amount of time, cost and manpower (Article 6.3)'.

Slovenia The Slovenian Personal Data Protection Act[74] states that 'an individual shall be identifiable when identifiable in a manner which does not incur large costs or require a large amount of time (Article 2.2)'.

C: Different Wording to the Directive and have their own Interpretation of both Article 2a and Recital 26 Those countries discussed below have interpreted Article 2(a) and Recital 26 in their laws.

Austria The Austrian Federal Act Concerning the Protection of Personal Data[75] states that data are only indirectly personal for a 'controller… , a processor …, or recipient of the transmission … when the Data relate to the subject in such a

---

[71] Act of the 4 April 2000 on the Protection of Personal Data and on Amendment to Some Related Acts, Czech Republic.
[72] Federal Data Protection Act of the 20 December 1990 (BGBl. I 1990 S. 2954), as amended (last amendment on the 14 January 2003), Germany.
[73] Act of the 29 August 1997 on the Protection of Personal Data, Journal of Laws of the 29 October 1997, No. 133, item 883 with later amendments, Poland.
[74] Data Protection Law No. 59/99, Slovenia.
[75] Federal Act concerning the Protection of Personal Data (Datenschutzgesetz 2000— DSG 2000), Austria.

manner that ... [they]... cannot establish the identity of the data subject by legal means (Section 4.1)'.

Finland The Finnish Personal Data Act[76] defines personal data as 'any information on a private individual and any information on his/her personal characteristics or personal circumstances, where these are identifiable as concerning him/her or the members of his/her family or household; (Section 3.1).' There is no mention of direct or indirect identification. In practice the authorities do consider personal data as anonymous when the data holder cannot identify them. Therefore, in the case of indirect identification, it only matters what information the data controller has possession of, not any third parties.[77]

Ireland There is a similar position held in Ireland's Bill of Law to Finland—indirect identification is only possible by the data controller.

Latvia The Latvian Data Protection Act[78] states in Section 2(1) that a data subject is a '... natural person who may be directly or indirectly identified using data available within a data processing system...'. This may not be a qualifying statement in relation to Recital 26, but appears to place some limits on what type of data can be used to identify the data subject—it must be available within a data processing system or a '...structured body of personal data ...'.

The Netherlands In the law, there is nothing mentioned about direct or indirect identification, but the legal guidance refers to this, and states that measures followed to identify an individual should be reasonable.[79]

Norway There is no mention of identification at all in the Act, which is also the case in Bulgaria.

The UK There is a similar position held in the UK to Ireland and Finland—indirect identification is only possible by the data controller. The 1998 UK Data Protection law states that personal data relates to a living individual who can be identified 'a) from those data or b) from data and other information in possession of, or likely to come into the possession of the data controller' (Section 1(1)).

Conclusion There are countries who interpret these provisions at both ends of the scale. In Sweden for example, and perhaps Denmark, the wide interpretation of the Directive means that as *anyone* can potentially indirectly identify the data subject it is therefore difficult to anonymize information. Countries such as Ireland, Finland and the UK have given a very narrow scope to the concept of indirect information,

---

[76] Personal Data Act (523/1999), Finland.
[77] From personal correspondence with Dr Lasse Lehtonen (email on 9 April 2003).
[78] Personal Data Protection Act adopted by the Saeima on the 23 March 2000, Latvia.
[79] Ministry of Justice/CBP *Guidelines for Personal Data Processors (Personal Data Protection Act)* (2001), 12, The Netherlands.

relating this solely to the means that the data controller or holder can use to identify the information—therefore meaning that coded information is potentially not personal information. In reality, it seems that a more pragmatic approach than those countries with the wide definitions, and a more permissive approach than those with the narrow definition is needed. Those countries which incorporate part of Recital 26 into the law outline the cases when the measures taken to identify the data subject are unreasonable—and these are often related to incurring large amounts of time, cost or manpower to identify the data subject.

Anonymization

Introduction Building on those questions and problems outlined above, this section will focus more directly on issues surrounding anonymization itself. In relation to this, firstly the definition of anonymization will briefly be considered, then the process of anonymization will be explored in relation to whether it can be considered a process subject to the respect of data protection principles (a problem often ignored). Following this, a case-study will be explored in relation to anonymization which hopefully highlights some of the key issues in this area, including analysis of the case where a data controller may collect data knowing he or she will later anonymize the data before using it for undisclosed purposes.

The definition of anonymization The main body of the Directive does not mention anonymization, except in Recital 26, where it states that for the Directive not to apply, data must be 'anonymized in such a way that the data subject is no longer identifiable'. The last data protection principle does make a reference to it, by stating that data should be 'kept in a form which permits identification for no longer than is necessary' (Article 6). Data protection law in the countries surveyed sometimes contains reference to anonymization, for example the Czech Republic defines anonymization as data which cannot be related to an identified or identifiable data subject in their original form, or following processing thereof.[80] Germany includes a definition of 'depersonalisation' in Section 3(6) of the Federal Data Protection Law[81], where it '...means the modification of personal data so that the information concerning personal or material circumstances can no longer or only with a disproportionate amount of time, expense and labour be attributed to an identified or identifiable individual'. It also includes a definition of pseudonymization, which is 'the replacement if the name and other identifying attributes with a view to making it impossible or significantly more difficult to identify the data subject...' (Section 3(6)(a)). Spain defines a 'dissociation procedure' which is any processing of personal data carried out in such a way that

---

[80] Act of the 4 April 2000 on the Protection of Personal Data and on Amendment to Some Related Acts, Czech Republic, Article 4(c).
[81] Federal Data Protection Act of the 20 December 1990 (BGBl. I 1990 S. 2954), as amended, last amendment on the 14 January 2003, Germany.

the information obtained cannot be associated with an identified or identifiable person.[82]

Anonymization as a process In the Directive, processing personal data means:

> any operation or set of operations which is performed upon personal data, whether or not by automatic means, such as collection, recording, organization, storage, adaptation or alteration, retrieval, consultation, use, disclosure by transmission, dissemination or otherwise making available, alignment or combination, blocking, erasure or destruction; (Article 2b).

It is a pertinent question as to whether this definition includes the process of anonymization itself. If anonymization is a process, then the principles in the Directive will need to be followed in respect of it. Deryck Beyleveld and David Townend argue that anonymization is itself a process which should be governed by the data protection principles.[83] Treating anonymization as a process could change practice in many countries; certainly it would not be as easy to anonymize information to avoid applying data protection principles. This is a critical point in the interpretation of the Directive, and in relation to issues raised in the following case-study, which is in relation to new purposes and informing the data subject. It was a major point made by the pan-European company IMS Health and The European Privacy Officers Forum in the recent consultation exercise that there are large and important questions in this area, which may in the end be for the European Court of Justice to rule upon.[84,85]

Many country reports also have commented on the area, for example, Mette Hartlev states in her report on the Danish regulations that anonymization should be viewed as a process because as 'making data anonymous could have consequences for the protection of the data subject's rights it seems plausible that this particular processing of data is covered by the Act'.[86] This is a position not undisputed in Denmark, where Peter Blume,[87] one of the 'leading Danish scholars in the field of data protection law has taken the position that the Act does not apply to the process of making the data anonymous'.[88] Ants Nõmper from Estonia outlines that:

---

[82] Article 3(f), Organic Law 15/1999 of 13 December on the Protection of Personal Data, Spain.

[83] Deryck Beyleveld and David Townend 'When is Personal Data Rendered Anonymous? Interpreting Recital 26 of Directive 95/46/EC' (2004) 6 *Medical Law International* 2: 73–86.

[84] IMS Health, 2002, n. 68 above, 4.

[85] European Privacy Officers Forum, *Comments on Review of the EU Data Protection Directive (Directive 95/46/EC)*, 2002, 4. Available online from: http://europa.eu.int/comm/ internal_market/privacy/docs/lawreport/paper/epof_en.pdf (last accessed on 27 October 2003).

[86] Professor Mette Hartlev, n. 44 above, 60–61.

[87] P. Blume, 'Personoplysningsloven' (*The Act on Processing of Personal Data*), (2000) *Greens§jura*, 44.

[88] Professor Mette Hartlev, n. 44 above, 61.

Although anonymization may be considered as processing of personal data, it can be argued that anonymization does not require the consent of the data subject. A processor of personal data does have an obligation to delete or make inaccessible all personal data that is not necessary for the achievement of lawful purposes of the processor (Article 18(1) of the Act). This obligation must be fulfilled irrespective of data subject's consent, although, if we look for instance at the definition of data processing under Estonian law or under the Directive, deletion of data or making the data inaccessible is also defined as data processing. Given the fact that anonymization of data is comparable to deletion of data and rendering data inaccessible, I am of the opinion that anonymization may therefore be carried out without consent of the data subject.[89]

Hermann Kühn, from Germany, expounds the view that 'anonymising personal data is regarded as a modification of personal data which itself is only lawful if this particular kind of processing is "necessary to safeguard justified interests of the data controller and there is no reason to assume that the data subject has an overriding legitimate interest in his data being excluded from processing or use" (§ 28.1 Nr. 2 FDPA)'.[90] The situation in Estonia and Germany generally means that anonymization is treated as a process, but a special process which does not need the data subject's consent as long as they would not have an interest in *not* having their data anonymized. This shows there are different opinions across Europe and that this issue requires clarification.

Anonymization and new purposes: a case-study   This case-study was designed to assess whether knowing at the time of collection that the data will be anonymized and then further used for new, incompatible, purposes means that the data subject should be informed of these at the time of data collection. In regards to the scenarios which follow: Person A is the data controller, Person B is the data subject, Person C is a third party processor, Purpose X is that which the data subject is informed about and Purpose Y is a new, incompatible, purpose.

Scenario one: If A wishes to use this data for new purposes Y, but will only do so after the data have been rendered anonymous, does A have to comply with the principles of protection with respect to purposes Y (and, in particular, with Article 10 and the information provisions)? *Scenarios two and three:* Suppose A discloses information taken from the data to C for purposes Y in a form in which the data subject is not identifiable by C, in:

- scenario two: A retains the information in personal form,
- scenario three: A does not retain the information in personal form.

---

[89] Ants Nõmper, n. 38 above, 77.

[90] Dr Hermann Christoph Kühn 'The Implementation of the Data Protection Directive 95/46/EC in Germany' in D. Beyleveld, D. Townend, S. Rouillé-Mirza, J. Wright (ed.), *Implementation of the Data Protection Directive in Relation to Medical Research in Europe* (Aldershot: Ashgate Publishing Ltd, 2004), 121–140, 127.

Comments were then invited on how this affects the need of A and C to comply with the principles of protection with respect to new purposes Y. These scenarios are discussed separately below.

Scenario one: information before anonymization The limited answers from the countries to this case-study reveal the confusion surrounding this issue. The answer from most countries to scenario one was that if a controller knows at the time of collection that information will be anonymized and then used for a certain, known, purpose, the data subject should be informed of this at that time. If this does not happen then it can be said to deviate from several key data protection principles, including the right to have information processed fairly and lawfully (and therefore the right to information), and the purpose-specification principle. Recital 26, and the fact that the Directive does not apply to anonymized data, does not appear to be applicable *until* the data becomes anonymous.

In the UK, the Court of Appeal case *Regina v Department of Health ex parte. Source Informatics Ltd*[91] would seem to allow scenario one to occur without informing the data subject; specifically, when the doctor is obtaining patient data for prescriptions, he or she knows that information will be anonymized by the pharmacist and passed to a company, Source Informatics, for use in gathering information on prescribing habits which it will sell for a profit. This, however, is not informed to the patient at the time of collecting the data. This situation appears to contradict the Directive in which (unless a legal exemption is provided) the data controller both ensures that the data are collected for specified, explicit and legitimate reasons and *not further processed in a way incompatible with those purposes* (Article 6(1)(b)) and that at the time of collection the data subject is informed of the *purposes of the processing for which the data are intended* (Article 10(b)). If the doctor or pharmacist knows such of a purpose, this should be disclosed. It does not mention anywhere in the Directive that this situation changes when it is known the data will be anonymized prior to the processing.

Scenarios two and three: disclosing information to third parties In both these scenarios, the third party (C) will never be able to inform the data subject, as he or she does not hold the data in personal form. Part of the reason the Directive does not apply to anonymized data is that some duties cannot be enacted by anyone who holds such data.[92] This does not preclude the third party using relevant security measures and informing the Data Protection Commission, for example.

In most countries it is agreed that, in scenario two, both the data controller and the third party holds information in a personal form and that the information the third party holds is indirectly identifiable. It is agreed that both parties should respect the data protection principles, to the extent they can, and that it is the responsibility of the original data controller to inform the data subject with respect to both the disclosure itself and the new purposes.

---

[91] *Regina v Department of Health ex parte. Source Informatics Ltd.* [2001] QB 424.
[92] See D. Beyleveld, 'The Duty to Provide Information to the Data Subject: Articles 10 and 11 of Directive 95/46/EC', Chapter 6 of this volume.

In scenario three, it may depend on exactly *when* the data are anonymized by the data controller (similar to scenario one), as the answer will change depending on whether the information was held in a personal form when disclosed to the third party. If it were anonymized and then it was decided to disclose it to a third party for a new purpose, it was generally agreed that in such a situation the Directive and the principles do not apply to either the data controller or the third party. However, if the data were still held in personal form on disclosure, then the data controller (as seen in the first scenario) should inform the data subject of the disclosure *and* the new purpose.

Transitional Provisions with Regards to Manual Processing

Transitional provisions in the Directive Studying the implementation of transitional measures is confusing because the Directive contains four different transitional provisions, not all of which relate to manual processing.

The first one concerns the implementation of the Directive by Member States, which has to be made within three years from the date of adoption of the Directive, therefore before the 24 October 1998.[93] The second transitional provision states that processing already under way on the date the domestic law was adopted must comply with it within three years of this date. The third provision concerns manual processing and is analysed here.[94] Finally, the fourth transitional provision concerns processing made for the purpose of historical research, which is also exempted from Articles 6, 7 and 8 of the Directive in certain situations.[95] Taking this into account, it can be confusing to analyse the domestic laws and define which of these transitional provisions the countries have implemented.

Implementation or effect of the transitional provision of the Directive with regards to manual processing The scope of data protection law with regard to the types of processing operations covered has changed in the last 20 years. Some of the first domestic data protection laws enacted in Europe only concerned the processing of data held in automatic files. Directive 95/46/EC widened the scope of data protection law to also cover the processing of data held in manual filing systems. In order to accompany this change, the Directive provides a transitional provision in Article 32(2) giving Member States the possibility to exempt the processing of personal data already held in manual filing systems on the 24 October 1998 from Articles 6, 7 and 8, until the 24 October 2007. Article 6 of the Directive outlines the principles relating to data quality, Article 7 defines the criteria for legitimate processing and Article 8 establishes the processing conditions for sensitive data. The question addressed here will therefore be whether the countries, in writing the domestic law, have used this provision to temporarily exempt manual processing, as is provided in Article 32(2) of the Directive.

---

[93] Directive 95/46/EC, Article 32(1).
[94] Directive 95/46/EC, Article 32(2).
[95] Directive 95/46/EC, Article 32(3).

First of all, it can be noted that some of the domestic laws do not mention any transitional exemptions concerning manual processing at all. This is the case for instance in the Belgian, Danish, German, Dutch, Finnish and Estonian law. However, the countries which do not provide an exemption specifically for manual processing, provide other transitional exemptions, which include manual processing. It seems that Malta is the only country where the law does not provide transitional exemptions either for manual or automatic processing.

It appears that only two countries, France and Sweden,[96] have adopted exactly the same transitional provisions concerning manual processing as those provided by the Directive. In both cases, manual processing already under way at the time of adoption of the domestic law is exempted from compliance with the national provisions implementing Articles 6, 7 and 8 of the Directive until October 2007.

Other domestic laws which provide transitional exemptions for manual processing do not repeat the Directive exactly. In some cases, domestic law can still be considered as respecting the Directive because the exemption lasts for less than three years, so the law is complying with the second transitional exemption of the Directive (processing already underway must comply with the Directive within three years).[97] This is the case, for instance for Cyprus, which exempts manual processing, in Article 28(3) of its Data Protection Law, from respecting the obligation to notify and the right to inform the data subjects. The right to inform the data subjects corresponds to Article 10 of the Directive. Article 10 is not covered by the provisions from which manual processing can be exempt as regards to Article 32(2) of the Directive, but it is covered under exemption two as long as it was already underway. However, in Cyprus, the exemption to the right of information only lasts for three years, not until 2007 as the transitional exemption concerning manual processing provides in the Directive. Thus, the provision of the Cypriote law is covered by Article 32(2)(1) of the Directive.

Some of the other countries provide transitional exemptions concerning manual processing which are broader or different than those in Article 32(2) of the Directive. For example, the Spanish law exempts manual processing until the 24 October 2007 from complying with the Data Protection Act except with the right of access.[98] The Directive mentions that exemptions can only be made from Articles 6, 7 and 8, and so it is clear that the Spanish exemptions are broader than those of the Directive. Portugal exempts manual processing from complying with the domestic provisions equivalent to Articles 6, 7 and 8 of the Directive and from the right of access and the obligation to inform until the 26 October 2003.[99] This is

---

[96] Article 16-II of French Bill of Law voted by the Senate on the 1 April 2003, on protection of individuals with regard to processing of personal data and modifying Law no. 78–17 of the 6 January 1978; Section 51(3) of the Swedish Personal Data Act (1998:204) of the 29 April 1998.

[97] Directive 95/46/EC, Article 32(2).

[98] First additional provision of the Spanish Organic Law 15/1999 of the 13 December on the Protection of Personal Data.

[99] Transitional provisions of the Portuguese Act no. 67/98 of the 26 October 1998 on the Protection of Personal Data.

also broader than the provisions of the Directive, as are the transitional provisions in the UK law.

The majority of the countries studied here and almost all the NAS countries did not enact a transitional exemption concerning manual processing which lasts until 2007. The usual transitional provisions which can be found in the domestic law last for three years or less and concern any processing already under way at the date of the adoption of the domestic law. The provisions from which manual processing are exempted can be different from one country to the other. The obligation to inform and the principles of lawfulness are often mentioned. The obligation to notify the processing to the Supervisory Authority is very often exempted in the transitional provisions of the pre-2004 NAS[100] and in the transitional exemptions of some of the EU and EEA countries.[101]

Duties Imposed on the Controller and Rights Granted to Data Subjects in Europe

Articles 6, 7 and 8 of the Directive provide the data protection principles and the processing conditions imposed on any controller. In relation to them, this part of the chapter focuses on the condition of consent generally, the conditions applying to the processing of sensitive data in the case of public interest, the use of a national identification number and finally on the conditions applying to processing for the purposes of historical research. In relation to the rights granted to the data subject under the Directive, this chapter will focus on two of these rights: the right to information and the right to object. First, it analyses the right to information and the case of change of purpose. Secondly, it will outline the existence and the meaning of the right to object for 'compelling legitimate grounds'.

Consent: Definitions, the Notion of Explicit Consent and the Possible Hierarchy of Consent in the Processing Conditions

Introduction   The Directive defines consent as a freely given, specific and informed decision (Articles 2(h)), which according to the processing conditions for personal data under Article 7(a) should be given unambiguously. In the case of processing sensitive data, Article 8(2)(a) states that the data subject should give his or her 'explicit consent', a phrase that is not directly defined in the Directive.

The first question this section will address is whether the general definition of consent across countries is the same as that in the Directive. The second is what is required to turn this into explicit consent. Finally, this section will look at the consent requirement in relation to the other processing conditions, and whether they are interpreted as being open alternatives (any condition may be used), or partially lexically ordered (some kind of priority is given to consent).

---

[100] In the Latvian, Czech, Bulgarian Data Protection Acts.
[101] In the Norwegian and Dutch Data Protection Acts.

The definition of consent when processing personal data   The summary below shows the difference in wording of the definition of consent requirements when processing personal data:[102]

- Freely given, specific and informed and unambiguous (the same as the Directive) in Belgium, Netherlands, Spain, Sweden, and Malta.
- Freely given, specific and informed in Denmark, Estonia,[103] Lithuania, Norway and Portugal.
- Freely given, informed, specific and explicit in Greece.
- Freely given and unambiguous in Latvia.
- Informed and specific in Czech Republic.
- Express, unambiguous, free, specific, and informed in Luxembourg.
- Voluntary, detailed, conscious, and unambiguous in Finland.
- Free, informed and explicit in Germany.
- Specific, written, freely given, express and informed in Italy.
- Explicit in Ireland.
- '[A] declaration of will by which the data subject signifies his/her agreement to personal data relating to him/her being processed; the consent cannot be alleged or presumed on the basis of the declaration of will of other content' in Poland.
- Not defined in France, UK, Bulgaria and Hungary.

These differences show a need for the Directive's requirements on consent to be elucidated, with a particular focus on what each of the terms means, and how important they are. It is clear from the above examples of the different definitions of consent, that there is variation between countries. There are some countries that have implemented the wording in the Directive directly, but even here there could be differences in the way it is implemented in practice. Some of the countries appear to have extended the requirements of the Directive, for example, Germany and Italy, whose law includes the stipulation that consent for processing personal data must also be written, a condition never mentioned in the Directive, even in relation to sensitive personal data. In some cases the requirements of the Directive have been narrowed, for example in the Czech Republic, where there is no mention of the consent needing to be either freely given, or voluntary. In some countries, there is no mention of the condition that consent be informed, for example, in Greece, Latvia, Finland, Ireland and Poland. Finally, in the law in some countries, there is not even a definition of consent (a solution is presumably given in the relevant guidance to the law, which has no actual legal standing), such as in UK, Bulgaria, Lithuania and France (where the CNIL—the French Supervisory Authority—have given a definition).

---

[102] Which could, in part, be due to the English translation of the law.

[103] Consent is described in Section 12(1) of the Personal Data Protection Act 2003, (RT[1] I 2003, 26, 158), as '...a freely given specific and informed indication of the wishes of a data subject by which the data subject signifies his or her agreement to personal data relating to him or her being processed'.

The definition of consent when processing sensitive personal data   The question here is first, how did the law interpret the provision for explicit consent, and secondly, how is it interpreted in practice? What is required to turn into explicit consent a freely-given informed indication by which the data subject unambiguously signifies his or her agreement to the processing of personal data relating to him or her? The summary below shows some of the main terms used in the various national laws in relation to the type of consent requirements for processing sensitive data:

-   Explicit consent in Portugal, Sweden, UK and Malta.
-   Express consent in Finland, France and the Netherlands.
-   Written consent in Belgium, Greece, Bulgaria, Hungary, Latvia, Lithuania[104] and Poland.
-   Express reference in Germany.
-   Explicit and written in Spain.[105]
-   Approval of Supervisory Authority in Italy.
-   Specific reference and written in the Czech Republic.
-   Same as that for personal data (explicit) in Ireland, Denmark and Estonia.
-   Same as that for personal data (express) in Luxembourg.
-   Same as that for personal data (not express or explicit) in Norway.

In some of these cases it is clear exactly how the national law has interpreted the requirements for explicit consent, in others it is not. The interesting question here is how the countries interpret such terms as 'explicit' and 'express' in practice. In the reports compiled in the companion volume,[106] the authors are often unsure as to the interpretation of explicit consent. This is the case in Sweden, Malta, Finland, Ireland, and Luxembourg. Portugal interpreted explicit consent as written consent, at least for health data[107], and the French Supervisory Authority interprets express consent as written.[108] In Italy, consent must be given in writing, as well as approval should be given by the Garante (Supervisory Authority).[109] A very common answer to what makes consent explicit is that it should be written, but a more literal

---

[104] The Lithuanian Law on Legal Protection of Personal Data (as amended on 21 January 2003) states in Article 2, paragraph 11 '... consent with regard to special categories of personal data must be expressed clearly – in a written form, its equivalent or any other form giving an unambiguous evidence of the data subject's free will'.

[105] However, some types of sensitive data require different treatment—it is only written for personal data which reveals ideology, trade union membership, religion and beliefs (Article 7.2 of Organic Law 15/1999 on the Protection of Personal Data). Personal data referring to racial origin, health or sex life may be processed with explicit consent (Article 7.3).

[106] D. Beyleveld, D. Townend, S. Rouillé-Mirza, J. Wright (ed.), *Implementation of the Data Protection Directive in Relation to Medical Research in Europe* (Aldershot: Ashgate Publishing Ltd, 2004).

[107] European Commission, 2003, n. 16 above, 12.

[108] However in France (see n. 47), on the Internet, written consent can be substituted by a double-click (one for consent, and another to expressly consent).

[109] Isabelle de Lamberterie, n. 47 above.

interpretation would be that it requires some kind of affirmative action (not necessarily written) that is very specific, where the data subject actively indicates consent. This definition would certainly benefit from further explanation from the EC. The countries outlined below are a selection of those that did not follow the interpretation of explicit consent as written.

Denmark: In Denmark, explicit consent (given both for personal and sensitive personal data), means that there needs to be some affirmative action, for example, the data subject saying or writing 'yes, I consent'. The consent should not be tacit or indirect.[110]

The Netherlands: The Data Protection Authority's guidance[111] states that for explicit consent, the data subject must have expressed his will explicitly, by some affirmative action, and that this is (even) stronger than unambiguous consent. Explicit consent does not directly require it to be written.[112]

The UK: The Information Commissioner's Legal Guidance[113] states that the explicit consent needed for processing sensitive data means that the consent must be 'absolutely clear' and should cover, as appropriate; specific details of the processing, the type of data to be used, purposes and any specific aspects of the processing which may affect the individual (for example, disclosures). This indicates that explicit can be interpreted here as meaning 'absolutely clear'.[114]

Hierarchy of consent in relation to conditions for processing Articles 7 and 8 lay down the conditions to be met for legitimate processing; in the case of personal data, one or more from Article 7 should be met, and for sensitive data (most view as additionally), one from Article 8. In both cases, the first condition when such data can be processed on the list is either unambiguous (Article 7) or explicit consent (Article 8). The conditions are separated by *or*, which generally means in law that they are open alternatives—and that the conditions can be appealed to separately. However, a question that arises here is whether, when one of the other processing conditions is satisfied, and consent is not impracticable or inappropriate

---

[110] Professor Mette Hartlev, see n. 44 above, 62–63.

[111] Ministry of Justice/CBP, 2001, n. 79 above, 50.

[112] Jessica Wright and Jeroen Terstegge 'The Implementation of Directive 95/46/EC in Dutch Law and Medical Research' in D. Beyleveld, D. Townend, S. Rouillé-Mirza, J. Wright (ed.), *Implementation of the Data Protection Directive in Relation to Medical Research in Europe* (Aldershot: Ashgate Publishing Ltd, 2004), 273–288.

[113] UK Information Commissioner, *Data Protection Act 1998: Legal Guidance* (Version 1), (1998), 30, para. 3.1.5.

[114] Deryck Beyleveld, Andrew Grubb, David Townend, Ryan Morgan, and Jessica Wright 'The UK's Implementation of Directive 95/46/EC' in D. Beyleveld, D. Townend, S. Rouillé-Mirza, J. Wright (ed.), *Implementation of the Data Protection Directive in Relation to Medical Research in Europe* (Aldershot: Ashgate Publishing Ltd, 2004), 403–428, 425–426.

to achieve, it should still be sought. This would indicate a partial lexical priority for consent.

The UK report contains a very interesting discussion on this question in relation to that of human rights and the jurisprudence of the European Court of Human Rights. It mentions that

> in, for example, *MS v Sweden,* it is clear that the European Court of Human Rights considers the processing of any data on a person's health without consent to engage Article 8(1) ECHR and require a justification in terms of Article 8(2) of the Convention. And while neither the UK Act nor the Directive explicitly states that consent must take lexical priority, neither instrument says anything that does precludes such an interpretation, which renders an interpretation of lexical priority for consent possible in the terms of the Human Rights Act 1998. [115]

This statement would mean that generally, in the terms of the European Convention on Human Rights (the Convention), consent would appear to have a lexical priority (at least for health data), unless there is a justification under Article 8(2) of the Convention. If Article 8(2) of the Convention applies to the other processing conditions in Articles 7 and 8, then these will be justified as applying even when consent is readily available. It is beyond the scope of this chapter to discuss whether the processing conditions are justifiable under Article 8(2) which states that the right to respect for private and family life, home and correspondence applies

> ...except such as is in accordance with the law and is necessary in a democratic society in the interests of national security, public safety or the economic well-being of the country, for the prevention of disorder or crime, for the protection of health or morals, or for the protection of the rights and freedoms of others (Article 8(2)).

Keeping in mind the fact that the Directive was based around these principles, it is not objectionable to claim that this is also the case in the Directive itself. What follows is a discussion of the position the countries hold in relation to whether it is felt the processing conditions either a) view them as open alternatives or b) give consent a priority.[116]

Open alternatives   This is the position held in the majority of countries, for example; Denmark, Finland, Germany, Ireland, Italy, Luxembourg, The Netherlands,[117] Portugal, Sweden, the UK, Bulgaria, Latvia, Malta and Poland. In practice, this means that as long as one processing condition is satisfied from the national provisions equivalent to Articles 7 and 8, consent does not have to be

---

[115] Deryck Beyleveld, Andrew Grubb, David Townend, Ryan Morgan and Jessica Wright, n. 114 above, 417.

[116] It is important to note that some countries are missing from this discussion as the position on this question was not certain.

[117] However, in relation specifically to disclosure and medical research, consent is always required. This has few exceptions, see Jessica Wright and Jeroen Terstegge, n. 112 above.

obtained, even if it is practicable and not a disproportionate effort. As discussed earlier, this position could be incorrect in the light of the European Convention on Human Rights. In Cyprus, the law is interesting because although it highlights consent in Section 5(1) as required for processing of personal data to take place, it then in Section 5(2) lists exemptions to this provision. This also occurs in Czech law and shows that consent is the main rule, but can have exemptions. This seems to be more classed as an 'open alternative' structure, but also appears to give consent a priority. It is uncertain where Cyprus and the Czech Republic should be categorized.

Give consent a priority There are many countries where the processing conditions are viewed to be partially lexically ordered, for example; Belgium, Cyprus, the Czech Republic (questionable, see above), Greece and Norway. In Greece there is an emphasis on consent in Article 5 of the Data Protection Law,[118] but there are still (exceptional) exceptions to this following the Directive in the subsequent Articles.[119] T. Garanis-Papadatos and D. Boukis state in the Greek report[120] that the conditions for legitimate processing are treated as being partially lexically ordered. In Norway, the conditions for legitimate processing are treated as lexically ordered—therefore there is an emphasis on consent and statutory authority for the processing as the main rule and the rest of the conditions are treated as open alternatives. In Section 11(1), Estonian law,[121] states that '[p]rocessing of personal data is permitted only upon data subject's consent, unless otherwise set forth in law'. These are strong words, and are added to emphasize that consent has a clear priority in relation to other alternatives.[122] In Belgium, it is 'necessary to get consent unless this would be impracticable or inappropriate',[123] which indicates partial lexical ordering.

Conclusions on the hierarchy of consent It is questionable to what extent consent has a priority in the processing conditions. It is arguable that, according to EC law, consent is required unless it is impracticable or inappropriate to achieve it (a position reflected in at least Belgium). There are only a few countries who hold this view, but other countries, however, go half-way and emphasize consent as the

---

[118] Law 2472/1997 on the Protection of Individuals with regard to the Processing of Personal Data (as amended by Laws 2819/2000 and 2915/2001), Greece.

[119] Tina Garanis-Papadatos and Dimitris Boukis 'Report on Data Protection Law 2472/97 in Greece' in D. Beyleveld, D. Townend, S. Rouillé-Mirza, J. Wright (ed.), *Implementation of the Data Protection Directive in Relation to Medical Research in Europe* (Aldershot: Ashgate Publishing Ltd, 2004), 141–156.

[120] Tina Garanis-Papadatos and Dimitris Boukis, n. 119 above, 146.

[121] Personal Data Protection Act passed 12 February 2003 (RT[1] I 2003, 26, 158), Consolidated Version, Estonia.

[122] From correspondence with Ants Nõmper, Estonian member of the PRIVIREAL project.

[123] Professor Herman Nys 'Report on the Implementation of Directive 95/46/EC in Belgian Law' in D. Beyleveld, D. Townend, S. Rouillé-Mirza, J. Wright (ed.), *Implementation of the Data Protection Directive in Relation to Medical Research in Europe* (Aldershot: Ashgate Publishing Ltd, 2004), 29–41, 36.

main rule with the other conditions being listed as exemptions. However, many countries do not give consent any priority at all, and simply have it top of a list of conditions. It seems that some clarification is required generally about whether consent should indeed be given a direct priority. It can be noted that many countries have separate rules and laws relating to consent and medical research, which very often require that consent *is* obtained in this case—this is at least the case in Finland, the Netherlands and Sweden.

The Prohibition of Processing Sensitive Data and Exemption in the Public Interest

Introduction Public interest is a concept which is not defined in the Directive but which is nevertheless used to exempt certain processing operations from particular provisions of the Directive. One of them is Article 8(4) which exempts, under certain conditions, the processing of sensitive data for substantial public interest from the prohibition of processing sensitive data. This will be studied hereafter.

The Directive also has Articles concerning public security or safety. Article 3(2) exempts from the whole Directive matters of public security, defence, state security, and activities relating to criminal law, the areas where the EC has no jurisdiction. Another provision of the Directive, Article 13, allows countries to exempt processing made for the purposes of national security, defence, and public security from Article 6(1) amongst other provisions. Article 13 of the Directive does not include an exemption to the provisions of Articles 7 or 8 directly but it does indirectly as it exempts from Article 6(1) which includes that data should be processed fairly and lawfully—and Articles 7 and 8 are requirements for lawful processing. In consequence, when a country provides an exemption to the processing of sensitive data for public interest, it is not clear if the country implements Article 3(2), Article 13 or Article 8(4) of the Directive. Thus, any exemptions found to the prohibition of processing sensitive data in the domestic laws in relation to state security etc. could only possibly be attributable to the 'substantial public interest' provision of Article 8(4) of the Directive. Examples of those countries with such exemptions are Belgium (State Safety under Article 3(4)), Bulgaria (national security and national defence under Article 21(2)(6), Cyprus (National needs/security under Article 6(2)(g)), Czech Republic (national security Article 3(6)), Germany (serious threat to public security (Section 13(2)(5)) or it is urgently necessary in order to avert serious prejudice to the public interest or to safeguard important public interest concerns (Section 13(2)(6)) and necessary on compelling grounds relating to defence or the fulfilment of multilateral or bilateral obligations of the Federal Government in the area of crisis management or conflict prevention or for humanitarian measures (Section 13(2)(9))), Greece (national security, criminal or correctional policy, offences, public health or public control on social welfare service (Art. 7(2)(e))), Italy (Some types of criminal data can be processed with an authorization from the Supervisory Authority, which must confirm the 'substantial public interest' addressed by the processing (Article 24.1)).

Implementing Article 8(4) specifically Some of the provisions of the domestic laws seem to be specifically implementing Article 8(4) of the Directive. Article 8 of the Directive prohibits the processing of special categories of data. However, Articles 8(2) to 8(5) mention several exemptions to this principle, and specifically, Article 8(4) states that:

> [s]ubject to the provision of suitable safeguards, Member States may, for reasons of substantial public interest, lay down exemptions in addition to those laid down in paragraph 2 either by national law or by decision of the Supervisory Authority.

Thus, the question is whether the EU, EEA and NAS countries included this possibility given by the Directive to create other exemptions in the substantial public interest to Article 8, and another question is what is generally considered as being a reason of substantial public interest.

First of all, it appears that Austria, Finland,[124] Greece, Italy, Latvia, and Lithuania do not set out a provision concerning the possibility to create new exemptions to the prohibition of processing sensitive data for substantial public interest. In other countries such as Denmark, France, Germany, Luxembourg and Poland, the domestic laws only mention the possibility of creating such exemptions in this case but no example or interpretation of what 'substantial public interest' means is given in the law, so no further exemptions can be seen and the possibility is left open for future interpretation. In Denmark however, Section 10 of the Act concerning research provision is an example of what 'substantial public interest' means.

In the other countries, the data protection law sets out different cases where sensitive data can be processed for reasons of substantial public interest. From a general point of view, it appears that substantial public interest is interpreted as in the interest of society, for State security or for public safety. For example, the Czech law seems to interpret the notion of public interest in providing that sensitive data can be processed if it is necessary to eliminate an imminent danger to the data subject's property or for the purpose of social security.[125] Some countries give more details. In Ireland the processing of sensitive data is exempted from prohibition in numerous instances and in particular when processing concerns taxes or social welfare payments.[126] The 2002 Irish Bill also mentions damage to the property or health of the data subject in 2B(1)biii. Lithuania also, although perhaps not directly related to substantial public interest, includes social care information as an exemption when related to social insurance or other social care purposes, but

---

[124] However, the EC's 'Analysis and Impact Study on the Implementation of Directive EC 95/46/EC in Member States' mentions the possibility for the Finnish supervisory authority to allow processing of sensitive data in certain circumstances, as for examples, for the maintainance of records by banks and insurance companies, n. 16 above, 15.

[125] Act of the 4 April 2000 on the Protection of Personal Data and on Amendment to Some Related Acts, Article 9(b) and 9(c) Czech Republic.

[126] Data Protection (Amendment) Act, 2002 (No.6 of 2003), Article 2B (1)(b) xii and xiii, Ireland.

only between social care providers.[127] Portugal mentions legal or criminal issues as an interpretation of substantial public interest. Finally, 'legal' medicine, the disclosure of diseases, or donor registers and archiving are examples quoted in different legislation as being of substantial public interest. In Estonia for instance, the processing of data concerning health or genetic information without the consent of the data subject is possible if it is assigned by law to a controller for public interest. This means that in all these cases, and other cases which could be decided by the Supervisory Authority in certain countries, the prohibition of the processing of sensitive data could be lifted. The chapter includes a focus on the interpretation of exemption for substantial public interest in relation to medical research.

Protection of Sensitive Data and National Identification Numbers

Introduction   Article 8 of the Directive is devoted to the processing of special categories of data, and Article 8(7) states that:

> Member States shall determine the conditions under which a national identification number or any other identifier of general application may be processed.

This provision seems to be compulsory and, as a consequence, domestic laws should have a provision concerning the processing of an identification number. Such an identification number is considered, in particular, as permitting the identification of a data subject (Article 2 of the Directive).

A personal identification number can be either national, also of 'general application', or can be devoted to only one sector (bank, health, social security, etc.). The Directive concerns the first kind of personal identification number. Such a number of general application can be defined as 'a unique means of identifying an individual in an administrative file'.[128] A general identification number can be used not only by the public sector but by the private sector as well. The same number can be used as a tax number, a social security number, a passport number and as a number used by the private sector. A general identification number has the advantage to render the management of administration more efficient, to save costs and to reach a good level of accuracy in the identification of the data subject. However, a general identification number leads to particular risks, in giving such a huge power of identification to the administration which can match up different information on the data subject by using only one number. In studying the establishment of such an identification number, the Constitutional Court of Germany stated that a universal personal identification number 'would constitute a possible attack on human dignity by opening up possibilities of social control through increased possibilities for file-interconnection and individual and group

---

[127] Law Amending the Law on Legal Protection of Personal Data of the 11th June 1996, No. I-1374 Vilnius (As amended on the 21 January, 2003 No. IX-1296), Article 9, Lithuania.
[128] Study prepared by the Committee of experts on data protection (CJ-PD) under the Authority of the European Committee on Legal Co-operation (CDCJ), *The Introduction and Use of Personal Identification Numbers: The Data Protection Issues* (1991), Strasbourg.

profiling.'[129] Moreover, a general identification number could be used with other techniques of identification, such as genetic fingerprints and other systems of biometry. Such a combination would increase the possibility of identifying the data subject and of processing sensitive data.

The aim of this study is to know whether the countries surveyed have implemented Article 8(7) of the Directive in their domestic laws and then to outline what these domestic provisions state on this topic.

Implementing Article 8(7) First of all, it can be noted that Bulgaria, the Czech Republic, Germany, Greece and Spain do not provide any statements concerning the establishment of an identification number in their data protection law, and so do not provide any conditions for the processing of a national identifier (or other). However, Spain has regulated the use of its national identification number in the Decree of 12 August 1982[130] in which it is stated that: '...With the purpose of making all administrative procedures quicker and easier, the I.D. number will be a general numerical identifier' (Article 4). It is also established that 'during its emission the right to privacy will be preserved and it will be supported by electronic systems of gathering, processing and transmitting information, trying to give the highest guarantees of accuracy, data untransferability and number unity'.

Greece once had a national identification number, which has been abolished by Law 1988/91. Even more interestingly, the Czech Republic has a National Identification Number, which is used in different sectors; for example in the health sector to identify patients, but no provision on this topic can be found in its law. In this case, only the general provisions of the Data Protection Law apply to the processing of this number.

Secondly, amongst the other countries, a minority have provisions on the processing of the identification number in an Act other than the national Data Protection Act,[131] and a majority have implemented Article 8(7) of the Directive by adding such a provision in their Data Protection Act.[132]

Some of the countries provided that the consent of the data subject must be obtained in the case of processing a general identification number[133] or that the right to information of the data subject has to be complied with.[134] In Denmark, explicit consent is required where the processing is undertaken in the private sector, except in relation to the exemptions in Section 11(2) of the Act.[135]

---

[129] See n. 128 above.

[130] Professor Carlos Maria Romeo Casabona and Pilar Nicolás 'The Implementation of Directive 95/46/EC in Spain' in D. Beyleveld, D. Townend, S. Rouillé-Mirza, J. Wright (ed.), *Implementation of the Data Protection Directive in Relation to Medical Research in Europe* (Aldershot: Ashgate Publishing Ltd, 2004), 358–380, 369.

[131] Belgium, Ireland, Portugal, Latvia, Poland and Hungary.

[132] Denmark, Finland, France, Italy, Luxembourg, The Netherlands, Norway, Sweden, UK, Estonia, Lithuania, Malta and Romania.

[133] This is notably the case of Denmark, Estonia, Lithuania, Malta, Norway and Sweden.

[134] Latvia.

[135] Act on Processing of Personal Data No. 429 of 31 May 2000, Denmark.

However, all these countries also provide some exemptions where obtaining consent is not necessary. This is generally the case where processing of the identification number is required by law,[136] when the processing is made for research or statistical purposes,[137] or when the data are not collected from the data subject.[138] Other countries enumerate the purposes for which processing of an identification number can be undertaken. For instance, Finland allows such processing for health care research or scientific activities, Ireland allows it in the taxation, welfare, education and local activities sectors and Lithuania for use by institutions, agencies and firms involved in granting of loans, recovery of debts, insurance or leasing, health care and social insurance, institutions of social care, educational institutions and institutions of science and learning.

Some other countries, more generally, state that an identification number can be used only if the law provides for this.[139] In France the processing of an identification number has to be authorized by the Supervisory Authority when the controller is in the private sector, and by a decree taken in Conseil d'Etat after an opinion of the Supervisory Authority when the controller is in the public sector. The processing of a general identifier is in this case very regulated. On the contrary, in Luxembourg and Poland, the provisions are less strict on this topic. The identification number is considered as another piece of personal data and is required to comply with the Data Protection Law.

Finally, it should be observed that some laws contain a provision concerning a general identification number but no such number exists, for the time-being, in the country. This is the case in Italy and the UK where the laws only mention the possibility of the existence of such a number. The Portuguese law makes provisions for identification numbers, *but* states that identification number of general application are not permitted as it would be contrary to the Portuguese Constitution.

In conclusion, regulation of a general identification number is not harmonized in Europe, probably because the Directive does not mention any compulsory rules to follow on this topic. However, the Directive does mention it under Article 8, which means it should be considered and protected as sensitive data. Some of the European countries are very reluctant to even create a national or general identification number, whereas some others consider it as basic personal data. However, it appears that an important number of countries require the consent of the data subject to be obtained to allow the processing of personal data in a general identification number and mention strict conditions where exemptions are possible.

Exempting Historical Research from Articles 6, 7 and 8 of the Directive

Introduction   Looking at the transitional exemptions contained in the Data Protection Directive, it appears that Article 32(3) permits Member States, subject

---

[136] Estonia, Lithuania and Malta.
[137] Denmark and Lithuania.
[138] Norway.
[139] Ireland, Malta and The Netherlands.

to suitable safeguards, to exempt data kept for the sole purpose of historical research from Articles 6, 7 and 8 of the Directive.[140] These provisions concern the principles relating to data quality, the criteria for making data processing legitimate and for the processing of special categories of data. Following the exemption of Article 32(3), Members States had the possibility to exempt processing for the purpose of historical research from these provisions without any time limit. It is interesting to evaluate how the EU and EEA countries have used this exemption and to know whether the NAS countries were influenced by this provision when writing their data protection law.

Interpretation of historical research   First of all, it is necessary to know how 'historical research' is interpreted through the different countries. In the large majority of countries, the data protection law does not define 'historical research'. The Italian law is the only one giving a definition of this term. Thus, 'historical research' includes 'studies, investigations, research and documentation concerning characters, events and situation of the past'.[141] Apart from this, some of the reports written for the project give an interpretation of this term. The majority of these interpretations agree that 'historical research' concerns retrospective research. This is the interpretation given by the Finnish, Latvian and Polish reports.[142] The Latvian interpretation talks about archives as being 'historical research'.[143] On the other hand, the UK interpretation specifies that 'historical research' should be interpreted differently than processing for 'historical purposes', assuming that research is one of the different purposes existing in relation to processing for historical purposes.[144] An interesting interpretation to draw attention to is that of the German law. Following this interpretation, 'historical research' only concerns research on living persons and does not apply to research on dead persons. This

---

[140] Directive 95/46/EC, Article 32(3): 'By way of derogation from paragraph 2, Member States may provide, subject to suitable safeguards, that data kept for the sole purpose of historical research need not be brought into conformity with Articles 6, 7 and 8 of this Directive'.

[141] Italian Legislative Decree no. 281/1999, Section 1(2), letter b).

[142] See Dr Lasse A. Lehtonen 'The Implementation of EU Directive 95/46/EC and the Protection of Sensitive Health Data in Medical Research in Finland' in D. Beyleveld, D. Townend, S. Rouillé-Mirza, J. Wright (ed.), *Implementation of the Data Protection Directive in Relation to Medical Research in Europe* (Aldershot: Ashgate Publishing Ltd, 2004), 87–95; Inga Cabe, 'The Implementation of Directive 95/46/EC into National Legislation With Regard to Medical Research in Latvia' in D. Beyleveld, D. Townend, S. Rouillé-Mirza, J. Wright (ed.), *Implementation of the Data Protection Directive in Relation to Medical Research in Europe* (Aldershot: Ashgate Publishing Ltd, 2004), 209–218; and Dr. Paweł Łuków, 'Personal Data Protection and Medical Research in Poland' in D. Beyleveld, D. Townend, S. Rouillé-Mirza, J. Wright (ed.), *Implementation of the Data Protection Directive in Relation to Medical Research in Europe* (Aldershot: Ashgate Publishing Ltd, 2004), 307–318.

[143] Inga Cabe, see n. 142 above.

[144] Deryck Beyleveld, Andrew Grubb, David Townend, Ryan Morgan and Jessica Wright, n. 114 above.

interpretation is a probable consequence of the fact that the German data protection law does not apply to dead persons.[145] In consequence, a provision in the Act only concerns living persons even when it mentions historical issues. To summarize, it appears that historical research is interpreted in the majority of data protection laws as retrospective research.

Exemptions for historical research   The second step of this analysis is to know whether the European countries used the provision set out in the Directive to exempt processing made for purposes of historical research from respecting the principles equivalent to Articles 6, 7 and 8 of the Directive in their data protection law.

After consideration of the domestic law reports, it appears that about half of the countries do not provide an exemption to the principles mentioned above in the case of processing for the purposes of historical research. A minority of countries repeat the Directive in their law and adopt the same kind of exemptions. This is the case in Ireland and Latvia, for example. Finally the countries provide exemptions concerning processing for the purposes of historical research but these exemptions do not cover all the principles in Articles 6, 7 and 8 of the Directive, only partly using the exemptions offered by the Directive. In studying what exemptions are usually granted to processing for historical research, it is revealed that a usual method is to exempt this processing from the principle stating that personal data should not be kept for longer than necessary. This is the case in the Czech Republic, France, Italy and Sweden, although France only allows this exemption where processing is made for the purpose of keeping data for historical research. The Czech law adds that this keeping is only allowed for archival purposes. Usually changing the purpose is prohibited in the Directive and the domestic laws when the new purpose of the processing is incompatible with the original one. Once again, several countries, using the exemption provided in Article 6(b) of the Directive, exempt processing from this prohibition when the controller changes the purpose of his or her processing to a purpose of historical research. This is the case, for instance, in Poland and Spain. German law, however, provides this exemption only for the publication of the results of research on contemporary history.[146]

Historical research and suitable safeguards   After having found out which countries have implemented or used the exemption provided in Article 32(3) of the Directive, it appears necessary to check if the different countries have complied with the condition of providing suitable safeguards. It seems that some of the countries did not set out any provision for safeguards concerning this exemption. This is the case for instance in Finland, Germany, Portugal and Ireland. In Ireland,

---

[145] Dr Hermann Christoph Kühn, see n. 90 above.
[146] Paragraph 40.3 of the German Federal Data Protection Act of the 20 December 1990 (BGBl. I 1990 S. 2954), as amended, last amendment on the 14 January 2003.

suitable safeguards will be provided in future regulations.[147] In other countries, the laws require that the controller take measures to ensure the security, secrecy, confidentiality or storage of the personal data.[148] These measures should be considered as suitable safeguards in the case of processing personal data for the purpose of historical research. Another kind of suitable safeguard is the principle of not using the data to make individual decisions regarding the data subject and is provided in the Italian and the Maltese laws. Finally, Luxembourg and Denmark point out the importance of the role of the Supervisory Authority in safeguarding the rights of data subjects. In Luxembourg, the Supervisory Authority is the only body which can authorize processing for historical research purposes when it does not comply with data protection law.[149]

To summarize, it appears that the exemptions provided by Article 32(3) of the Directive have been used in about half of the countries studied here, but in different ways. The problem appearing here is that countries using this exemption do not always provide suitable safeguards, as the Directive requires. This can be interpreted as being an incorrect implementation of this provision.

Right to Information and Change of Purpose

The Directive mentions the information to be given to the data subject in Articles 10 and 11. The right to information is probably the most important right given to data subjects. When the data subject is informed about the processing of his or her own personal data, he or she can then exercise the other rights provided by the Directive, notably checking that the law is respected and that the controller does not surpass his power. Moreover, the data subject needs to be informed about the processing in order to give his consent, when this is a requirement of the law. Thus, the Directive mentions the different information which has to be provided to the data subject. However, the Directive makes a distinction between the information to provide where the personal data have been collected directly from the data subject (Article 10) and where the data have not been collected from the data subject (Article 11). In both situations the types of information to be provided are almost the same. To summarize what this information is, it can be said that the controller or his representative has to inform the data subject of the identity of the controller, the purpose of the processing, the recipients of the data, whether replies

---

[147] Dr Deirdre Madden and Dr Maeve McDonagh 'Implementation of Directive 95/46/EC in Relation to Medical Research in the Republic of Ireland' in D. Beyleveld, D. Townend, S. Rouillé-Mirza, J. Wright (ed.), *Implementation of the Data Protection Directive in Relation to Medical Research in Europe* (Aldershot: Ashgate Publishing Ltd, 2004), 175–192.

[148] See examples given in the domestic reports for Denmark (Mette Hartlev, see n. 44 above), Poland (Dr. Paweł Łuków, n. 142 above), Spain (Professor Carlos Maria Romeo Casabona and Pilar Nicolás, see n. 130 above), Sweden (Professor Elisabeth Rynning, see n. 70 above).

[149] Article 42(3) of the Luxembourg Law of the 2 August 2002 on the Protection of Persons with regard to the Processing of Personal Data A—Number 91 13 August 2002.

to the questions are obligatory or not and the existence of the right to access and to rectify data.

However, when data are not collected from the data subject, the controller has to give this information 'at the time of undertaking the recording of personal data or if a disclosure to a third party is envisaged, no later than the time when the data are first disclosed'. Nothing is mentioned in Article 10 about *when* the information has to be provided if the data have been collected from the data subject and then, after this, the controller envisages a disclosure to a third party. Thus, it seems that the information to be provided in the case where the data have been collected from the data subject and then the controller changes the purpose of the processing, has been left for the Members States to resolve.

However, when looking at Recital 39 of the Directive it appears that

> [d]ata can be legitimately disclosed to a third party, even if the disclosure was not anticipated at the time the data were collected from the data subject' and that 'the data subject should be informed when the data are recorded or at the latest when the data are first disclosed to a third party.

Thus, it seems that this situation is foreseen by the Directive and even if the controller changes the purpose of his or her processing, he or she should provide information to the data subject.[150] Another analysis is also possible. First, it can be noted that Recital 39 does not state that in the case where a controller changes his or her purpose after having collected data from the data subject, 'the data subject should be informed when the data are recorded or at the latest when the data are first disclosed to a third party.' Recital 39, in fact, only mentions the case where the controller makes an unanticipated disclosure of the data to a third party. This would mean that Recital 39 only concerns the unanticipated disclosure of data to a third party and not every change of purpose. Thus, it would mean that the Directive does not provide for the situation where data are collected from the data subject and then the controller changes the purpose of the processing (to another one than the disclosure to a third party). It could also be said that Article 10 applies to this case anyway, because this Article does not state when information has to be given to the data subject. Indeed, it states that 'the controller [...] must provide a data subject [...] the following information, except where he already has it' and then mentions: 'the purpose of the processing for which the data are intended'. Thus, if a controller who has collected data from a data subject for a first purpose, decides after a while to change the purpose of the processing, it appears that there is a new purpose intended—of which the data subject has to be informed.

In conclusion, it could be said that information has in any case to be provided to the data subject and that in the case of a disclosure to a third party, the controller has to provide information 'when the data are recorded or at the latest when the data are first disclosed to a third party'.

---

[150] See on this matter D. Beyleveld, 'The Duty to Provide Information to the Data Subject: Articles 10 and 11 of Directive 95/46/EC', Chapter 6 of this volume.

Now the second step of this analysis is to study how the countries surveyed have implemented the information provisions.

First of all, it can be observed that a majority of countries have implemented the information provision as it is written in the Directive, without giving more details. In this case, it is not possible by studying the domestic laws to know what information should be provided to a data subject when the controller wants to change the purpose of his or her processing after having collected data from the data subject. However, the domestic provisions are not exactly similar to those of the Directive and some peculiarities can be noted.

When has information to be provided to the data subject in the case where data have been collected from the data subject? In the Directive, Article 10 does not provide any time-limit for informing the data subjects whereas Article 11 states that information has to be provided 'at the time of undertaking the recording of personal data or if a disclosure to third party is envisaged, no later than the time when data are first disclosed'.

The study of the domestic laws shows that in the Article 10 case (where data are collected from the data subject), some countries require that information should be provided to the data subject no later than the time the data were obtained—that is to say the time of collection. This is the case in Belgium, Austria, Cyprus, Denmark, Finland, Germany, Greece, Luxembourg and the Netherlands. In other countries, no time-limit is mentioned in the case where data are collected directly from the data subjects. This is the case in Latvia, Lithuania, Malta, Norway, Poland, Portugal, Romania and Sweden. Many of the countries do not therefore provide any time-limit for informing the data subject. This could leave the question of knowing whether the data subject still has to be informed in the case of change of purpose open. However it can be said that since information has to be provided, especially concerning the purpose of the processing, and no time-limit is given to do so, this information should still have to be provided even after a change of purpose. Nothing in the Directive says that information should not be provided to data subjects after a change of purpose and the general statement of Article 10 leads one to interpret it as applying to any case.

Anyway, some peculiarities still have to be noted. In Ireland and the UK, the laws provide that information has to be given 'as far as practicable' which is difficult to interpret or can be interpreted in a very flexible way. In Bulgaria, there is no distinction between the cases of Articles 10 and 11 of the Directive. In both cases information has to be given to the data subject before the processing of data. In the Czech Republic and Italy, information has to be provided prior to commencing the processing. An interpretation of this provision could lead one to say that information still has to be given to the data subject in the case of change of purpose since it is prior to a new processing. In Hungary, information has to be given to the data subject before the data are collected.[151]

---

[151] DPA Art. 6. (2) as amended by the Parliamentary Act No. LXXII of 1999, Hungary.

In the Slovakian law it is said that information has to be provided only if it is requested from the data subject and within 30 days of the request. In Slovenia, information has to be provided in writing when the processing is on the basis of written consent and there is no other provision concerning the right to information. It is obvious that these countries do not comply with the provisions of the Directive on the right to information where information is supposed to be provided to the data subjects without any conditions.

When has information to be provided to the data subject in the case where data have not been collected directly from the data subject? The majority of the countries repeat the Directive in providing that information should be given at the time of undertaking the processing or at the time of the first disclosure of the data to a third person.[152] Some countries do not make a distinction in their law between the cases of Articles 10 and 11 of the Directive. Indeed, in Bulgaria, Hungary, Slovakia and Slovenia, the provided time-limit applies to the cases where data are collected from the data subject as well as the cases where data are not collected from the data subject (see above). The Austrian law does not mention when information should be provided in the case of Article 11 of the Directive. In the Czech Republic, information should be provided 'without delay'. In Latvia, information has to be provided prior to disclosure to a third person and in Poland 'immediately after the recording of personal data'. In Spain, it is mentioned that information should be provided within three months of the recording of data when data are not collected directly from data subjects and in the UK information must be provided 'as far as practicable'. These countries do not implement the Directive properly and have a provision slightly different from that which the Directive requires. In the three countries mentioned above (Czech Republic, Latvia and Poland) and Spain and the UK, the domestic law could allow the controller to take a certain amount of time before informing the data subject or not informing him or her at all.

What types of information have to be provided? It is interesting to study whether the countries surveyed provide the same type of information to be given to the data subject as the Directive. The information the Directive requires to be provided has been noted above.[153] Only five of the countries surveyed provide exactly the same information as the Directive requests to be given to the data subject.[154] However, the level of compliance with the Directive is higher if the information mentioned in Article 10 is the only case taken into account, that is to say, when the domestic laws provide information mentioned in Article 10 but not information concerning the categories of data mentioned in Article 11. Indeed, 13 countries have implemented Article 10 in respect of the information mentioned but not Article

---

[152] This is the case in Belgium, Cyprus, Denmark, Finland, France, Luxembourg, Lithuania (at the time of the disclosure in the case of purpose of direct marketing), Malta, The Netherlands, Norway, Greece, Ireland, Italy, Portugal, Romania and Sweden.
[153] See pages 163–164 above.
[154] This is the case of Belgium, Denmark, Ireland, Luxembourg and Malta.

11.[155] Finland and Estonia do not appear to mention information to be given in relation to whether replies to the questions of the data controller are obligatory or voluntary. Moreover, Germany, Hungary and Lithuania do not mention the information about the existence of a right of access and a right to rectify data. Slovakia, as well as the information mentioned above, does not provide information concerning the recipients of the data. The Netherlands, Hungary and the UK only mention the information with regard to the identity of the controller and the purpose of the processing and leave open the choice of further information necessary to enable processing in respect of the data subject to be fair.[156] Anyway, even if it can be said that these countries do not repeat the Directive on this point, it has to be recalled that providing all of this information does not seem to be compulsory in the Directive since it is stated, 'Member States shall provide that the controller or his representative must provide any further information such as' etc (Article 10(c) and 11(c)). Thus, Member States have the option to provide more information but the types of information mentioned in Article 10(c) and 11(c) of the Directive are just examples. Slovenia can be regarded as not providing the same rights to information as the Directive since the Slovenian law states that the only information to be provided are the purpose of the processing and the duration of storage of data and do not include information about the identity of the controller.

Which exemptions from the right to information do the domestic laws provide?
Article 11(2) provides two exemptions to the right to information in the case where information has not been collected from the data subject. The first one concerns 'processing for statistical purposes or for the purpose of historical or scientific research, where the provision of such information proves impossible or would involve a disproportionate effort' and the second concerns the case where recording or disclosure is expressly laid down by law.

A majority of countries provide these two exemptions and thus repeat the Directive.[157] However some of these countries do not make a distinction between the Article 10 and 11 cases of the Directive, which means that the exemptions would also apply in the case where data are collected from the data subject, which is not provided in the Directive.

Amongst the countries that do not provide the first exemption are Bulgaria, Greece, Hungary, Slovakia and Slovenia. The second exemption is not provided by Cyprus, Greece, Luxembourg, Portugal, Slovakia, Slovenia and Sweden. Some interesting points can be added to this analysis. In four domestic laws,[158] there is an exemption to the right to information in the case of processing made for

---

[155] This is the case of Bulgaria, Cyprus, Czech Republic, France, Greece, Italy, Latvia, Norway, Poland, Portugal, Romania, Spain and Sweden.
[156] Schedule 1 Part II Paragraph 2 (3) of the UK Data Protection Act 1998, 1998 Chapter 29.
[157] This is the case in Austria, Belgium, Czech Republic, Denmark, Estonia, Finland, France, Germany, Ireland, Italy, Latvia, Lithuania, Malta, The Netherlands, Norway, Poland, Romania, Spain and the UK.
[158] Cyprus, Greece, Portugal and Romania.

journalistic purposes and in nine countries[159] for public, defence, security or judicial purposes. In Luxembourg, a similar exemption is provided in the case of financial interest and in Poland the controller is exempted from the right to information if he or she 'does not intend further processing after single use'.[160] These exemptions provided by the above-mentioned countries seem to be related to the implementation of Article 13 of the Directive, which provides numerous cases of exemptions, notably to Articles 10 and 11 of the Directive.

In conclusion, it can be noticed that the exemption provisions of Article 11 of the Directive have been implemented in the countries by adopting provisions where the exemptions found are larger than those in the Directive. The countries have not limited themselves to the two cases provided by the Directive but added some other ones which could be said to be due to the implementation of Article 13 of the Directive. Thus, the right to information seems to be more easily exempted in the countries surveyed than in the Directive, which could be interpreted as a diminution of rights for the data subject. However, once again, if these exemptions were considered as resulting from the implementation of Article 13, then the Directive would be said as being well implemented.

After having analysed how the information provision has been implemented in the domestic law, another question arises about the consequences of a change of purpose.

Shall the controller inform the data subject when he/she changes the purpose of the processing when data have been directly collected from the data subject? There is no general answer that can be found in the domestic laws but in some of the countries a solution to this problem is given by interpretations of the laws.

For example, an interpretation of the Portuguese law[161] leads to the conclusion that information *should* be given in the case of a change of purpose, because Article 28 of the Portuguese law states that in the case of a new purpose, the processing needs to be authorized by the Supervisory Authority. The Authority thus checks that the rights of the data subject are respected in which is included the right to information. However in this case, only the information which has changed has to be provided to the data subject. In Finland, a practical interpretation of the law[162] allows one to say that information should be provided to the data subject in the case of a change of purpose, and when data are collected directly from the data subject, at the time of the disclosure of the data to a third party. The question then is whether information should also be provided where the controller changes the purpose of his or her processing but continues to process the data him or herself. The answer seems to be that the controller would have to inform the data subject only if the new purpose is not compatible with the purpose of the initial data processing. Later processing for a scientific research project would always be

---

[159] Cyprus, Denmark, Estonia, Finland, France, Greece, Italy, Luxembourg and Portugal.

[160] Article 25-2-4) of the Polish Act of the 29 August 1997 on the Protection of Personal Data, Journal of Laws of the 29 October 1997, No. 133, item 883 with later amendments.

[161] Helena Moniz and Catarina Sarmento e Castro, n. 62 above.

[162] Dr Lasse A. Lehtonen, n. 142 above.

considered to be compatible with the initial processing in Finland[163] as in most of the countries, following the data protection principles of the Directive. In Germany, the collection of data is unlawful if the data subject can prove that he/she would not have agreed to the collection if he or she had known the use of his/her data.[164] Thus, in practice it is advisable to inform the data subject about a change of purpose and maybe to ask for a new consent in order to avoid the processing operation being unlawful.

In Poland, it seems that the consent given to processing extends to the future uses of data if the purpose remains unchanged.[165] This would mean that in the case of a change of purpose, renewal of the consent has to be obtained and as the consent has to be informed, further information would also have to be given to the data subject.

In conclusion, it can be noted that the interpretation of the domestic laws leads one to consider that information should be provided to the data subject in the case of a change of purpose where the data have been collected from the data subject. This rule would particularly apply when the change of purpose amounts to a disclosure of data to a third person. However, the domestic laws seem to provide more exemptions to the right to information than the Directive in Articles 10 and 11. Thus, the implementation of the information provision seems to have been less strict than the Directive requires unless one considers the countries which have used such exemptions have implemented Article 13 of the Directive which exempts the controller from the information provision in a lot of cases.

Right to Object and Compelling Legitimate Grounds

Introduction Alongside the right to information, the Directive provides the right to object in Article 14 to protect data subjects. The first paragraph of this Article states:

> Member States shall grant the data subject the right:
> (a) at least in the cases referred to in Article 7 (e) and (f), to object at any time on compelling legitimate grounds relating to his particular situation to the processing of data relating to him, save where otherwise provided by national legislation. Where there is a justified objection, the processing instigated by the controller may no longer involve those data.

The Directive states that at least in two cases, data subjects shall have the right to object. The cases this relates to are Article 7(e) (processing made in the public interest) and Article 7(f) (processing made for legitimate interests).[166] The question

---

[163] Paragraph 7 of the Finnish Personal Data Act (523/1999).

[164] Dr Hermann Christoph Kühn, n. 90 above.

[165] Article 23-2 of the Polish Act of the 29 August 1997 on the Protection of Personal Data, *Journal of Laws* of the 29 October 1997, No. 133, item 883 with later amendments.

[166] Directive 95/46/EC, 'Article 7 (e) processing is necessary for the performance of a task carried out in the public interest or in the exercise of official Authority vested in the controller or in a third party to whom the data are disclosed; or

is whether the European countries have implemented or introduced such a right for the data subjects in their domestic law. This right is very important in practice, as it enables the data subjects to have control over the processing of their data. It seems particularly important to provide such a right to the data subjects when processing is made in the public interest or for legitimate interests. It could be said, for instance, that medical research is made in the public interest or can be termed as being a legitimate interest. In these cases, granting a right to object to data subjects seems to be of real importance to insure a balance of interests between controller or a third party and data subjects. However, the right to object can only be used if the data subject exercises it on 'compelling legitimate grounds'. This notion is not defined and this section tries to report the explanations given in the domestic reports for the meaning of this notion.

Implementing the right to object It appears that two domestic laws do not provide a right to object to the data subjects. This is the case in the Czech Republic and in Estonia where the laws provide more a right to access and to rectify than a right to object. This is obviously not respecting the principles set out by the Directive.

A minority of countries do not follow the Directive when they do provide a right to object to the data subject. The right to object in these countries is often limited to specific cases and in general includes the right to object when personal data are processed for direct marketing. Thus, these countries can be said as implementing more Article 14(b) than 14(a) of the Directive. Countries in this case include Finland (right to object granted in case where processing is made for direct sales, polls and professional or genealogy registries),[167] Greece (right to object in case where processing is made for selling or promoting goods and services),[168] Norway (right to object in case where processing is made notably for direct marketing[169]), Sweden (right to object in case where processing is made for direct marketing or where consent was a prerequisite to the lawfulness of the processing[170]), Hungary (right to object if the processing is used or transmitted for commercial purposes), Latvia (right to object in case where processing is made for commercial purposes[171]) and Lithuania (right to object in case where processing is made for commercial purposes[172]). These countries do not implement Article 14(a)

(f) processing is necessary for the purposes of the legitimate interests pursued by the controller or by the third party or parties to whom the data are disclosed, except where such interests are overridden by the interests for fundamental rights and freedoms of the data subject which require protection under Article 1 (1)'.

[167] Article 30 of the Finnish Personal Data Act (523/1999).

[168] Article 13 of the Greek Law 2472/1997 on the Protection of Individuals with regard to the Processing of Personal Data (as amended by Laws 2819/2000 and 2915/2001).

[169] Section 26 to 28 of the Norwegian Act of the 14th April 2000 No. 31 relating to the processing of personal data (Personal Data Act).

[170] Section 11 and 12 of the Swedish Personal Data Act (1998: 204) of the 29 April 1998.

[171] Article 19 of the Latvian Personal Data Protection Act adopted by the Saeima on the 23 March 2000.

[172] Article 21 of the Lithuanian Law Amending the Law on Legal Protection of Personal Data of the 11th June 1996, No. I-1374 Vilnius (As amended on the 21 January, 2003 No.

of the Directive and can be said as providing a very limited right to object to data subject.

Finally, the majority of the countries surveyed[173] provide in their domestic laws a general statement on the right to object implementing Article 14(a) of the Directive. These countries, even if they do not mention the cases of Article 7(e) and (f) as Article 14(a) does, can be said as implementing the Directive since they provide a general right to object to the data subject. Only three countries mention the cases of Article 7(e) and (f) of the Directive as particular cases where the right to object should be provided to the data subjects. They are Malta,[174] the Netherlands[175] and the UK.[176]

Sometimes domestic laws specify the cases where the right to object cannot be used by the data subjects. For instance, when the processing is made for a legal reason[177] or for the vital interest of the data subject,[178] when the data subject has given his consent to the processing[179] or when it results from an express disposition of the law[180] the data subject cannot object to the processing.

Compelling legitimate grounds Finally, only a few reports give an interpretation of the meaning of 'compelling legitimate grounds'. The Directive states that the right to object has to be exercised on 'compelling legitimate grounds'—but what does it really mean?

The majority of domestic laws contain a provision stating that the data subjects can exercise their right to object for any processing if one condition applies. In general this condition is a serious and legitimate reason,[181] a very strong

---

IX-1296).

[173] Bulgaria, Belgium, Denmark, France, Germany, Ireland, Italy, Luxembourg, Poland, Portugal and Spain.

[174] Article 11(1) of the Maltese Data Protection Act of the 22 March 2002 to make provision for the protection of individuals against the violation of their privacy by the processing of personal data and for matters connected therewith or ancillary thereto. ACT XXVI of 2001, as amended by Act XXXI of 2002.

[175] Article 40 of the Dutch Personal Data Protection Act—Rules for the protection of personal data 25 892—Passed Upper House on the 3 July 2000 (Stb. 2000, 302).

[176] Section 10 of Data Protection Act 1998, Chapter 29, UK.

[177] Bill of Law voted by the Senate on the 1 April 2003, on protection of individuals with regard to processing of personal data and modifying Law no. 78–17 of the 6 January 1978, France.

[178] Data Protection (Amendment) Act, 2002 (No. 6 of 2003), Ireland and Data Protection Act 1998, 1998 Chapter 29, UK.

[179] Data Protection (Amendment) Act, 2002 (No. 6 of 2003), Ireland and Data Protection Act 1998, 1998 Chapter 29, UK.

[180] Bill of Law voted by the Senate on the 1 April 2003, on protection of individuals with regard to processing of personal data and modifying Law no. 78–17 of the 6 January 1978, France and Federal Data Protection Act of the 20 December 1990 (BGBl. I 1990 S. 2954), as amended, last amendment on the 14 January 2003, Germany.

[181] Belgian, French, Italian Data Protection Acts: Law of December 8, 1992 on Privacy Protection in relation to the Processing of Personal Data as modified by the law of December 11, 1998, Belgium, the Bill of Law voted by the Senate on the 1 April 2003 on

reason to object,[182] that the processing causes a substantial damage and distress to the data subject[183] or if data processing serves the sole interest of the data controller or processor.[184] These reasons appear to be an interpretation by the domestic law of 'compelling legitimate grounds'.

It appears that in the main this provision is interpreted in the reports as being situations where the data subject suffers from damage or detrimental consequences because of the processing of his or her personal data. The German view is that it is when the data subject's situation is adversely affected by the use of the data and his interest outweighs the interest of the lawful user. The same kinds of interpretation are given in the Irish and Portuguese reports.[185] However, in the Maltese and Polish reports the interpretation which is given for 'compelling legitimate grounds' is the infringement of the fundamental rights of the data subject.[186]

Conclusions and the right to object   In conclusion on the implementation of the right to object through the European countries, one of the first things to notice is that there is no harmonization on the attribution of such a right to the data subjects. A minority of countries give a restricted right to object to the data subject or no right to object at all whereas a majority of countries provide a general right to object to the data subject. However, the majority of the countries providing this right consider that the data subject must have a legitimate reason to object to the processing, even if interpretation of the meaning of legitimate reason seems to be dissimilar between the countries. Such an absence of harmonization in the implementation of the right to object through the European countries is understandable since the Directive mentions that such a right is conditioned by national legislation (Article 14(a)), which can provide other than that stated in the Directive. However, as the right to object is one of the most important rights granted to the data subjects in data protection law, it can be considered as irregular that the data subjects do not receive the same degree of protection all over Europe.

Safeguards and other Means of Protection by the Standards of the Directive

The Directive mentions a lot of safeguards or measures that can guarantee the respect of the standards of data protection. Amongst them, the creation of a

---

Protection of Individuals with regard to Processing of Personal Data (modifying Law no. 78–17 of 6 January 1978), France and Law no. 675 of 31 December 1996 on the Protection of Individuals and other Subjects with regard to the Processing of Personal Data, Italy.
[182] Act No. 429 of the 31 May 2000 on Processing of Personal Data, Denmark.
[183] Data Protection (Amendment) Act, 2002 (No. 6 of 2003), Ireland and Data Protection Act 1998, Chapter 29, UK.
[184] Parliamentary Act No. XLVIII of 2003, Hungary.
[185] Dr Deirdre Madden and Ms Maeve McDonagh, n. 147 above, and Helena Moniz and Catariena Sarmento e Castro, n. 62 above.
[186] Dr. Pierre Mallia, Prof. Ian Refalo, Prof. Maurice Cauchi and Mr. Etienne Calleja, n. 59 above and Dr. Paweł Łuków, n. 142 above.

Supervisory Authority in each country to which is granted specific powers is probably the most important. The Directive also provides rules applying in the case of a breach of data protection law. This part of the chapter will focus first on the concept of safeguards and then on the submission of cases to the Supervisory Authority or to Courts, on the liability of the controller and on the sanctions applying in case of breach of the law in the countries surveyed. Finally, the Directive provides a special regime for the transfers of data to third countries. This study will focus on similar regimes existing in the domestic data protection laws.

Interpretation of the Concept of Safeguards in the European Countries

The Data Protection Directive mentions several times that Members States can adopt exemptions to the provisions of the Directive if they provide 'appropriate', 'adequate', 'adequate legal', 'suitable', 'suitable specific' safeguards, or 'take suitable measures'. The Directive does not give definitions *per se* of these safeguards but it is possible to find general explanations of how this concept should be interpreted in some provisions.

-   Recital 29 states that the suitable/appropriate safeguards in relation to the further processing of information for historical, statistical or scientific purposes (Article 6(1)(b)) must, in particular, 'rule out the use of data in support of measures or decisions regarding any particular individual'. This is also referred to in relation to the adequate legal safeguards required when data processed solely for scientific research (or statistics) is exempted from several Articles of the Directive using Article 13(2).
-   Recital 34 states that the specific and suitable safeguards needed in relation to the exemption in the public interest to the ban on processing sensitive personal data (Article 8(4)) must 'protect the fundamental rights and privacy of individuals'. Recital 46 states that in order to protect the rights and freedoms of individuals 'appropriate technical and organizational measures be taken …taking into account the state of the art and the costs of their implementation in relation to the risks inherent in the processing and the nature of the data to be protected…'.
-   Article 15(2)(a) which provides for a derogation to the ban on using information for automated individual decisions in the case that there are 'suitable measures to safeguard his legitimate interests' outlines that these can be measures 'such as arrangements allowing him to put his point of view' forward.
-   Article 26(2) in relation to the authorization of data transfer to a third country, states that it can be transferred where the controller adduces adequate safeguards, which may, in particular, result from 'appropriate contractual clauses'.

The difference between the safeguards used is the situation in which it is required, perhaps apart from the case relating to exemptions under Article 13(2), where it includes the word 'legal' as a qualifier. This means that, practically, the different types of safeguard depend on exactly *what* is being safeguarded. It is therefore interesting to know how EU and EEA countries, as well as the NAS, have interpreted this fundamental notion of safeguards in their domestic data protection law.

One of the possible interpretations of 'safeguards' given in the domestic laws is anonymization, codification of the personal data or the use of security measures to protect personal data. For instance, the Belgian, Danish (anonymization of data to the public, not always the researchers), German, Norwegian, Czech, Latvian and Lithuanian laws state that anonymization of personal data is considered as a safeguard. The particular role of the Supervisory Authority is also considered as a safeguard in countries as Belgium, Estonia, Luxembourg and Norway, where the notification of processing or the prior authorization of the Supervisory Authority are interpreted as safeguards. In Ireland, the role of the Supervisory Authority is to define safeguards in relation to the vulnerability of data subjects and the circumstances of the provision of data. In Italy and Malta, respecting codes of conduct and good practice seem to be considered as safeguards. These three interpretations of safeguards, anonymization, intervention of the Supervisory Authority and respecting codes of conduct, seem to match with one of the explanations found in the Directive, which states that a safeguard should protect the fundamental rights and the privacy of individuals. Indeed, these three kinds of measures do help enable protection of the fundamental rights and privacy of individuals. The anonymization process protects the data subject's privacy by rendering personal data non-identifiable, the Supervisory Authorities ensure the controller respects the data subjects' rights and the establishment of codes of conduct to promote the respect of these rights as well.

The domestic laws have also interpreted safeguards as the use of contractual clauses in the case of transfer of personal data to third countries as the Directive mentions. More generally, the domestic laws have merely expressed that safeguards mean respect of the principles of data protection law and the protection of privacy and fundamental rights, without giving more details of how to meet such protection. Thus what can be learned from this is that anonymization and other security measures, as well as the intervention of the Supervisory Authority, are considered through the different countries of Europe as being safeguards.

Creation of the Supervisory Authorities through Europe

Directive 95/46/EC provides requirements with regard to the creation of a Supervisory Authority in each Member State in Article 28(1):

> Each Member State shall provide that one or more public authorities are responsible for monitoring the application within its territory of the provisions adopted by the Member States pursuant to this Directive. These authorities shall act with complete independence in exercising the functions entrusted to them.'

The EC analysis and impact study[187] explains the role of the Supervisory Authority:

> The roles they have to play accordingly range from ombudsman, auditor, consultant, educator, policy advisor, negotiator, enforcer to international ambassador. The first role, as perhaps the more classical one, is essential, although there seems to be an evolution towards an increasingly pro-active rather than reactive role.

Supervisory Authorities did not exist in every country before the enactment of laws implementing the 1995 Directive. As outlined in the introduction of this chapter, the majority of the NAS countries and three pre-2004 Member States; Austria, Greece and Italy, created a Supervisory Authority for the first time in enacting their latest data protection law. The other Member States, who adopted such a Public Authority in law before the Directive, generally gave more powers to their Supervisory Authorities by implementing the Directive. For instance, the Netherlands gave it more power to impose administrative sanctions and fines and France allowed it to investigate, issue warnings and to impose sanctions. In Latvia, the most recent amendment of the Latvian law authorizes the Inspectorate to impose administrative penalties for violation of personal data processing. It can be noted that the main change in allocating more powers to the Supervisory Authority is the accordance of powers to impose sanctions for violations of the data protection law.

Powers granted to Supervisory Authorities

The Directive states in Article 28(2) that:

> [e]ach Member State shall provide that the Supervisory authorities are consulted when drawing up administrative measures or regulations relating to the protection of individuals' rights and freedoms with regard to the processing of personal data.

Powers of the Supervisory Authority shall be investigated separately below.

Giving advice and recommendations The study of the domestic law reports shows that some of the countries[188] endow the Supervisory Authorities with the power to give advice or provide recommendations either on its own initiative or on request.

Moreover, in some of the countries surveyed, (for example, the Czech Republic, France and Greece), the laws give the Supervisory Authority the power to issue regulations, whereas this is not envisaged in the Directive. However, the Directive does not state that the Supervisory Authority must not be given such a

---

[187] EC *Analysis and Impact Study on the Implementation of Directive EC 95/46/EC in Member States*, (2003) n. 16 above, 38.
[188] Belgium, the Czech Republic, Denmark, Estonia, Finland, France, Germany, Greece, Lithuania, Luxembourg, the Netherlands, Norway, Malta, Poland, Portugal and Spain.

power. Thus, according such a power to the Supervisory Authority cannot be considered as not complying with the Directive.

Power of investigation   Paragraph 3 of Article 28 of the Directive states that each Authority shall be endowed with investigative powers, effective powers of intervention and power to engage in legal proceedings.[189] Most of the countries studied here have given their Supervisory Authorities the power of investigation. This power means that the Supervisory Authorities have the power to access data, to search the premises of the data controller, and in some cases to seize information necessary for their investigations. For instance, in the UK, the Information Commissioner (the Supervisory Authority) has the power to seize information after obtaining a warrant issued by a judge. As a consequence, the power of investigation defined by the Directive as the power of access to data and the power to collect information seems to be well implemented by almost all the countries.

Power of intervention   The power of intervention of the Supervisory Authority is provided by the Directive as a power to deliver opinion and to order the blocking, erasure or destruction of data, imposing a temporary or definitive ban on processing, and of warning or admonishing the controller. The majority of the countries provide their Supervisory Authority with the power to give orders, rectify, erase or block data processing. Thus, the provisions of the Directive concerning the power of intervention of a Supervisory Authority seems to be well implemented by the majority of the countries.

Supporting security measures   Some of the countries also mention that their Supervisory Authority has a duty to support the taking of security measures to protect personal data. For instance, Denmark and Poland provide that the Supervisory Authority's powers include ordering a data controller to supply security measures to protect personal data. The Swedish and the Estonian data protection laws state that the Supervisory Authority has the power to decide on or implement technical or security measures in order to protect personal data. The Directive does not mention the taking of security measures as a duty or a power of the Supervisory Authority. However, this power seems to be a practical application

---

[189] Directive 95/46/EC, Article 28(3): 'Each Authority shall in particular be endowed with:
- investigative powers, such as powers of access to data forming the subject-matter of processing operations and powers to collect all the information necessary for the performance of its Supervisory duties,
- effective powers of intervention, such as, for example, that of delivering opinions before processing operations are carried out, in accordance with Article 20, and ensuring appropriate publication of such opinions, of ordering the blocking, erasure or destruction of data, of imposing a temporary or definitive ban on processing, of warning or admonishing the controller, or that of referring the matter to national parliaments or other political institutions,
- the power to engage in legal proceedings where the national provisions adopted pursuant to this Directive have been violated or to bring these violations to the attention of the judicial authorities'.

of Article 28(1) of the Directive stating that Member States shall provide that the Supervisory Authority monitors the application of the provisions adopted pursuant to the Directive. Then, the creation of security measures seems to support the respect of the data protection law and is encouraged by the Supervisory Authorities.

Power to engage in legal proceedings   Finally, the third power stated in Article 28(3) of the Directive is the power to engage in legal proceedings. Half of the domestic laws reports surveyed state that the Supervisory Authority in the country concerned is endowed with the power to bring a case to Court. It is quite difficult to be sure that only this proportion of countries gave such a power to their Authority. However, if it were really the case, it would mean that the Directive is not well implemented on this particular point. The EC analysis and impact report[190] states on this point that:

> Some authorities are bodies that prosecute and where appropriate sanction the violations of the law with no referral to the Courts. (...) Some authorities just have the power to investigate and to bring the violations to the attention of the judicial authorities.

Power to impose sanctions   The power to impose sanctions is used to make the controller comply with the law. This power is not provided in Article 28 of the Directive with the other powers given to the Supervisory Authority, but separately in Article 24 of the Directive. This Article does not name the bodies to be endowed with this power:

> The Member States shall adopt suitable measures to ensure the full implementation of the provisions of this Directive and shall in particular lay down the sanctions to be imposed in case of infringement of the provisions adopted pursuant to this Directive.

Depending on the countries, sanctions can be imposed by only the Courts, or the Courts *and* the Supervisory Authority. It appears, after an analysis of the domestic law reports, that only half of the domestic laws give the Supervisory Authority the power to impose fines or administrative sanctions in the case of a violation of the law. However, as the power to impose sanctions is not one which is required to be given to the Supervisory Authority following the Directive, it is quite understandable to see a difference on this matter between the countries. It was the countries' decision to decide whether such a power should be given to the Supervisory Authority.

Duty to draw-up an annual report   Article 28(5) of the Directive states that the Supervisory Authority shall draw up a report on its activities at regular intervals.

---

[190] EC *Analysis and Impact Study on the Implementation of Directive EC 95/46/EC in Member States*, (2003) n. 16 above, 40.

Such a provision has been implemented in almost all the countries where an annual report has to be written by their Supervisory Authority.

Conclusions In conclusion, it appears that the majority of the countries surveyed provide the same powers to their Supervisory Authority as those provided by the Directive. The only doubt concerns the attribution of the power to engage in legal proceedings. However, it has to be noted that some countries grant their Supervisory Authority powers which are not mentioned in the Directive, such as the power of taking security measures.

The Supervisory Authority and its Role in Protecting the Standards of the Data Protection Law: Prior Checking of Processing Operations.

The Data Protection Directive states in Article 20 that Members States shall determine the processing operations likely to present risks to the rights and freedoms of data subjects and organize the checking of these operations prior to the start of the processing. The question is then whether this 'prior checking' provision has been implemented in the domestic laws. Medical research and prior checking is considered specifically in the next chapter of this volume.

In which countries does prior checking exist? In analysing the domestic data protection laws, it appears that a large majority of the countries in the European Union and in the NAS provide a prior checking provision. However, in Bulgaria and Poland, there is no provision in the law saying that the Supervisory Authority should check any particular kind of processing before they start. In a few countries there is no special provision concerning prior checking but it could be envisaged in the future. For instance, in Belgium, a provision states that the King and the Supervisory Authority can establish prior checking for processing operations that are a threat for the rights and freedoms of data subjects. However, for the time-being, such prior checking has not been established. In Finland, Article 43 of the Personal Data Act[191] states that the Supervisory Authority can grant permission for processing made in order to protect the vital interests of the data subject, when the controller is a Public Authority, in order to realise a legitimate interest of the controller, or in the case of the processing of sensitive data. However, nothing states that such permission should be granted prior to the start of the processing. It can therefore be said that the countries which do not provide a prior checking provision do not well implement the Directive.

What does prior checking involve? Prior checking is provided in the majority of the domestic laws for particular types of processing; however, this prior checking can have different forms. Sometimes the law states that a licence or a permit has to be given to the controller by the Supervisory Authority, as is the case in Cyprus

---

[191] Personal Data Act (523/1999), Finland.

and Greece.[192] In other countries the Supervisory Authority has to give a judgement (Slovakia) or an appraisal (Germany) of the proposed processing operations. In France, the procedure of prior checking is very precise and described in the Bill of Law as being different according to the type of processing. An authorization from the Supervisory Authority is usually required, but in the case of processing on behalf of the State, prior checking has to be undertaken by a Minister or the Conseil d'Etat (the highest administrative Court) after an opinion given by the Supervisory Authority.[193] This discussion shows that the procedure of prior checking which was not described in the Directive has been interpreted and established in different ways throughout European countries.

What are the cases in which prior checking is required? The Directive says that prior checking shall be established by the Member States where the processing operations are likely to present specific risks to the rights and freedoms of the data subjects. It is interesting to see how the European countries have interpreted this in their domestic law.

One of the cases where domestic law establishes the necessity of a prior checking is in relation to the processing of sensitive data. In a lot of countries this kind of processing is subjected to the prior checking of the Supervisory Authority. Usually even if such prior checking is provided in the law, some exemptions exist. This is the case in the German law[194] or in Norway where the law states that licensing is required from the Supervisory Authority for the processing of personal data except, for example, where an informed consent has been obtained.[195]

In general, the domestic laws evoke different types of processing where prior checking is required and it is possible to observe two major types. It is often found in the law that in the case of a change of purpose, processing must be prior checked by the Supervisory Authority. This is the case for example in Luxembourg and Portugal.[196] This is also the case in the Netherlands if the new purpose involves linking the identification number to other data. To summarize, it appears that processing being at risk for the rights and freedoms of the data subjects has generally been interpreted as the processing of sensitive data or a change of purpose. These two cases are themselves pointed out in the Directive as being of a

---

[192] Article 8 (3) (a) of the Cypriote Processing of Personal Data (Protection of Individuals) Law 138 (I) 2001 and Article 7-3 of the Greek Law 2472/1997 on the Protection of Individuals with regard to the Processing of Personal Data (as amended by Laws 2819/2000 and 2915/2001).

[193] Articles 26 to 29 of the French Bill of Law voted by the Senate on the 1 April 2003, on protection of individuals with regard to processing of personal data and modifying Law n. 78-17 of the 6 January 1978.

[194] Paragraph 4d(5) of the German Federal Data Protection Act of the 20 December 1990 (BGBl. I 1990 S. 2954), as amended, last amendment on the 14 January 2003.

[195] Section 33 of the Norwegian Act of the 14 April 2000 No. 31 relating to the processing of personal data (Personal Data Act).

[196] Article 28, 1(d)I of Act no. 67/98 of 26 October 1998 on the Protection of Personal Data, Portugal.

particular risk for the data subjects. Thus, this interpretation seems to be coherent with the meaning of the Directive.

Two cases can be noted where prior checking seems to be compulsory for every type of processing operation. In Latvia, *all* processing appears to have to be checked by the Supervisory Authority.[197] In Germany, the law in Bavaria provides prior checking for all of the first instances of processing, however it should be noted that in Bavaria the law only applies to Public Bodies and enterprises in this State. At least in Latvia, the domestic law goes further than the Directive by extending the necessity of prior checking to *all* kinds of processing.

There are no real differences appearing between the EU countries and the NAS in the implementation of the Directive concerning the prior checking provisions.

Breach of Data Protection Law: Bringing a Case, Liability and Sanctions

The next step after elaborating the principles of data protection is the adoption of measures to ensure that the law will be respected. In order to apply the law, provisions must be made concerning who can bring a breach of the law to the attention of the Supervisory Authority and/or the Courts. The liability of the controller also has to be defined to know whether it is absolute or not in case of a violation of the law. The data subject needs to know what type of judicial remedies are available in order to act and the controller has to know which sanctions can be imposed on him in the case of a breach of the law. For each of these questions it will be analysed what happens in the countries studied. The provisions of the domestic law will then be compared with what is envisaged in the Directive.

Who can bring the case to the Supervisory Authority and/or to the Court? In the case of a breach of data protection law, the Supervisory Authority in each country can have the role of hearing a claim and investigate the case to resolve it. The question here is which persons or body can bring such a breach to the attention of the Supervisory Authority.

Following the domestic law reports, it appears that either a) only the data subject or b) anyone including the data subject can complain to the Supervisory Authority. Case a) is the situation in the minority of countries, for example in the Czech Republic. On the contrary, for the majority of the countries, anyone can complain to the Supervisory Authority, case b). This is the position of Norway and Finland, who state that breaching the data personal law is a criminal offence and thus, anyone can bring it to the attention of the Supervisory Authority. However in some of the countries like France, Luxembourg and the Netherlands, the person who lodges the complaint must have an interest to act. This means that someone cannot make such a claim if he has not suffered in some way from the violation of the law, or if he will gain no benefit from proper respect of the law. In Italy only the data subjects and associations representing them can bring breach of law to the

---

[197] Article 22 (2) of the Latvian Personal Data Protection Act adopted by the Saeima on the 23 March 2000.

attention of the Supervisory Authority. In other cases where a domestic law states that only the data subject can complain, the law adds that any other person can approach the Supervisory Authority to inform it about a violation of the law. This means that the Supervisory Authority can take up a case in its own initiative. This is the case for example in Denmark.

To summarize, it appears that the majority of the countries state that anyone, or at least anyone having an interest to act (or representing someone having an interest to act) can bring a violation of the data protection law to the attention of the Supervisory Authority.

Is this majority position a relevant implementation of the Directive? Article 28(4) of the Directive states that

> [e]ach Supervisory Authority shall hear claims lodged by any person, or by an association representing that person, concerning the protection of his rights and freedoms in regard to the processing of personal data. The person concerned shall be informed of the outcome of the claim.

Paragraph 3 of this Article states that the Supervisory Authority shall have 'the power to engage in legal proceedings where the national provisions adopted pursuant to this Directive have been violated or to bring these violations to the attention of the judicial authorities'. Thus, a relevant implementation should be to allow anyone or any association representing him or her to lodge claims to the Supervisory Authority concerning the protection of his rights and freedoms. The position of the majority of the countries giving this possibility to anyone interested in acting seems to be in accordance with the Directive. On the contrary, the countries giving only this right to the data subject have narrowly interpreted the Directive.

Who can bring a violation of the law to the attention of the Supervisory Authority has been discussed. Now it is studied who, in the countries surveyed, can bring such a violation to the attention of the Courts.

Here it can be noted that a large majority of the countries, give anyone having an interest[198] or having suffered from damage[199] the ability to complain to the Courts. In Sweden, only the data subject can complain to the Courts to obtain compensation for damages and violation of personal integrity. In Finland, as violation of the data protection law is a criminal offence, anyone can lodge a complaint to the Public Prosecutor. Once again the Czech Republic seems to allow the right to complain to the Courts only to the data subject. More specifically, some countries[200] empower the Supervisory Authority to bring a violation of the law to the attention of the Courts. This conforms with the requirements of the Directive which states in Article 28(3) that the Supervisory Authority shall have 'the power to engage in legal proceedings where the national provisions adopted pursuant to this Directive have been violated or to bring these violations to the attention of the

---

[198] In France and Luxembourg.
[199] In Germany, Hungary, the Netherlands or the UK.
[200] Belgium, France, Luxembourg, Portugal and Poland.

judicial authorities'. Apart from this provision, nothing is mentioned in the Directive regarding the person who can complain to the Courts. It seems that such a question is linked to the usual way of access to the Courts in each country.

What type of liability does the controller have?   The question of the liability of the controller is important since it determines whether the person having suffered from damage would be able to receive compensation from the controller or any person violating the data protection law. If the liability of the controller is absolute, he or she would be responsible of any violation of the data protection law even if the damage arises independently of his or her behaviour. On the contrary, if the liability of the controller is non-absolute, then the controller can invoke facts to prove that he or she is not responsible for the event giving rise to the damage. Analysis of the domestic law reports shows that almost all the countries studied have a non-absolute liability system. Among the countries which have been studied, only the Irish, Bulgarian and Italian data protection laws state that the controller has a strict liability when the law is violated. However, concerning Ireland, this strict liability is only required where the controller discloses personal data without authorization. All other cases where the law is violated in Ireland hold a non-absolute liability for the controller.

The type of non-absolute liability is different from one country to the other. For some of them,[201] the controller is not liable for the event giving rise to damage if the damage cannot be imputed to him or her. In other countries,[202] the controller is not liable if he can prove that he did not act negligently or intentionally. In Denmark the controller is not liable if he can prove that the damage could not have been averted through the diligence and care required.

The Directive states in Article 23(2) that the Member States shall provide that '[t]he controller may be exempted from this liability, in whole or in part, if he proves that he is not responsible for the event giving rise to the damage'. The Directive says 'shall provide...' and thus, the exemption from liability given to the controller does not seem to be optional. It seems that an accurate implementation of the Directive should mention this exemption. A domestic law imposing a strict liability to the controller in the case of breach of the data protection law could not be considered as an accurate implementation of the Directive at first glance, however, it does say that the non-absolute liability clause 'may' be implemented. It does appear that almost all the countries comply with the Directive on this point, considering the Directive does not mention what 'to be responsible for the event giving rise to the damage' means. Both the interpretations mentioned above, ('damage imputed to the controller' or 'controller having acted with negligence and intentionally'), are possible.

What are the sanctions for breaching the law?   The Directive provides a very general statement concerning sanctions. Indeed, Article 24 states:

---

[201] Belgium, France (interpretation of the law), the Netherlands, Norway, Spain, Sweden, the Czech Republic, Estonia, Latvia.
[202] Finland, Germany, Greece, Ireland, Norway, The UK and Poland.

The Member States shall adopt suitable measures to ensure the full implementation of the provisions of this Directive and shall in particular lay down the sanctions to be imposed in case of infringement of the provisions adopted pursuant to this Directive.

Nothing in the Directive is said on the type of sanctions which should be given and in which situation.

Analysis of the different types of sanctions in the countries studied shows that there is a broad range of sanctions in the data protection laws across Europe. Penalties can be imposed by the Courts or by an Administrative Authority.

First of all, some of the countries do not have any sanctions outlined in their law. This is the case in Finland, Ireland, Latvia and Lithuania. However, in these cases the sanctions provided in the Civil or Criminal Code can be applicable.

Secondly, some countries only provide fines. Bulgaria and UK provide for fines of up to €2 500 and £5 000 respectively. Some countries also provide for 'small' sanctions such as the obligation to do public service[203] or short imprisonment sanctions such as up to six months[204] or one year.[205] On the next level up, a lot of domestic laws provide for up to two or three years of imprisonment as well as fines, which can go up to €1.8 million in Germany. The strictest countries are France and Spain where the imprisonment sanctions can reach five and seven years respectively. Thus, it can be observed that there is a big difference between the countries. The fines can be relatively small or very big and the imprisonment can go from six months to seven years. Despite this, a majority of countries can be seen as providing for at least up to two years imprisonment in the case of violation of the data protection law.

The domestic laws also provide for sanctions other than just fines and imprisonment. Thus, the Courts can impose the confiscation or the erasure of the data.[206] In Italy, the Court can require the publication of the judgment in the press. Finally, the controller can be disqualified, as is the case in Denmark or Spain.

Moreover, in some countries the domestic laws provide sanctions which can be imposed by the Supervisory Authority itself. These sanctions are usually fines or the withdrawal of the authorization[207] for processing.

Penalties imposed in case of violation of the data protection law can also be based on the Penal Code, which is applicable, for instance, in Belgium, Denmark, France, Greece and Portugal.

Transfer of Personal Data to Third Countries Ensuring an Adequate Level of Protection and Exemptions to this Principle

The transfer of personal data to third countries is dealt with in Article 25 of the Directive, which states in principle that transfer of personal data to third countries

---

[203] In Hungary.
[204] In Malta and Netherlands.
[205] In Luxembourg.
[206] In Belgium.
[207] For instance in France or Greece.

is allowed only where the country ensures an adequate level of protection. The third countries are defined to be those outside of the European Economic Area. Article 26 of the Directive provides certain derogations to this principle. One of them is the derogation stated in Article 26(2), which states:

> ... a Member State may authorize a transfer or a set of transfers of personal data to a third country which does not ensure an adequate level of protection within the meaning of Article 25 (2), where the controller adduces adequate safeguards with respect to the protection of the privacy and fundamental rights and freedoms of individuals and as regards the exercise of the corresponding rights; such safeguards may in particular result from appropriate contractual clauses.

The question asked to the countries studied here was whether the Member States implemented this derogation and whether the NAS countries have such an exemption provided in their law.

Some of the countries do not implement or do not provide a provision similar to that in Article 26(2) of the Directive. In Latvia, for instance, the law does not provide any other derogation than that of Article 26(1) of the Directive. No additional derogation for transfers is envisaged. In other cases,[208] the exemption of Article 26(2) is provided but the domestic law does not mention the necessity for the controller to provide additional safeguards, which is a condition of the use of this exemption in the Directive. In other countries,[209] the domestic law repeats Article 26(2) of the Directive but does not describe the cases in which such a derogation is possible and what kind of safeguards should be provided.

Finally, other countries implement Article 26(2) of the Directive and provide an indication of what are the safeguards required in such a case. As provided in the Directive, France, Sweden and the Czech Republic impose on the controller the use of contractual clauses as additional safeguards where transfers other than those provided in their law is allowed. The Estonian law states that encoding data allows it to be transferred to countries without an adequate level of protection. The Lithuanian law states that security measures should be provided. Italy asks for codes of conduct to be respected (so far, such codes of conduct have not been approved for medical and scientific research in Italy).

In most of the countries, derogatory transfers have to be approved by the Supervisory Authority, which in some case has to check the level of data protection in the third country and gives permission for the transfer. However, in Sweden this role is given to the Government.

It can be observed that only a few of the countries do not mention the necessity of additional safeguards in this case. Among them can be cited Bulgaria, Greece, Poland or Spain. Greece and Spain might be considered as offering additional safeguards as some conditions must be followed for the Supervisory Authority to give its authorization. The large majority of EU and EEA countries

---

[208] Bulgaria, Greece, Latvia, the Netherlands and Poland.
[209] Belgium, Ireland, Finland, Italy, Germany, Luxembourg, Malta, Norway, Portugal and the UK.

and the NAS have implemented or provided the exemption mentioned in Article 26(2) of the Directive and some of them indicate the types of safeguards to be provided by the controller.

Conclusions

Many areas are identified in this Chapter where further clarification is needed over the definitions or scope of the law.

- Does the natural person concept include the dead?
- What does 'reasonable means' in Recital 26 indicate in relation to indirect identification?
- Does it matter who can identify the data subject indirectly?
- Is anonymization a process which should fall under the scope of the Acts?
- What does explicit consent mean, and how is it different from normal consent?
- The terms within the definition of consent in the Directive need to be further defined.
- Should consent, according to EC law, have priority over other processing conditions?
- The definition of public interest.
- Should a general identifying number be considered as sensitive personal data?
- The definition of historical research.
- What happens to information provision in the case of a change of purpose?
- When, time-wise, does information have to provided to the data subject in the Article 10 case?
- The definition of compelling legitimate grounds in relation to the right to object.
- What types of safeguard are most appropriate in each situation?
- Which body should have the power to impose sanctions?
- What does prior-checking involve?
- Who can complain to the Courts when there is a breach of the data protection law?
- The type of sanctions to be imposed in each situation.

These sorts of clarifications also represent the areas where many of the laws throughout Europe and the NAS differ in their interpretation. To further assess compatibility with the Directive on these matters is difficult due to this ambiguity. Suffice to say, practices differ enough to raise questions in relation to the ability of these laws to provide an efficient and similar pan-European data protection regime good enough to provide consistent protection from one country to another, and to remove the barriers it aims to remove.[210]

Adequate implementation of the Directive   This paper also attempts to highlight any issues of inadequate implementation of the Data Protection Directive in the EU and EEA Member States, as well as how well the standards present in the Directive are reflected in the laws of the NAS. For the sake of this discussion, this issue will simply be discussed, in relation to all countries, in terms of complying with the Directive.

It is often difficult to assess compliance due to the fact that the law *can* be interpreted in different ways, or the Members have a certain flexibility with some provisions. What follows is a summary of the major areas we have identified where some issues of non-compliance could be interpreted:

- Some of the countries include 'legal persons' within the scope of the law where the Directive does not mention it. These countries are Austria, Italy, Luxembourg and Denmark (only in part of its legislation).
- In some countries the implementing laws are stated to only apply to the living. This appears to be a narrow interpretation of 'natural person'. These countries are Ireland, Sweden, and the UK.
- As for the interpretation of the provisions relating to indirect identification and who can identify the data subject indirectly, some countries have interpreted that only the data controller can identify a data subject indirectly. This seems to be potentiality too narrow an interpretation. These countries are Ireland and UK in law, and Finland in practice.
- Some countries in practice exclude the process of anonymization from the requirements of the implementing Acts.
- Some countries have broadly implemented the transitional manual processing exemptions, which are from Articles 6, 7 and 8 of the Directive, and include exemptions from other parts of their Acts. These countries are Spain (from all the Act except the right of access) and Portugal (includes exemptions from the rights of access and information).
- In some cases there are no distinctions between the types of consent to be given when processing personal and sensitive data. However, in particular, Norway keeps a similar definition of consent as found in the Directive for personal data, for both personal data and sensitive personal data processing.

---

[210] Directive 95/46/EC, Recital 1: 'Whereas the objectives of the Community, as laid down in the Treaty, as amended by the Treaty on European Union, include creating an ever closer union among the peoples of Europe, fostering closer relations between the States belonging to the Community, ensuring economic and social progress by common action to eliminate the barriers which divide Europe, encouraging the constant improvement of the living conditions of its peoples, preserving and strengthening peace and liberty and promoting democracy on the basis of the fundamental rights recognized in the constitution and laws of the Member States and in the European Convention for the Protection of Human Rights and Fundamental Freedoms'.

- EC law appears to require that consent should be given a priority in the processing conditions. This concept is not followed in most of the countries.
- Some Member States did not include conditions under which a national identification number (or any other identifier of general application) may be processed. Countries not to include these are: Bulgaria, the Czech Republic and Greece.
- In relation to the exemption for historical research from Articles 6, 7 and 8 of the Directive, some countries do not appear to provide the safeguards required in Article 32(3) of the Directive.
- The provision of information is sometimes incorrectly implemented in relation to when information is provided. This is the case in at least Slovakia and Slovenia.
- Some countries have interpreted the information provision to include the Directive's Article 11(2) exemption to both types of information provision.
- Some countries do not include the Article 11(2) exemption for processing for statistical, historical or scientific purposes, when it is impossible or involves a disproportionate effort at all, to either information provision. These countries include Bulgaria, Greece, Hungary, Slovakia and Slovenia.
- Some countries do not provide the exemption provided in Article 11(2) of the Directive for disclosures expressly laid down by law. These countries are: Cyprus, Greece, Luxembourg, Portugal, Slovakia, Slovenia and Sweden.
- In many cases, the exemptions to the Article 11 provisions seem to be larger than provided in the Directive.
- A minority of countries do not include an Article 14 right to object for any reason; this is the case in the Czech Republic and Estonia.
- Some countries do not appear to implement the right to object found in Article 14(a) of the Directive, this is the case in Finland, Greece, Hungary, Latvia, Lithuania, Norway and Sweden.
- Some countries do not appear to have allowed the Supervisory Authority the power to engage in legal proceedings.
- Bulgaria and Poland do not include any provision for prior checking or the possibility of prior checking in National law.
- Some countries only endow the data subject themselves with the right to inform the Supervisory Authority or Courts of a breach of the law, which seems to be a narrow interpretation of the Directive. This is the case at least in the Czech Republic.
- Some countries do not provide sanctions in their law directly, this is the case in Finland, Ireland, Latvia and Lithuania.
- In relation to transferring data to third countries, some countries do not implement the requirement of using adequate safeguards. These countries appear to be Bulgaria and Poland.

Chapter 11

Comparative Study on the Implementation and Effect of Directive 95/46/EC on Data Protection in Europe: Medical Research

Ségolène Rouillé-Mirza and Jessica Wright[*]

Contents

---

[*] Co-ordinating Co-workers, PRIVIREAL, University of Sheffield, UK.

Introduction

This chapter of the comparative analysis will focus on those provisions of the Directive applying in particular to medical research. Medical research itself is held in high respect generally in Europe, and this is reflected in the Directive. The Charter of Fundamental Rights of the European Union[1] states in Article 35 that a high level of human health protection shall be ensured through Union policies and activities, while the Declaration of Helsinki[2] states that '[m]edical progress is based on research which ultimately must rest in part on experimentation involving human subjects'. This indicates the significance of at least some forms of medical research in relation to health care, and the importance of improving it. There is an interaction between on the one hand the rights of the individual to the protection of their medical information, and on the other the need for medical research to further science, knowledge, and health-care. Within its regime, the Directive makes two specific provisions that relate to medical research without referring to it specifically: first, it requires added protection for 'sensitive data', and medical information relating to an identified or identifiable individual is clearly sensitive data as it concerns health; and second, through its treatment of 'scientific' research. The balance between the individual's rights and the greater public interest is reflected in the exemptions within the Directive. It is interesting to note how far these exemptions are taken, not only within the Directive itself, but by the different countries implementing it which all have some degree of choice over the way they word their national laws. In some countries it can be seen that there are more exemptions for scientific research, or sometimes even medical research is mentioned directly, than can be seen to be provided within the Directive. This could be in opposition to the rights an individual has, or the duties a controller has, under the Directive in relation to the protection of their sensitive health data. This raises many interesting questions relating to how far the countries take the exemptions for such research, and whether this is further than the Directive itself would seem to allow. Some countries could also be seen to be stricter than the

---

[1] Charter of Fundamental Rights of the European Union, *Official Journal of the European Communities*, 2000/C, 364/01.
[2] The World Medical Association Declaration of Helsinki; Ethical Principles for Medical Research Involving Human Subjects, 2002 version, as available from the webpage: http://www.wma.net/e/policy/b3.htm (accessed on 24 July 2003).

Directive in relation to such sensitive data and this could provide a barrier to medical research. This study therefore allows for a discussion of these aspects of medical privacy, and provides an original comparison of the provisions across Europe.

This section will first focus on the scope of certain concepts in relation to medical research, followed by consideration and comparison of exemptions in relation to medical research. Finally, the safeguards and other means of protection of the standards of the Directive particularly in relation to medical research will be considered. Conclusions are drawn at the end of the chapter.

The Scope of Certain Concepts in Relation to Medical Research

The scope of some general concepts will be explored here in relation to medical research; first anonymization will be considered in relation to medical research. This will be followed by an assessment of whether human biological samples are treated as personal data. This is important given the increasing use of such samples in medical research generally; it is therefore useful to elucidate the country positions in relation to the standards of the Data Protection Directive and implementing laws.

Anonymization and Medical Research

Anonymization of data is important in relation to medical research, firstly as a safeguard to protect the privacy of the research participant and secondly because it means that the body conducting the research will not have to comply with data protection legislation, saving the resources and money needed to do this. In relation to anonymization relating to 'scientific' and therefore presumably medical research, countries like Greece mention that processing of sensitive data is allowed for research and scientific purposes as long as, among other things, anonymity is maintained.[3] Bulgarian law states that it is not necessary to inform the data subject when data are processed for scientific purposes and the data are anonymous,[4] and in such cases the processor should also inform the Supervisory Authority, who will not allow such processing if it is not anonymous (Article 25(4)). In the Human Gene Research Act in Estonia, there is an exact description of when data are considered as anonymized enough for principles not to apply: when information is issued in coded form and refers to at least five donors.[5]

---

[3] Law 2472/1997 on the Protection of Individuals with regard to the Processing of Personal Data (as amended by Laws 2819/2000 and 2915/2001), Article 7(2)f, Greece.

[4] Data Protection Act adopted by Parliament on the 21 December 2001 and published in the State Gazette on the 4 January 2002, Bulgaria, Article 20(2)2.

[5] Ants Nõmper 'Personal Data Protection Regulation in Estonia and Directive 95/46/EC' in D. Beyleveld, D. Townend, S. Rouillé-Mirza, J. Wright (ed.), *Implementation of the Data Protection Directive in Relation to Medical Research in Europe* (Aldershot: Ashgate Publishing Ltd, 2004), 73–85.

Anonymization of data is very often a safeguard imposed on data being processed for medical research which is subject to one of the exemptions in the Directive. The potentially large scope of indirect identification makes it difficult to know when, taking into account 'reasonable means', data becomes truly anonymized. This can make it difficult to conduct medical research as anonymization can be a requirement when using the exemption—and how properly to anonymize the data is difficult.

IMS Health[6] considered some of the issues raised in relation to identification and anonymization and research in the recent consultation on the implementation of the Directive.[7] IMS Health focused on the interpretation of indirect identification and applying the law to the process of anonymization. It recognized that a strict interpretation of the definition of personal data will mean data are personal if in any way identifiable. It states that '[t]he concept of personal data should rather be defined pragmatically, as per Recital 26…'. It states that it should not be so difficult to anonymize data as to do it '… may for example require the destruction of valuable identifiable data sets residing outside the control of the anonymising organisation'. Better that it is anonymized in such a way that 'all means *likely reasonably* to be used to identify the data subject will fail.' IMS Health states that the value of anonymization is lost as companies are discouraged from using this as a privacy enhancing technology, as it potentially requires an excessive amount of resources. IMS Health then considered what would happen if anonymization is also a process in the law.[8] It argues that if this is a process to protect privacy it should not have the law applied to it and that a 'purposive view of this Recital [26] leads one strongly to the opinion that the Directive should have no more application to the operation of anonymising data than to the use or disclosure of anonymous data'.[9] IMS Health would hope that anonymization is not a process in order to save valuable resources for the researchers and to preserve its use as a privacy enhancing technology.

These points are important for health data, and for research, as making anonymization a) difficult and b) a covered process, could hinder the types of health data collection or research that often uses such procedures. If performing European-wide research it will also be important to know how anonymization can be achieved in each country, and what the requirements are. Ideally, to perform such research this would be the same in every country. As Chapter 10 illustrates, the general differences seen in relation to indirect identification throughout the countries leads one to be unsure about the data protection requirements when processing anonymized data. For example, research which takes place with coded

---

[6] A company which collects data from hospitals, general practice and pharmacies across the European Community.

[7] IMS Health *European Commission Review of the EU Data Protection Directive (Directive 95/46/EC)*, 2002, 2–5. Available online from: http://europa.eu.int/comm/internal_market/privacy/docs/lawreport/paper/imshealth_en.pdf (last accessed 9 September 2003).

[8] Discussion in the previous chapter (pages 145–146) also considers applying the law to the processing of anonymization.

[9] N. 8 above.

information. In some countries, if the individual processing the data does not hold the code themselves, it is not personal data (for example, in Finland, Ireland and the UK where it is information that the present data controller holds or may hold which is important). In other countries, the fact that such a reversible code exists at all means that someone can identify the individual, and means that it is definitely personal data (for example in Norway and Sweden). Guidance is therefore needed on whether coded data used in research should still be seen as, and treated as, personal data in Europe, and what the requirements are surrounding anonymization.

Are DNA Samples (or Human Biological Samples) Treated as Personal Data?

Introduction An interesting question arising generally when discussing medical research and medical information is whether genetic information is personal data, and whether human biological samples (hair, urine, cells etc.) containing DNA can be considered as personal data. The Directive does not mention DNA, genetic information or biological samples specifically, and guidance does not elucidate their position directly—so it would seem to be the responsibility of the individual countries to make the decision on these matters. What follows in this part of the chapter is first a brief discussion of DNA, genetic information and samples and to what extent 'data' protection can be afforded to them. The second part will then look at practice and differing views on this subject across the countries surveyed for this project.

The nature of DNA and human biological samples Could DNA or human biological samples themselves be classed as personal data? Deoxyribonucleic acid (DNA) is a type of biological data made up of combinations of four nucleotide bases called adenine, guanine, cytosine and thymine (at some stages uracil replaces thymine). It is these bases that, depending on their positions and resulting code, provide the genetic blueprint for the body. Human biological samples themselves contain DNA, but have to undergo a relatively complex process to extract it and obtain any information from it meaningful to a human being. The type of information DNA holds, after analysis, can be on the order of the bases themselves, information on disease carrier status, the probability of having a late-onset genetic condition, or information on physical characteristics.[10] DNA can also be processed to produce a type of identifier for inclusion on a forensic DNA database. Other types of genetic information can arise either through observation of the individual (the girl has blue eyes) or from medical analysis (that person has AB blood group).

A working document issued by the EC considers that 'in regulating genetic data, consideration must also be given to the legal status of DNA samples'.[11] The

---

[10] For more information see L. Lehtonen 'Genetic Information and the Data Protection Directive of the European Union', Chapter 8 of this volume.

[11] European Commission Article 29 Data Protection Working Committee 'Working Document on Genetic Data' (2004), as available from the webpage: http://europa.eu.int /comm/internal_market/privacy/docs/wpdocs/2004/wp91_en.pdf (last accessed on 29 June

aforementioned working document also considers that the Directive clearly already regulates genetic data as far as the person concerned is identified or identifiable, and it may be sensitive data as far as it could be either health data, or data on ethnic origin. It remains to be seen exactly how much consideration should be given, and whether the same law should be applied to samples as genetic information itself. A good classification is needed as to at exactly what stage the human biological sample may become genetic information—is it when the DNA has been isolated from the sample, when analysis upon it has taken place, or when interpretation of the analysis has taken place? Similarly, when would genetic information cease to be regulated, and is it always sensitive? It would seem absurd to, for example, class the colour of one's hair as sensitive information when it is observable to anyone who passes by. This shows the problems inherent with even defining genetic information.

The level of protection required raises issues for forensic DNA databanks containing 'DNA fingerprints' or potential identifiers—these databases exist in countries including the UK, Denmark, France, Germany, Austria and the Netherlands.[12] Other types of genetic databases include those used for medical research which currently only contain small amounts of sequence information, most likely not enough to identify an individual. However, new types of profiling like SNP (single nucleotide polymorphism) techniques can be used on a much smaller sample size or sequence, and is already being used in a forensic capacity for identification purposes. In general, research projects, hospital records or criminal databanks do not contain full or even large parts of DNA sequence from individuals but, if the technology were available and easy to use, they could do, and this would lead to some important questions relating to privacy. It is interesting to note that in almost all cases where DNA profile or sequence information is stored automatically, the original DNA sample is also kept manually. It is a characteristic of DNA that the information contained within it does not change with age. It is a type of 'data' very amenable to storage and future uses as technology progresses. It is then a sensitive subject to discuss whether DNA itself or human biological samples are personal information *by themselves*, as there may be profound affects on scientific research when they could, for example, no longer be simply anonymized by removing the name or address—leading to the consequence that it would always have to be processed in accordance with the data protection principles.[13]

Practice and differing views relating to samples (DNA and biological) as personal data Very often the situation in the individual country is unclear in relation to either genetic information or samples. Some countries do provide some reference to either the 'genetic code' (Poland, in relation to special categories of data),

---

2004), 5.

[12] See for example, J. Kimmelman, 'The promise and perils of criminal DNA databanking' (2000) 18 *Nature Biotechnology* 7, 695–696.

[13] Of course, medical research is often exempt from certain provisions under the banner of 'scientific research'.

'genetic identity' (Luxembourg in relation to factors which can, by reference to, identify the individual), 'genetic data' (France, in relation to needing an authorization from the Supervisory Authority), or 'inherited characteristics' (the Netherlands, in relation to processing sensitive data), in their data protection legislation, but the situation remains unclear in relation to samples themselves. In Portugal there is legislation covering storage of biological samples and databases containing genetic information for clinical purposes. Databases containing genetic information not for clinical purposes are not covered, and therefore authorization from the Supervisory Authority is generally required—so some genetic information is covered by data protection legislation.

In Lithuania, whether or not samples fall under the data protection legislation is unclear, but another Act—the Law on Ethics of Biomedical Research[14]—does provide some guidance in relation to informed consent provisions. The situation in Norway also remains unclear, although draft legislation[15] is in preparation which intends to cover 'the collection, storing and use of biological material, especially blood samples, for business and research purposes'.[16] This law may or may not refer to data protection legislation as that, for example, in Latvia does. In Latvia, Article 9 of the Law on Human Genome Research[17] states that in relation to research, biological materials should be treated as personal data.[18] This is only as long as the biological material contains information that could reasonably be used by *anyone* to identify individuals who donated them or to whom they relate (a problem discussed in the above sections).[19]

Latvia is an example of a category of countries where the data protection legislation does not directly cover DNA or biological samples, but there are other laws which may protect them either through appeal to data protection legislation (currently rare), or by creating alternate protection. Latvia appears to be the only country in the first category, but there are many countries with laws or constitutions protecting samples without referring to data protection. In Finland there is a law regulating the Medical Use of Organs and Tissues[20] which, though it does not refer to samples as personal data, does impose some processing

---

[14] Law on Ethics of Biomedical Research as of the 11 May 2000, no. VIII-1679, Vilnius, Lithuania. See specifically Articles 3 and 8.

[15] Draft law on Biobanks, presented in 2001, Norway. See Sverre Engelschion, 'The Implementation of Directive 95/46/EC in Norway, Especially with Regard to Medical Data' (2002) 9 *European Journal of Health Law* 189–200.

[16] Asta Cekanauskaite and Professor Eugenijus Gefenas 'The Implementation of Directive 95/46/EC in Relation to Medical Research in Lithuania' in D. Beyleveld, D. Townend, S. Rouillé-Mirza, J. Wright (ed.), *Implementation of the Data Protection Directive in Relation to Medical Research in Europe* (Aldershot: Ashgate Publishing Ltd, 2004), 219–228.

[17] Law on the Research of Human Genome, 2003, Latvia.

[18] Inga Cabe 'The Implementation of Directive 95/46/EC into National Legislation With Regard to Medical Research in Latvia' in D. Beyleveld, D. Townend, S. Rouillé-Mirza, J. Wright (ed.), *Implementation of the Data Protection Directive in Relation to Medical Research in Europe* (Aldershot: Ashgate Publishing Ltd, 2004), 209–218.

[19] Inga Cabe, n. 18 above.

[20] Act 101/2001 on the Medical Use of Organs and Tissues, 2 February, 2001, Finland.

conditions.[21] In Greece, the Council of Europe's Convention on Human Rights and Biomedicine[22] is integrated into domestic law by law 2619/98. This law gives certain provisions which relate to genetics, but not directly to samples.[23] The newly amended Greek Constitution includes Article 5.5, which contains a provision for the protection of genetic identity:

> All persons shall enjoy full protection of their health and genetic identity. All persons shall be protected with regard to biomedical interventions as provided by law.

The Greek Constitution also provides for protection of the personality (Article 9A) and human value (Article 2.1). In relation to this, the Data Protection Authority has given the opinion[24] that analysis of human genetic material is a 'radical offence of personality in essence, as it reveals data of the past and the future' (heredity, predisposition for diseases, etc) (paragraph D7). A similar provision about protecting genetic identity can be found in the Portuguese Constitution.[25]

The only country to extend protection to define tissue samples as personal data under data protection legislation without clarification, by a decision of the commissioner, is Denmark.[26] The Information Commissioner in Denmark also states that tissue banks are considered as a manual register.[27] Countries that extend protection where the sample is identifiable are Ireland (only when identifiable by data controller), and Sweden (and this does not apply to tissue collections). The Bulgarian and Slovenian reports state that, in practice, human biological material is considered to be personal data.[28] Countries that do not appear to extend protection

---

[21] Dr Lasse A. Lehtonen 'The Implementation of EU Directive 95/46/EC and the Protection of Sensitive Health Data in Medical Research in Finland' in D. Beyleveld, D. Townend, S. Rouillé-Mirza, J. Wright (ed.), *Implementation of the Data Protection Directive in Relation to Medical Research in Europe* (Aldershot: Ashgate Publishing Ltd, 2004), 87–95.

[22] Convention for the protection of Human Rights and dignity of the human being with regard to the application of biology and medicine: Convention on Human Rights and Biomedicine. ETS No.: 164, Council of Europe.

[23] For example, the prohibition of genetic discrimination (Article 10) and the provision that genetic tests are only undergone for medical purposes (Article 11). See Tina Garanis-Papadatos and Dimitris Boukis 'Report on Data Protection Law 2472/97 in Greece' in D. Beyleveld, D. Townend, S. Rouillé-Mirza, J. Wright (ed.), *Implementation of the Data Protection Directive in Relation to Medical Research in Europe* (Aldershot: Ashgate Publishing Ltd, 2004), 141–156.

[24] Data Protection Authority Directive 115/2001 on the worker's file, Greece.

[25] Tina Garanis-Papadatos and Dimitris Boukis, n. 23 above.

[26] Professor Mette Hartlev 'The Implementation of Data Protection Directive 95/46/EC In Denmark' in D. Beyleveld, D. Townend, S. Rouillé-Mirza, J. Wright (ed.), *Implementation of the Data Protection Directive in Relation to Medical Research in Europe* (Aldershot: Ashgate Publishing Ltd, 2004), 57–71, 60.

[27] Professor Mette Hartlev, n. 26 above, 60.

[28] Sylvia Tomova 'Implementation of Directive 95/46/EC in Relation to Medical Research in Bulgaria' in D. Beyleveld, D. Townend, S. Rouillé-Mirza, J. Wright (ed.), *Implementation of the Data Protection Directive in Relation to Medical Research in Europe* (Aldershot: Ashgate Publishing Ltd, 2004), 43–46, 46, and Alenka Selih 'Implementation of

in any form to samples are the Czech Republic, Spain and the UK.

Conclusions In most countries samples are not acknowledged to be covered under data protection legislation. This situation in some countries (e.g. Denmark) is different because the Supervisory Authority issued specific instructions on this matter. This issue would benefit from clarification or advice from the European Commission as the importance of this area cannot be underestimated.[29],[30] There are resounding implications for medical research which uses samples or genetic data, and there are numerous issues to be considered. Examples included in some reports are the use of genetic data and samples for forensic, insurance or employment purposes. These issues will be discussed in further volumes related to this project.

Exemptions in Relation to Medical Research

The Directive mentions general standards on data quality in Article 6, conditions for processing sensitive data in Article 8, the right to information in Articles 10 and 11 and the right of access in Article 12. These principles are exempt under certain conditions, also mentioned by the Directive. None of the exemptions directly concern medical research but it is possible to consider medical research as included in some of these conditions. Thus, this section analyses the domestic data protection laws to see whether they use the exemptions provided by the Directive to exempt processing made for the purposes of medical research. It first focuses on exemptions created for medical research using Article 13, and then on those from the purpose principle—data protection principle 6(b). It then goes on to look at whether exemption from the prohibition on processing sensitive personal data

---

Directive 95/46/EC in Slovenia' in D. Beyleveld, D. Townend, S. Rouillé-Mirza, J. Wright (ed.), *Implementation of the Data Protection Directive in Relation to Medical Research in Europe* (Aldershot: Ashgate Publishing Ltd, 2004), 347–355, 355.

[29] The EC Article 29 Data Protection Working Party issued on 17 March 2004 a 'Working Document on Genetic Data', see n. 10 above. This Working Document does state that samples, e.g. found at the scene of a crime, may constitute personal data following the Directive 'as far as it may be possible to associate samples of DNA with a given person'. It outlines the importance of considering the legal status of DNA samples when regulating genetic data. The issues which should be addressed are considered to be '… data subjects' rights to the management of such samples, as well as to destruction and/or anonymisation of the samples after obtaining the required information'.

[30] UNESCO adopted a Declaration on Human Genetic Data at the 32nd session in 2003. The available draft declaration treats 'biological samples' and 'human genetic data' separately, and covers the treatment of genetic data extensively. In the proposed Article 17, '[s]tored biological samples may be used to produce human genetic data with the prior, free, informed and express consent of the person concerned'. There are some exemptions to this provision, for example if national legislation or regulation provides that the data deduced will have significance for medical and scientific research or public health purposes, but this must follow the consultation processes set up in Article 6(b), which includes consulting an ethics committee.

applies to medical research (there are exemptions for preventative medicine and medical diagnosis) and whether the public interest exemption applies to medical research. Finally, this section will consider exemptions to the right to information for statistical, historical or scientific research and its application to medical research.

To what Extent and to what Effect has Article 13 been used to Exempt from the Data Protection Principles and the Rights of Information and Access for Medical Research (and what Provision for Checks has been made)?

Introduction   This section considers Article 13 of the Directive and firstly, exemptions to the principles relating to data quality generally (Article 6), and secondly the right to information and the right of access in relation to medical research specifically. The provision for checks on the lawfulness of such processing in countries will then be studied.

Article 13 of the Directive allows the Members States to adopt legislative measures to restrict the obligations and rights provided for in Articles 6(1), 10, 11(1), 12 and 21. These Articles include the data protection principles, the right to information, right to access and the publicization of processing operations— effectively, many of the rights of the data subject. Article 28(4) of the Directive stipulates that each Supervisory Authority shall 'hear claims for checks on the lawfulness of data processing lodged by any person when the national provisions adopted pursuant to Article 13 of this Directive apply'. This means the data subject still has a right to request that the Supervisory Authority check the processing is lawful, even when Article 13 conditions apply.

The main question to be considered here is how far Article 13(1) of the Directive (not including Article 13(2) and exemptions to the right of access for scientific research or creating statistics) can be and has been applied to exempt medical research from the Articles mentioned *supra*. In order for Article 13(1) to exempt medical research, one of the following categories of data would need to be invoked:

(a)   national security;
(b)   defence;
(c)   public security;
(d)   the prevention, investigation, detection and prosecution of criminal offences, or of breaches of ethics for regulated professions;
(e)   an important economic or financial interest of a Member State or of the European Union, including monetary, budgetary and taxation matters;
(f)   a monitoring, inspection or regulatory function connected, even occasionally, with the exercise of official authority in cases referred to in (c), (d) and (e);
(g)   the protection of the data subject or of the rights and freedoms of others.

The only category which would seem appropriate to use to exempt medical research is 13(1)(g)—that to protect the data subject or the rights and freedoms of others. However, as Deryck Beyleveld states in his Chapter relating to the duty to provide information to the data subject[31] other provisions could also be appealed to:

> For example, there might be cases where medical research to develop biological weapons or, more plausibly, to defend against them, could be necessary for (a)–(c). Provision (d) could be appealed to in relation to the investigation of fraud in medical research. Medical research is also, arguably, an important economic or financial interest of the Member States. In so far as (c)–(e) apply, (f) applies.

But how could medical research fall under Article 13(1)(g)? In relation to the protection of rights and freedoms, it could be argued that the results of medical research can protect the data subject and that medical research is both a *right* and a *freedom*, generally. As Roberto Lattanzi notes in his paper on processing personal data for medical and scientific research in Italy:

> Indeed, the conflicting values involved in this issue rank among the most important ones that are recognised and protected by our legal system. They consist, on the one hand, in freedom of science (Article 33(1) of the Constitution), the duty to encourage scientific research development and progress that is committed by the Constitution to the State (as per Article 9(1) and 4(2) of the Constitution, respectively) and, with regard to the specific issue of medical research, in the social community's interest in detecting the cause of disease—ultimately in the right to health as a community interest enshrined in Article 32(1) of the Constitution. On the other hand, they consist in the protection of personal rights and human dignity, which unquestionably have been granted recognition not only as related to individual issues—through specific legislation concerning principles referred to in the Constitution—, but actually in Article 2 of the Constitution.[32]

Medical research could be regarded as either a societal right or good (the community's interest in detecting the cause of disease—public health or the interest in knowledge accumulation), a right to freedom of speech for the scientists, or perhaps as a right to physical integrity (and therefore privacy), well-being or healthcare of an individual. In any case, there seems to be a sound basis that medical research could be a right, even if it is not mentioned directly in the European Convention on Human Rights (ECHR).[33] The main barrier to medical research being carried out under these banners is the right of the individual potentially involved in the research to privacy (be that physical integrity or informational privacy); which is a difficult hurdle to overcome. The argument can

---

[31] D. Beyleveld, 'The Duty to Provide Information to the Data Subject: Articles 10 and 11 of Directive 95/46/EC', Chapter 6 of this volume, 73.

[32] Dr. Roberto Lattanzi 'Procesing of Personal Data and Medical/Scientific Research within the Framework of Italy's Legal System' in D. Beyleveld, D. Townend, S. Rouillé-Mirza, J. Wright (ed.), *Implementation of the Data Protection Directive in Relation to Medical Research in Europe* (Aldershot: Ashgate Publishing Ltd, 2004), 193–208, 195–196.

[33] Convention for the Protection of Human Rights and Fundamental Freedoms as amended by Protocol No. 11, The Council of Europe, *Registry of the European Court of Human Rights*, February 2003, http://conventions.coe.int. (Last accessed on the 3 November 2003).

therefore result in the weighing-up of the different rights. As Deryck Beyleveld states '... at least in principle, medical research could be argued to be something that individuals have a right to that can be placed in the balance with data protection rights of the data subject'.[34]

It is also interesting to note that health care or well-being is commonly seen as a right.[35] Again, it does not figure *directly* in the ECHR, but it is found in Article 35 of the (not compulsory) European Charter on Fundamental Rights in the European Union. This Article is generally seen to confer a right to basic healthcare, but of course without some forms of research, healthcare often does not evolve. This is noted in the Declaration of Helsinki,[36] which states in Article 4 that '[m]edical progress is based on research which ultimately must rest in part on experimentation involving human subjects'. It is noted in Article 35 of the Charter on Fundamental Human Rights that individuals have the right of access to preventative healthcare—and it then states that a high level of human health provisions shall be ensured through Union polices and activities. To give an individual the best health-care possible, research should take place to push the boundaries and try new methods. Indeed, sometimes patients want to join clinical trials out of desperation to find a treatment for their illness[37]—it is difficult to argue that these people do not have a *right* to find out about clinical trials relating to their illnesses, and a *right* to partake in it, if it can offer them hope. If individuals also have a right to healthcare or well-being, surely anything which helps to realise that right, for example, medical research, becomes a means to realising that right, and therefore becomes at least a *part* or *condition* of the right itself. As Deryck Beyleveld states '[i]n essence, logic and fairness both demand that if a right is granted to someone ('Y') to something ('X') then Y must be granted a right to any necessary means to X as well'.[38]

The Charter of Fundamental Rights of the European Union[39] also states in Article 13 that scientific research should be free of constraint, and that academic

---

[34] D. Beyleveld, 'The Duty to Provide Information to the Data Subject: Articles 10 and 11 of Directive 95/46/EC', Chapter 6 of this volume, 73–74.
[35] See, for example, T. L. Beauchamp and J. F. Childress, *Principles of Biomedical Ethics* (5th edn., Oxford, UK: Oxford University Press, 2001), 242 and C. Fabre, *Social Rights under the Constitution* (Oxford, UK: Clarendon Press), 17–37.
[36] The World Medical Association Declaration of Helsinki; Ethical Principles for Medical Research Involving Human Subjects, 2002 version, as available from the webpage: http://www.wma.net/e/policy/b3.htm (accessed on 24 July 2003).
[37] See, for example, M. Lemonick and A. Goldstein, 'At your own risk', (April 22 2002), *Time Magazine* (US version).
[38] D. Beyleveld, 'The Duty to Provide Information to the Data Subject: Articles 10 and 11 of Directive 95/46/EC', Chapter 6 of this volume, 31.
[39] Charter of Fundamental Rights of the European Union, Charter of Fundamental Rights of the European Union, *Official Journal of the European Communities*, 2000/C, 364/01. Available from: http://ue.eu.int/df/docs/en/CharteEN.pdf (last accessed on the 3 November 2003).

freedom should be respected. It could therefore be said that scientific (or medical) research could be a freedom, at least when conducted in an academic environment.

In the light of this, it seemed appropriate to survey the countries to discover whether medical research had already been directly interpreted as falling under the Article 13(1)(g) exemption and then whether the law included provision for checks to be made by the Supervisory Authority. In relation to the exemptions for medical research from other Article 13(1) provisions, Article 3(2) of the Directive contains exemptions from the whole of the Directive for some similar provisions— '...public security, defence, State security (including the economic well-being of the State when the processing operation relates to State security matters) and the activities of the State in areas of criminal law...'. This means analysis of these types of exemption could be carried out under either Article. What follows is therefore an analysis of Article 13 and its implementation in Member States in relation to medical research, as far as can be reasonably interpreted within the laws and reports themselves.

Using the exemption to Article 6(1)   Article 6(1) of the Directive outlines the 'data protection principles' which are the responsibility of the controller to comply with (Article 6(2)) (or any body or person who determines the purposes and means of processing (Article 2(d)). These include the requirement that data be processed fairly and lawfully (Article 6(1)(a))—a requirement that can be viewed either broadly or narrowly, so it can mean *all* law must be complied with to satisfy this principle or that only some of the Directive's requirements are relevant. For processing to be lawful, according to Recitals 30–36, it must respect the conditions for processing in Articles 7 and 8. For it to be fair, according to Recital 38, it must respect the requirements for information in Articles 10 and 11. This means that when these principles are derogated from it could, in theory, have a burgeoning effect on many of the other requirements, if not all, of the Directive. It is provided for in Article 13(1) that exemptions can be made from Article 6(1), for those reasons mentioned above. What follows is an analysis of how Article 13(1) has been used, within the data protection law itself, to restrict the application of the data protection principles, with a particular focus on medical research as a conclusion.

Only ten of the 27 countries surveyed have an exemption in the enacting law from the data protection principles relating to those conditions set out in Article 13(1). Eight of these countries include such exemptions by exempting from the whole of the relevant Act (Denmark, Estonia, Ireland, Latvia, Lithuania, Malta, Netherlands, Romania). In a few cases it is stated in the Acts that the exempted categories are, in fact, regulated by other Acts (like Latvia in relation to State secrets, and the Netherlands which includes many examples). Five[40] surveyed

---

[40] But note that some countries include exemptions to the information provisions, which, for example, could be seen as an exemption from the fair processing aspect of the first data protection principle in the Directive (Article 6.1(a), Recital 38). The only country included in this respect is Ireland.

countries included direct exemptions from the data protection principles—the Czech Republic, Ireland, Malta, the Netherlands and the UK.

Exemptions to the Data Protection Principles for Medical or Scientific Research
There are exemptions directly in the Directive from certain data protection principles, which almost all countries include in their implementing laws, for example, that stating that further processing of data for historical, statistical or scientific purposes shall not be considered as incompatible with the initial purpose (Article 6(1)(b) of the Directive). This section, however, will not concentrate on these exemptions. It will instead concentrate on exemptions provided to the data protection principles for medical or scientific research which appear to stem from the Article 13(1) exemptions.

As discussed earlier, possibly the only way of including medical or scientific research under the Article 13(1) exemptions is to define it as 'the protection of the data subject or of the rights and freedoms of others' outlined in Article 13(1)(g). This raises the question of whether any country includes such an exemption from the data protection principles, or even a specific exemption in the implementing law which could be attributable to this? Three countries appear to include such an exemption:

Malta Includes an exemption to the data protection principles in Section 23(1)g of the Maltese Data Protection Act[41] for processing where necessary in the interest of such information being prejudicial to the protection of the data subject or of the rights and freedoms of others.

The Netherlands There is an exemption to the incompatibility principle to protect the rights and freedoms of others.

The UK Processing for health, education and social work can be exempted from the first data protection principle (as far as it requires compliance with information provisions) by the Secretary of State (Section 30). The Secretary of State can make further areas exempt from all or part of the first data protection principle's provisions that he considers necessary for the safeguarding of the interests of the data subject or the rights and freedoms of any other individual (Sections 38(1) and (2)).

Exemptions to the right to information using Article 13(1) and medical research
Compared to restrictions to the data protection principles, restrictions to the right to information (and the controller's duty to provide it), are relatively common. There are certain countries that include an exemption to the whole of the implementing law for categories such as national security, state secrets, defence, or criminal law,

---

[41] Data Protection Act of the 22 March 2002 to make provision for the protection of individuals against the violation of their privacy by the processing of personal data and for matters connected therewith or ancillary thereto. Act XXVI of 2001, as amended by Act XXXI of 2002, Chapter 440, Malta.

within the scope of said laws. Even within *these* laws, there are often still more limits placed on the right to information. There is already an exemption from the Article 11 information provision for processing for scientific research in Article 11(2), which states that where providing information to the data subject is impossible or would require a disproportionate effort, and appropriate safeguards are observed, the data controller or his/her representative would not have to provide any information. In fact, as discussed[42] in the previous chapter, some countries seem to have used this exemption from both Articles 10 and 11 information provisions. The discussion that follows here attempts to ignore these exemptions and focus on any which could relate to Article 13, firstly focusing on those derogations from the information provisions when relating to fundamental rights and freedoms of others, and secondly outlining some countries where there are interesting situations.

Firstly, there are eight countries which provide the opportunity for exempting from both the information provisions for the protection of the data subject or the rights and freedoms of others. These are: Denmark, Estonia, Hungary, Luxembourg, Malta, the Netherlands, Norway and Slovenia. Other countries include exemption to both information provisions for other issues that could be related, for example, 'national needs' in Cyprus, 'to protect constitutional interests' in Austria, and in relation to health, education and social work in the UK. As outlined above, this could possibly relate to medical research. There are some countries where there are interesting provisions, discussed separately below.

Czech Republic   There are exemptions from both the information provisions for information processed exclusively for scientific 'purposes' under Article 11(5)(a) of the Act on the Protection of Personal Data.[43] It is possible to assume that in this case this interpretation is brought directly from the Article 13 provision for protecting the rights and freedoms of others, and that medical research would be included as a scientific purpose. However, it is also possible that it is a wide interpretation of Article 11(2) of the Directive even though there is no mention of disproportionate effort.

France   There is an exemption in Article 57 of the Bill of Law[44] to both rights of information if, for legitimate reasons, the doctor views that the patient should be left ignorant of a severe diagnosis or prognosis.

Luxembourg   There are exemptions from both information provisions for scientific research in the Law on the Protection of Persons with Regard to the Processing of

---

[42] In Chapter 10 of this volume, 168–169.

[43] Act of the 4 April 2000 on the Protection of Personal Data and on Amendment to Some Related Acts, Czech Republic.

[44] Bill of Law voted by the Senate on the 1 April 2003, on protection of individuals with regard to processing of personal data and modifying Law no. 78–17 of the 6 January 1978, France.

Personal Data,[45] Article 27(3). However, as provisions are included relating to where it is impossible to notify, or involves a disproportionate effort, this is probably due to a wide interpretation of the Directive's Article 11(2) provisions.

The Netherlands Scientific research is exempt from provision of information when not obtained from the data subject (equivalent to Article 11 of the Directive), with no clause included for impossibility or 'disproportionate effort' according to Article 44 of the Personal Data Act.[46] This could be seen either to be related to the Article 13 exemptions for the protection of the rights and freedoms of others, or to be an wide interpretation to the Directive's Article 11(2) provisions.

Norway Includes an interesting exemption to the information provisions where it is inadvisable for the data subject to gain such knowledge, out of consideration for the health of the person concerned or for the relationships with persons close to the person concerned, outlined in Section 23(c) of the Norwegian Personal Data Act.[47] This may be relevant to medical research perhaps only when it is taking place for the benefit of a relative. Another interesting exemption is when it would be contrary to obvious and fundamental private or public interests to provide such information (this is mentioned above under the umbrella of 'fundamental rights or freedoms'), and is included in Section 23(f) of the Act. If medical research can be viewed as a public interest, this could apply.

Portugal There are waivers from both information provisions for processing for scientific research where there is a legal provision or a decision of the Supervisory Authority according to Article 10(5) and (6) of the Act on the Protection of Personal Data.[48] However, as provisions are included relating to where it is impossible to notify, or involves a disproportionate effort, this is probably due to a wide interpretation of the Directive's Article 11(2) provisions.

The UK There are exemptions in the Data Protection Act[49] Section 30(1) to both information provisions for 'personal data consisting of information as to the physical or mental health or condition of the data subject', when provided for by the Secretary of State.

Exemptions to the right of access using Article 13 for medical research Article 12 of the Directive includes provision that the data subject has the right to receive confirmation as to whether data are being processed about him/her, ask for the

---

[45] Law of the 2 August 2002 on the Protection of Persons with regard to the Processing of Personal Data A—Number 91 13 August 2002, Luxembourg.
[46] Personal Data Protection Act—Rules for the protection of personal data 25 892—Passed Upper House on the 3 July 2000. (Stb. 2000, 302), The Netherlands.
[47] Act of the 14 April 2000 No. 31 relating to the processing of personal data (Personal Data Act), Norway.
[48] Act no. 67/98 of the 26 October 1998 on the Protection of Personal Data, Portugal.
[49] Data Protection Act 1998, Chapter 29, UK.

logic behind automatic decisions, and also to request rectification, erasure or blocking when the data are incomplete or inaccurate. The data controller must also notify these changes to third parties, unless it is impossible to do so (Article 12(c) of the Directive). Article 13(1) allows exemptions too. Article 13(2) also provides for exemption when data are processed solely for scientific research or statistics, under certain conditions. In the implementing laws the right of access is often included as a separate provision from the right to rectification and notification to third parties. This section of the Chapter will largely concentrate on those Articles related to the right of access. This section will focus on exemptions which could relate to Article 13(1), first more generally, and then concentrating on interesting examples. Ten countries provide exemptions to the right of access to protect the rights and freedoms of others. These are: Bulgaria, Estonia, Finland, Hungary, Luxembourg, Malta, the Netherlands, Norway, Slovenia, and Spain. Interesting situations occur in the countries outlined below.

Bulgaria There is a definite restriction on the right of access for cases which relate to national health in Article 27 of the Bulgarian Data Protection Act.[50] This could relate to medical research where it is going to benefit national health.

Denmark There is an exemption to the right of access for scientific purposes[51] but this does not mention there should be no risk of breaching the privacy of the data subject, or that it will not be used to take measures in relation to the individual, as there should be. Therefore this exemption may not be a result of Directive Article 13(2). However, later in the Act it does state that processing carried out for scientific purposes should obtain the opinion of the Supervisory Authority (Section 45(1)).

Finland There is exemption from the rights of access where providing access to the data would cause serious danger to the health or treatment of the data subject or to the rights of someone else, in Section 27(1)2 of the Personal Data Act.[52] In addition, Section 27(1)3 exempts data in the file if it is used solely for scientific research.

Italy There is exemption from the right of access and rectification by legislative Decree no. 282/1999 if the outcome significantly affects the outcome of the research.

---

[50] Data Protection Act adopted by Parliament on the 21 December 2001 and published in the State Gazette on the 4 January 2002, Bulgaria.
[51] Act No. 429 of the 31 May 2000 on Processing of Personal Data, (Section 32(4)), Denmark.
[52] Personal Data Act (523/1999), Finland.

The Netherlands Scientific research is exempt from the right of access,[53] the only stipulation being that the controller (the institution or service) ensure that the data will only be used for these purposes.

Norway Includes an interesting exemption to the right of access where it is inadvisable for the data subject to gain such knowledge, out of consideration for the health of the person concerned or for the relationship to persons close to the person concerned. This is outlined in Section 23(c) of the Norwegian Personal Data Act.[54] Another interesting exemption is when it would be contrary to obvious and fundamental private or public interests to provide information, including the interests of the data subject himself, and is provided in Section 23(f) of the Norwegian Act. If medical research can be viewed as a public interest, this would apply.

Poland There is an exemption from right of access for scientific purposes if it involves disproportionate efforts (Art 32(4)).

Romania There are partial exemptions from the time-periods of the right of access: but information must still be provided, at the latest when the scientific research has finished and only if the data subject had given express consent for the research (Art 13(5)).

Spain There is an exemption included in Article 24(2) of the Spanish Law on the Protection of Personal Data[55] which states that the rights of access (and rectification etc) do not apply when 'superseded by reasons of public interest or the interests of third parties more worthy of protection'. There is also another exemption provided separately to the right of access for the protection of the rights and liberties of third parties in Article 23(1) of the Spanish law. The fact that the first exemption is provided separately is interesting and it also includes, as safeguards, first that a reasoned justification for this should be provided to the Supervisory Authority, and secondly that the data subject should be informed of his or her right to appeal to the Authority (Article 24(2)). Medical research could fit under the banner of both public interest and that to protect the interests of third parties more worthy of protection.

The UK The right of access is exempted in relation to health, if the Secretary of State so orders it, under Section 30 of the Data Protection Act.[56] Also research purposes are exempt from the Section 7 right of access under Section 33(4), as long as results not made available in a form identifying people.

---

[53] Personal Data Protection Act—Rules for the protection of personal data 25 892, Passed by the Upper House on the 3 July 2000 (Stb. 2000, 302), Article 44, The Netherlands.
[54] Act of the 14 April 2000 No. 31 relating to the processing of personal data (Personal Data Act), Norway.
[55] Organic Law 15/1999 of the 13 December on the Protection of Personal Data, Spain.
[56] Data Protection Act 1998, Chapter 29, UK.

Checks on the lawfulness Article 28(4) of the Directive provides that;

> ...Each supervisory authority shall, in particular, hear claims for checks on the lawfulness of data processing lodged by any person when the national provisions adopted pursuant to Article 13 of this Directive apply. The person shall at any rate be informed that a check has taken place.

This provision means that the Supervisory Authority shall hear claims specifically related to checking the lawfulness of data processing when the country has included some of the provisions from Article 13 in the implementing laws. Just before this provision it is stated, more generally, that each Supervisory Authority shall hear claims lodged by any person concerning the protection of his or her rights and freedoms in regard to data processing (Article 28(4)). This provision makes the more general point that data subjects may approach the Supervisory Authority in relation to any part of the relevant data protection legislation. This section will focus on whether the implementing laws have included a similar stipulation in relation to processing when Article 13 based exemptions are concerned.

In general, one of three options are followed, either:

a.   Provision for such checks are specifically provided, as in; Austria, Estonia, Luxembourg (right of access), Malta, Portugal and Spain.
b.   They are not, and only the more general provision relating to 'rights and freedoms' exists, as in; Belgium, Bulgaria, the Czech Republic, Denmark, Finland, France, Germany, Hungary, Ireland, Italy, Latvia, Lithuania, the Netherlands, Norway, Poland, Slovenia, Sweden and the UK.
c.   The Supervisory Authority authorizes or is informed about such processing in the first place, making the need for such a provision quite superfluous, as in; Cyprus, Denmark, Greece and Romania.

Article 28(4) of the Directive specifically states that the Supervisory Authority shall hear claims for checks on the lawfulness of the processing undertaken through an exemption using Article 13. If only the first part of this paragraph is implemented, there may be no provision for the Supervisory Authority to check claims related to the lawfulness of data processing, only those concerning the protection of rights and freedoms. Not including such a provision limits the rights of the data subject, as they cannot ask the Supervisory Authority whether or not a certain processing operation is actually lawful. It could be said that hearing claims concerning the protection of rights and freedoms in regard to data processing can encompass checks on the lawfulness, as if it does not protect the rights and freedoms as stipulated in the implementing law, it will not be lawful. It is therefore arguable whether including such a specific provision for lawfulness checks is important, as long as the more general provision is included.

Exemptions to the Principle of Not Further Processing in a way Incompatible with the Initial Purposes for Medical Research

Introduction One of the main data protection principles outlined under Article 6 of the Directive is that data should be:

> ... collected for specified, explicit and legitimate purposes and not further processed in a way incompatible with those purposes. Further processing of data for historical, statistical or scientific purposes shall not be considered as incompatible provided that Member States provide appropriate safeguards; (Article 6(b))

This data protection principle is often called the purpose-specification or purpose-limitation principle (or, in this analysis, the purpose principle). Consideration of this principle leads to a number of questions. The Directive only talks about 'incompatible processing', so what is compatible processing, and how can it be assessed? There is also a very important exemption for scientific purposes (and therefore medical research) from this principle, or rather not an exemption but a clarification: processing for scientific purposes is never incompatible to any initial purpose, provided there are appropriate safeguards. A final question is what are these appropriate safeguards? These are the questions that will be considered in the following section of this chapter.

The meaning of compatible and incompatible processing Recital 28 of the Directive repeats the provisions of Article 6b, and mentions that '...the purposes of processing further to collection shall not be incompatible with the purposes as they were originally specified'. At no point in the Directive is there a description of what is meant by incompatible or compatible processing, or what measures are needed to assess this. It is therefore interesting to observe how this provision was implemented in different countries, and therefore some of its possible interpretations.

Most of the countries use the term 'incompatible', following the Directive. However, some countries, while alluding to the purpose principle, do not use the word incompatible—rather, taking Germany as an example (others are Greece, the Czech Republic, and Latvia), the law states that:

> [t]he storage, modification or use of personal data shall be admissible where it is necessary for the performance of the duties of the data controller and if it serves the purposes for which the data were collected (Federal Data Protection Act,[57] Section 14(1)).

These countries simply tend to state that the data may only be further processed for the purposes for which they were originally collected. Therefore, where they include an exemption for scientific purposes, by nature of the provision, it has to be

---

[57] Federal Data Protection Act of the 20 December 1990 (BGBl. I 1990 S. 2954), as last amended on 14 January 2003, Germany.

an exemption, rather than simply a statement of incompatibility. However, in Greece, there seems to be no exemptions to the purpose principle, not even for scientific purposes. Greece does, however, allow the processing of sensitive data for research and scientific purposes as a processing condition.[58]

Two countries use the word 'compatible'—these are Hungary and Lithuania. Both countries do not further include a reference to scientific research in relation to this—and therefore they do not state that it is 'compatible' to further process data for scientific research. Bulgaria does not mention the term 'incompatible' or even allude to the purpose principle.

How do the countries interpret 'non-incompatibility'? There are only a few countries to mention this in the law. Many more rely on guidance, but the majority have neither law nor guidance to base judgments upon. The countries to mention it directly in the law are the Netherlands and Slovakia. Belgium, Norway and Portugal allude to it, but it is not clear whether the provisions can be interpreted more as safeguards or criteria for judgment. The Dutch law is the most explicit, stating:

> 2. For the purposes of assessing whether processing is incompatible, as referred to under (1), the responsible party shall in any case take account of the following:
> a. the relationship between the purpose of the intended processing and the purpose for which the data have been obtained;
> b. the nature of the data concerned;
> c. the consequences of the intended processing for the data subject;
> d. the manner in which the data have been obtained; and
> e. the extent to which appropriate guarantees have been put in place with respect to the data subject (Article 9.2, Personal Data Protection Act[59]).

The Slovakian Act on the Protection of Personal Data[60] states that:

> A controller must ensure that processing is not performed on personal data that
> a) by virtue of their scope and contents are incompatible with the given purpose of processing, whereas further processing of personal data for historical, statistical and scientific purposes shall not be considered as incompatible … (Article 7(3)(a))

The countries included in the PRIVIREAL project, demonstrate that there are several different ways of interpreting (or not) these provisions. The first group of countries simply repeat the wording of the Directive, so there is no guidance in the law itself on how to interpret this requirement. These countries include: Austria, Cyprus, Denmark, Ireland and Spain. The second group of countries conclude in the law that a purpose is compatible when a data subject can expect it. These

---

[58] Law 2472/1997 on the Protection of Individuals with regard to the Processing of Personal Data (as amended by Laws 2819/2000 and 2915/2001), Article 7(2)f, Greece.

[59] Personal Data Protection Act—Rules for the protection of personal data 25 892, passed by the Upper House on the 3 July 2000 (Stb. 2000, 302), The Netherlands.

[60] Act 52 on the Protection of Personal Data in Information Systems 1998, Slovakia.

countries include: Belgium, and Ireland and Sweden in guidance.[61] The third group of countries insist that a purpose is compatible if it is based on a legal provision: these countries include Belgium. The Irish report[62] contains an interesting discussion and a very interesting conclusion as to the definition of compatibility, in relation to guidance:

> With regard to the requirement of compatibility as required under Article 6(1)(b) and S.2(1)(c)(ii) of the Irish Act, the Irish Data Protection Commissioner's general attitude can be gleaned from Case Studies published in his annual reports (the Commissioner does not issue formal decisions). In Case No. 8 of 1996 the Commissioner said that he tended to take a restrictive view of the meaning of the word compatible and that he would be guided by the interpretation of the US Courts of the word 'compatibility' in the US Privacy Act. He referred in particular to the decision of the Court of Appeals for the Third Circuit in *Britt v Naval Investigative Service*[63] in which the Court held that compatibility required 'a concrete relationship or similarity, some meaningful degree of convergence, between the disclosing agency's purpose in gathering the information and its disclosure'. In another Case Study (No. 8 of 1999) the Commissioner said that in determining compatibility, a useful question is 'what would a data subject reasonably have expected to happen to his or her data at the time the data was obtained?

This statement reveals an interesting and direct definition of compatibility, and also refers to what the data subject would reasonably expect to happen to his or her data, a common interpretation. In other countries, things are different. In Finland, for example, guidance from the Data Protection Authority states that processing is compatible when it has the same purpose as the initial processing.[64]

The purpose principle and appropriate safeguards   As mentioned in Chapter 10, the only guidance this type of safeguard has received from the Directive is that it must, in particular, rule out measures or decisions regarding any particular individual. It seems that in most countries this is not observed. In some cases there are no safeguards referred to in the law, in some cases they are mentioned in the law but not defined, and in some cases the safeguards are highlighted and

---

[61] Professor Herman Nys 'Report on the Implementation of Directive 95/46/EC in Belgian Law' in D. Beyleveld, D. Townend, S. Rouillé-Mirza, J. Wright (ed.), *Implementation of the Data Protection Directive in Relation to Medical Research in Europe* (Aldershot: Ashgate Publishing Ltd, 2004), 29–41; Dr Deirdre Madden and Dr Maeve McDonagh 'Implementation of Directive 95/46/EC in Relation to Medical Research in the Republic of Ireland' in D. Beyleveld, D. Townend, S. Rouillé-Mirza, J. Wright (ed.), *Implementation of the Data Protection Directive in Relation to Medical Research in Europe* (Aldershot: Ashgate Publishing Ltd, 2004), 175–192; Professor Elisabeth Rynning 'Processing of Personal Data in Swedish Health Care and Biomedical Research' in D. Beyleveld, D. Townend, S. Rouillé-Mirza, J. Wright (ed.), *Implementation of the Data Protection Directive in Relation to Medical Research in Europe* (Aldershot: Ashgate Publishing Ltd, 2004), 381–402.

[62] Dr Deirdre Madden and Dr Maeve McDonagh, n. 61 above, 181.

[63] 886 F.2d 544; 1989 U.S. App. LEXIS 13826.

[64] Dr Lasse A. Lehtonen n. 21 above.

explained in the law. Of course, this depends on whether the particular country has an exemption for scientific purposes from the purpose principle to start with (which is, for example, not the case in Cyprus, Estonia, Greece, Hungary, Lithuania and Slovenia, although they outline it as a principle). It should be noted that all these countries except Estonia and Hungary include an exemption for (at least) scientific research from the sensitive data processing conditions. All of these provide safeguards in relation to this alternative exemption. These countries may believe that the further processing for such purposes is, in fact, incompatible with the initial purposes.

If we assume a situation where the country's law has both a purpose principle and a statement revealing the not-incompatible nature of historical, statistical and scientific research, we can discuss what kind of safeguards they apply. The category of countries that fit such a situation are those who provide an explanation of safeguards (appropriate or otherwise) in relation to this principle within national law.

The Czech Republic provides in Article 5(4) of the Czech Data Protection Act[65] that the data be made anonymous as soon as possible, and that the security measures remain strong. In France, the processing must respect the principles and procedures found in Chapters II, IV and Section 1 of Chapter V of the French Bill.[66] In Norway, the public interest in the research must outweigh the potential disadvantages, while in Malta Article 8 of the Data Protection Act[67] states that appropriate safeguards must be enacted when the data are kept for longer periods, and that the data are not used for decisions. Romanian law states that the data must comply with the provisions of the law and, in the UK, similar to the Irish provisions, it states that a) the data must not be processed to support measures or decisions in relation to the individual and b) it does not cause damage or distress to *any* data subject. Other countries also have safeguards in relation to this principle and medical research. They are Austria, Germany (which includes many safeguards), Latvia, Luxembourg, Netherlands, Poland, Portugal and Sweden. Those countries with a purpose principle, an exemption for science and no safeguards in the law appear to be Belgium, Finland, Italy, Slovakia and Spain. This position is not compliant with the Directive, which states that the scientific purpose *can only* be viewed as not incompatible with the initial purposes *provided* that the country furnish appropriate safeguards.

The fact that the Directive is not specific in relation to what types of safeguards must be provided, causes differences throughout the whole of Europe

---

[65] Act of the 4 April 2000 on the Protection of Personal Data and on Amendment to Some Related Acts, Czech Republic.
[66] Bill of Law voted by the Senate on the 1 April 2003, on protection of individuals with regard to processing of personal data and modifying Law no. 78-17 of the 6 January 1978, France.
[67] Data Protection Act of the 22 March 2002 to make provision for the protection of individuals against the violation of their privacy by the processing of personal data and for matters connected therewith or ancillary thereto, Act XXVI of 2001, as amended by Act XXXI of 2002, Malta.

and problems for every type of pan-European business. Some safeguards must be provided, and those countries that do not provide them do not properly implement the Directive.

Exemption to the Prohibition of Processing Sensitive Data when for the Purposes of Preventive Medicine and Medical Diagnosis: does it Cover Medical Research?

When talking about processing for the purposes of medical research, the first point which comes to mind is that the Directive prohibits the processing of sensitive data and this includes health data (Article 8(1)). Thus, processing this kind of data could be prohibited as it is both processing of sensitive data and unlawful. However, this would not take into account the exemptions provided by the Directive. Article 8 contains many exemptions to the principle of the prohibiting the processing of sensitive data. The most interesting exemption which could apply to medical research is that in Article 8(3):

> Paragraph 1 shall not apply where processing of the data is required for the purposes of *preventive medicine, medical diagnosis,* the provision of care or treatment or the management of health-care services, and where those data are processed by a health professional subject under national law or rules established by national competent bodies to the obligation of professional secrecy or by another person also subject to an equivalent obligation of secrecy (our emphasis).

In analysing this exemption, it can be noted that processing sensitive data is allowed when, in particular, the processing is undertaken for the purposes of 'preventive medicine' or 'medical diagnosis'. This provision does not mention the case of processing for the purpose of medical research. Thus, a question arises as to whether 'preventive medicine' and 'medical diagnosis' cover medical research. If they do, his could therefore allow the processing of sensitive data for the purposes of medical research. This question is of particular importance since medical researchers must at some stage process health or genetic data and perhaps other sensitive data. If this provision does not apply to medical research, it would mean that researchers would have to either anonymize the sensitive data or inform the data subject, or stop processing the data to carry-out the research. On the contrary, if the provision includes medical research, it would mean that the processing of sensitive data would be lawful as long as the controller respects the other provisions of the Data Protection Directive.

It is interesting to look at alternative European instruments to find out if anything concerns the processing of sensitive data for medical research. The Council of Europe provides in the Recommendation on the Protection of Medical Data[68] a section concerning scientific research in which it states:

---

[68] Council of Europe, Recommendation No. R (97) 5 of the Committee of ministers to Member States on the Protection of Medical Data, adopted on 13 February 1997.

[w]henever possible, medical data used for scientific research purposes should be anonymous.

However, after stating this principle, the Recommendation provides that the processing of medical data used in scientific research could be made if they respect rules further enounced in the Recommendation. This shows that the Council of Europe did not prohibit the processing of sensitive data for the purpose of medical research. However, it does not say whether 'preventive medicine' and 'medical diagnosis' cover medical research.

Do the (pre-2004) EU and EEA countries surveyed consider that 'preventive medicine' and 'medical diagnosis' covers medical research? Only three of the EU countries surveyed considered that medical research is covered by 'preventive medicine' and 'medical diagnosis' but four countries seem to exempt the processing of sensitive data for the purpose of medical research. In Ireland, Section 2B of the Bill of Law and the UK 1998 Act[69] lifted the prohibition of processing of sensitive data in the case of processing for medical purposes. Medical purposes include medical research, medical diagnosis and preventive medicine. Luxembourg exempts processing made for a purpose of medical diagnosis, preventive medicine and scientific research in biological and medical fields.[70] In Sweden it is said that the prohibition of processing of sensitive data does not apply when:

> Processing is required for purpose of medical diagnosis, preventive medicine, [...] or where those data are processed by a health professional subject...[71]

This means that in Sweden, processing of sensitive data can be undertaken for medical research with the only condition that health professionals carry this out. This seems to be a less strict provision than what is provided by the Directive because the Directive imposes two factors: the processing is made by a health professional *and* for a purpose of medical diagnosis or preventive medicine. Yet, the Swedish law used 'or' instead of 'and' allowing any processing of sensitive data to be made by a health professional. Moreover, Section 19 of the Swedish Law allows the processing of sensitive data for research and statistics purposes provided the interest of the society in the project is manifestly greater than the risk of improper violation of the personal integrity of the data subject.

The above-mentioned countries seem to have a very liberal approach of the processing of sensitive data for medical research in comparison with other countries in Europe.

In other countries, processing for medical research could be exempted provided it is considered as processing for scientific purposes, or for the purpose of medical diagnosis or preventive medicine.

---

[69] Data Protection Act 1998, 1998 Chapter 29, Schedule 3 paragraph 8(2), UK.
[70] Law of the 2 August 2002 on the Protection of Persons with regard to the Processing of Personal Data A—Number 91, 13 August 2002, Article 7, Luxembourg.
[71] Personal Data Act (1998:204) of the 29 April 1998, Section 18, Sweden.

For example, In Finland, the law does not have a provision similar to Article 8(3) of the Directive. Section 12 of the Finnish Data Protection Act contains exemptions to the prohibition of processing of sensitive data, and two exemptions can be observed: that for processing for historical, scientific or statistical research and that for processing for health care purposes.[72] The exemption for scientific research could include medical research, depending on the interpretation given to the provision. In this case the Finnish law would clearly allow the processing of sensitive data for medical research even without the data subject's consent.

In Belgium, Article 7 of the Data Protection Act repeats the Directive and does not mention medical research. However the Belgian Law provides the possibility of processing sensitive data for scientific research but only under the conditions established by the King in a decree agreed upon in the Council of Ministers after advice from the Commission for the protection of privacy.[73] In Denmark, the law also repeats the Directive and it seems that medical research is concerned by the provision only if medical research is made for preventive medicine or medical diagnosis. If medical research is not done for these purposes another provision of the Danish law applies.

Finally, in some of the countries, the provisions concerning medical research are independent from those concerning medical diagnosis and preventive medicine. For example, in Spain and Norway, under the interpretation of the laws given in the domestic reports, medical diagnosis and preventive medicine does not seem to include medical research. Some of the countries seem to apply specific conditions to the processing of sensitive data for medical research and do not consider that Article 8(3) of the Directive covers the case of medical research. This is the case in France and Germany.

In France, Article 8-II-5 of the Bill of Law implements perfectly Article 8(3) of the Directive by repeating it. Thus, this Article does not say more than the Directive on the inclusion of medical research by this provision. However, the Bill of law keeps Article 40 of the French 1978 Data Protection Act. This Article concerns the processing of personal data for research in the health sector. The processing of personal data for research in the health sector is allowed under specific conditions. One of which is that the results of the research cannot be disclosed if they enable the identification of data subjects.[74] The Act adds that when the research uses biological samples enabling the identification of the data subject, the prior and express consent of the data subject must be obtained. This seems to show that processing for medical research does not have the same rules as processing for medical diagnosis or preventive medicine. The processing of sensitive data for medical diagnosis or preventive medicine is allowed without the consent of the data subject, which is not the case for medical research. So, in

---

[72] Personal Data Act (523/1999), Section 12 paragraphs 6 and 10, Finland.

[73] Law of the 8 of December 1992 on Privacy Protection in relation to the Processing of Personal Data as modified by the law of the 11 of December 1998 implementing Directive 95/46/EC, Articles 6(g) and 7(k), Belgium.

[74] Law 78–17 of the 6 January 1978 on Informatics and Freedoms, Article 40(4), France.

France the rules are stricter for processing for the purpose of medical research than for the purpose of medical diagnosis or preventive medicine.

In Greece, medical research is also not covered by the implemented provision but by another one, which requires anonymization of the data. Portugal also provides a stricter regime for processing carried out for medical research. In this case, the data subject's consent and the Supervisory Authority's authorization must be obtained.

Do the (pre-2004) NAS countries surveyed consider that 'preventive medicine' and 'medical diagnosis' cover medical research? In Latvia, Section 11(5) of the Latvian Data Protection Act states that the prohibition of processing sensitive data is lifted when 'personal data processing is necessary for the purposes of medical treatment, is carried out by a medical practitioner or a medical treatment institution and an adequate level of protection of personal data is ensured'. This provision is close to Article 8(3) of the Directive and does not mention the case of processing made for the purpose of medical research. However several provisions concern processing for the purpose of scientific research. Section 17 of the Latvian Data Protection Act states that the provisions concerning the right to information and the right to object do not apply to processing made for scientific research purposes. This seems to give few rights to the data subjects. However, The Medical Treatment Law[75] states that information regarding a patient may be used in scientific research if the anonymity of the patient is guaranteed or his/her consent has been received. A regulation[76] states that the trial subject's identification data should be encoded and the Human Genome Research Law[77] states that tissue samples, DNA description, health description, etc. should be encoded to be used in genetic research. This procedure should also be checked by the State Data Inspectorate. This shows that Latvia grants a special protection to personal data used in medical research, notably by requiring its confidentiality or anonymization.

In Lithuania, Article 10 of the Data Protection Law repeats Article 8(3) of the Directive but adds a paragraph saying that the processing of personal data for medical research purposes is also regulated by other laws. This shows that medical research has its own juridical regime. In the present law on Ethics of Biomedical Research of Lithuania, an Ethics Committee has to decide whether the informed consent of the data subject is necessary for carrying out the processing of health or genetic data for a medical research purpose. However, the new Lithuanian law[78] states that the Data Protection Inspectorate shall not carry out a prior checking when the data controller is going to process personal data for health care or medical research purposes. These two examples show that processing of sensitive data for medical research is regulated apart from the processing for medical

---

[75] The Medical Treatment Law of the 12 June 1997, Section 50(4), Latvia.

[76] Regulation No.312, 12 September 2000, Procedure for clinical trials on medicines and pharmaceutical products and for observational studies, Latvia.

[77] Law on the Research of Human Genome, 2003, Latvia.

[78] Law Amending the Law on Legal Protection of Personal Data of the 11 June 1996, No. I–1374 Vilnius (As amended on the 21 January, 2003 No. IX-1296), Article 26, Lithuania.

diagnosis or preventive medicine, and that the law seems to be stricter in the case of medical research.

The Czech Law states, in Article 9(b), that sensitive data can be processed, amongst other reasons, to preserve the life or health of the data subject. An interpretation of this provision given in the domestic law report says that this includes processing for medical research.[79] Thus, the Czech Law would exempt medical research from the prohibition of processing sensitive data as a result of the reading of the provision concerning health care of the data subject. The Polish law[80] and the Romanian Law[81] also provide a provision similar to Article 8(3) of the Directive and consequently their provisions do not mention medical research. Contrary to the Czech Republic, we have found no interpretation of these provisions to confirm whether they could cover medical research.

Malta provides in Article 15 of its Data Protection Law a provision similar to Article 8(3) of the Directive, that is to say, one which does not refer to medical research. However, Article 16 states that sensitive data may be processed for research purposes provided the processing is necessary, notably, for public interest and the Supervisory Authority (acting on the advice of a research ethics committee) has approved the processing. While the domestic law report states that this provision is not in line with Article 8 of the Directive, this provision could be considered as complying with Article 8(4) of the Directive. In any case, Malta has not used Article 8(3) to exempt medical research.

In conclusion, it appears that the majority of the (pre-2004) NAS surveyed did not use Article 8(3) as a basis to exempt medical research from the prohibition to process sensitive data. Indeed, the law imposes certain safeguards in order for the controller to process sensitive data for medical research and this seems to be more the result of an interpretation of Article 8(4) of the Directive in relation to substantial public interest exemptions, which is discussed in the next section.

This part of the analysis has focused only on the provisions mentioning an exemption for the processing of sensitive data for the purpose of medical research *per se*, but it has to be recalled that a lot of countries exempt from the prohibition of processing, the processing of sensitive data for scientific purpose. Thus, the fact that a domestic law does not provide an exemption concerning the processing for purpose of medical research does not mean that such research would not be exempted as it may have a scientific purpose.

---

[79] Martina Kocourkova and Lukas Prudil 'Implementation of Directive 95/46/EC in the Domestic Law of the Czech Republic' in D. Beyleveld, D. Townend, S. Rouillé-Mirza, J. Wright (ed.), *Implementation of the Data Protection Directive in Relation to Medical Research in Europe* (Aldershot: Ashgate Publishing Ltd, 2004), 47–55, 50.

[80] Act of the 29 August 1997 on the Protection of Personal Data, *Journal of Laws* of the 29 October 1997, No. 133, item 883 with later amendments, Article 27(2), Poland.

[81] Law no. 677/2001 for the Protection of Persons concerning the Processing of Personal Data and Free Circulation of Such Data. Published in the Official Monitor of Romania, Part I, No. 790/12 December 2001, Article 7(2)g, Romania.

Exemption to the Prohibition of Processing Sensitive Data when they are for Public Interest in Relation to Medical Research.

The Directive provides different exemptions in Article 8 to the prohibition of processing sensitive data but none of them directly quote processing carried out for medical research. Article 8(3) of the Directive does not very often seem to have been interpreted by the domestic regulations assessed here as applying to medical research, with the result that often an exemption to the sensitive processing conditions could instead be interpreted as stemming from the public interest requirements. Article 8(4) of the Directive states:

> Subject to the provision of suitable safeguards, Member States may, for reasons of substantial public interest, lay down exemptions in addition to those laid down in paragraph 2 either by national law or by decision of the Supervisory Authority.

The European countries could have used this Article to exempt processing made for medical research from the prohibition to process sensitive data. It could be judged to be of substantial public interest to process sensitive data in order to undertake medical research, for example in the case of research on epidemiological diseases. A major question here is therefore whether the countries interpret medical research to be in the public interest? In general, one can say that it is difficult to assume that all medical research is in the public interest and, for example, it advantages more people than it disadvantages. For instance, one can consider the case of medical research undertaken for creating alternative versions of drugs already on the market, or slightly different versions for new patients. It is doubtful that the laws themselves will ever go into such intricate detail. Chapter 10 contains a more in-depth analysis of the meaning of public interest generally.

The majority of EU and EEA countries implement Article 8(4) by repeating the Directive but without giving any explanations of what could be interpreted as being of 'substantial public interest'. However, in certain countries, the provision on this matter contains references which could be interpreted as including medical research. For example, in Luxembourg, the Data Protection Act[82] states that the prohibition does not apply where the processing is necessary for reasons of public interest, especially for historical, statistical or scientific purposes. The Act adds that in such a case, the Supervisory Authority should give its prior authorization to the processing. If the Supervisory Authority interprets medical research as being of public interest and having a scientific purpose, then it could authorize the processing of sensitive data. It is difficult to know how the Supervisory Authority in Luxembourg would interpret this provision since its creation is very recent[83] and it has not been called upon to interpret this Article yet.

---

[82] Law of the 2 August 2002 on the Protection of Persons with regard to the Processing of Personal Data A—Number 91 13 August 2002, Article 6(g), Luxembourg.
[83] The National Commission in Luxembourg was created in 2002.

The same kind of provision exists in Norway[84] and Sweden[85]. In these countries, processing necessary for scientific research where the public interest clearly exceeds the disadvantages or risks it might entail for the data subject, could be exempted from the prohibition of processing sensitive data. Finally in the UK, Schedule 3 paragraph 10 of the Data Protection Act empowers the Secretary of State to remove the prohibition of processing sensitive data. A UK Data Protection Order states that the prohibition is removed where 'processing is necessary for research purposes that are in substantial public interest...'.[86] No examples are given by the Order, but one interpretation suggests that this applies to archiving. The Dutch law provides the same principle as the UK law by exempting from the prohibition processing made for the purpose of scientific research when the research serves a public interest.[87]

Thus, in the (pre-2004) EU and EEA countries, the exemption for substantial public interest has obviously not been used to exempt processing of sensitive data made for medical research at least directly in their domestic laws. However, in particular cases, a particular interpretation of the implementing domestic provisions could lead to an exemption of such processing. It can therefore be said that the allowance of the processing of sensitive data for medical research as being of substantial public interest is a real possibility.

In the surveyed (pre-2004) NAS, the situation is less clear with regards to the provision on the exemption for substantial public interest. Some of the countries have the same kind of provision as Article 8(4) of the Directive. This is the case in Malta and in Poland[88]. The case of the Estonian law is more interesting. It provides that processing concerning health or genetic information can be made without the consent of the data subject if the law assigns a public interest to a controller or a third person. The Romanian law also provides a general statement exempting from the prohibition the processing of health data necessary for the protection of public health. These general exemptions concerning health and genetic data could then be used to exempt processing made for the purpose of medical research in the case of public interest.

The influence of Article 8(4) in the data protection laws of the (pre-2004) NAS is not always obvious. However, certain provisions could be seen as being a result of the influence of this Article, as has been shown in the previous section of this Chapter.[89] It is not rare to see the NAS providing an exemption to the

---

[84]Act of the 14 April 2000 No. 31 relating to the processing of personal data (Personal Data Act), Section 9, Norway.

[85] Personal Data Act (1998:204) of the 29 April 1998, Section 19(1), Sweden.

[86] Statutory Instrument 2000 No. 417—The Data Protection (Processing of Sensitive Personal Data) Order 2000, Article 2 paragraph 9, UK.

[87] Personal Data Protection Act—Rules for the protection of personal data 25 892, passed by the Upper House on the 3 July 2000 (Stb. 2000, 302), Article 23(2)a, The Netherlands.

[88] Act of the 29 August 1997 on the Protection of Personal Data, *Journal of Laws* of the 29 October 1997, No. 133, item 883 with later amendments, Article 23.1(4), Poland.

[89] See Section above on the Exemption to the Prohibition of Processing Sensitive Data, 209–215.

prohibition of processing sensitive data for medical research for particular processing, which could be seen as being of public interest, and also when the safeguards required are in place.

Suitable safeguards The following are some examples of the 'suitable safeguards' the countries surveyed use in relation to scientific research and the implementation of Article 8(4) of the Directive which requires such safeguards. Safeguards are not always mentioned in the domestic laws in relation to the exemption for the public interest, but it is interesting to mention them as examples of how the concept of safeguards has been understood by the countries.

In Austria, there are strict rules and in some cases a permit is required from the Supervisory Authority for the processing of sensitive data for scientific research and statistics (pursuant to Sections 9(1)10 and 46 of the law[90]), and in Cyprus, for the processing of sensitive data for statistical, research, scientific and historical purposes, all measures taken must be for the protection of the data subject (Article 6(2)(h) of the law[91]). In Germany the advantages of the research project must outweigh the data subject's interest in opposing collection *and* the research purpose must not be achieved by other means without unreasonable effort (Section 13(2)(8)[92]), and in Greece anonymity is recommended for processing in scientific research *and* all processing of sensitive data must gain a permit. In Italy the Superior Health Council must issue an opinion before authorization is granted to process health data (Article 23(3)[93]), and in Lithuania identification should be made impossible *and* approval given when processing for scientific research (Article 12[94]). In Luxembourg, as outlined above, prior authorization is needed when processing for scientific research (Article 7(1)[95]), and in Sweden there are many safeguards including approval by a REC (Section 19[96]). The lack of specification in Sweden as to what type of safeguard to use may actually be useful as, depending on the substantial public interest, the country can decide what type of safeguard is relevant in the particular context. However, this malleability could also make it difficult for an international medical research organization correctly and accurately to follow the different requirements of the law in each country, thus perhaps causing a barrier to said research.

All other countries surveyed for this section also included safeguards to this provision where it was included in the law (including Belgium, Denmark, Estonia,

---

[90] Federal Act concerning the Protection of Personal Data (Datenschutzgesetz 2000—DSG 2000), Austria.

[91] The Processing of Personal Data (Protection of Individuals) Law 138 (I) 2001, Cyprus.

[92] Federal Data Protection Act of the 20 December 1990 (BGBl. I 1990 S. 2954), as last amended on the 14 January 2003, Germany.

[93] Law no. 675 of the 31 December 1996 on the protection of individuals and other subjects with regard to the processing of personal data, Italy.

[94] Law Amending the Law on Legal Protection of Personal Data of the 11 June 1996, No. I–1374 Vilnius (As amended on the 21 January, 2003 No. IX-1296), Lithuania.

[95] Law of the 2 August 2002 on the Protection of Persons with regard to the Processing of Personal Data A—Number 91, 13 August 2002, Luxembourg.

[96] Personal Data Act (1998:204) of the 29 April 1998, Sweden.

Finland, Hungary, Ireland, Malta, the Netherlands, Norway, Portugal, Romania and the UK). Bulgaria seems to be the only country that does not seem to have any safeguards to their included public interest provisions—therefore it does not properly reflect the standards of the Directive.

Exemption to the Right to Information in Articles 10 and 11 for Statistical, Historical or Scientific Research

The right to information is provided by the Directive in Articles 10 and 11. The general implementation of this right in the countries surveyed has been studied previously in Chapter 10 of this volume. Here, the focus is on the existence of exemptions to the right to information in the case of scientific research and the implementation of this exemption in the countries surveyed. The Directive provides in Article 11(2) an exemption when:

> …in particular for processing for statistical purposes or for the purposes of historical or scientific research, the provision of such information proves impossible or would involve a disproportionate effort…

It has to be noted that this exemption to the right to information in the Directive applies only when the data have not been collected directly from the data subject (the Directive Article 11 case).

In the EU, EEA and NAS, it appears that 14 countries[97] mention in their domestic law that the right to information does not apply when processing is undertaken for the purpose of scientific research or for a scientific purpose. However, not all of these 15 countries provide this exemption exclusively when data are not obtained from the data subject. Some countries do not make any distinction between the case of Article 10 and that of Article 11 of the Directive. In the Netherlands, even if Article 11(2) is implemented in the domestic law, the Medical Treatment Contracts Act states that medical data are particularly protected and that an informed consent (involving information to be provided to the data subject) has to be obtained from the data subject before the disclosure of such data outside a medical team.

France, interestingly, provides an exemption to the right to information in the case of storage of the data for historical, statistical or scientific purposes when data have been collected for another purpose.[98] The French law also provides an exemption where the provision of information proves impossible or would involve a disproportionate effort. Thus, the French implementation is slightly different to the provisions of the Directive by adding an exemption (case of storage) to the right to information in the case of processing for scientific purpose. In Portugal,

---

[97] These countries are Austria, Belgium, Cyprus, the Czech Republic, Germany, Ireland, Latvia, Luxembourg, Malta, the Netherlands, Poland, Portugal, Romania, and Spain.

[98] Bill of Law voted by the Senate on the 1 April 2003, on protection of individuals with regard to processing of personal data and modifying Law no. 78-17 of the 6 January 1978, Article 32-II, France.

certain disclosures of personal data must be made by force of law even without informing the data subject in the cases of compulsory declaration of infectious and contagious diseases and communication of health expenses to the social security system.[99]

Several of the other countries do not mention the case of scientific research as a case where the exemption applies, but this does not mean that, to the contrary, the right to information has to be provided in this case. In general, these countries have implemented Article 11(2) of the Directive by mentioning that the exemption applies where the provision of information proves impossible or would involve a disproportionate effort without adding that this is particularly the case for processing for scientific research. This is the case for Denmark, Finland, Italy, Lithuania, Norway and the UK. For instance, in Finland, interpretation of the exemptions for processing where data are collected on the basis of law leads one to conclude that the exemption applies to the registries made with patients records from public healthcare. In Norway, the law is interpreted as going further than the Directive with regards to the exemption from the right to information provision. This exemption applies to six national health registers.[100] In the UK, it is said in the 1998 Act that the Secretary of State could create an exemption for data processing related to the physical or mental health condition of the data subjects.[101] Finally, in Denmark, an interpretation of the 'travaux préparatoires' leads to the conclusion that there is only a very limited obligation to inform the data subject when the data have been collected for scientific purposes.

In Bulgaria, Estonia, Greece, Hungary, Slovakia and Slovenia, the situation seems to be different since the exemption from the right to information where the provision of such information is impossible or would involve a disproportionate effort is not implemented in their domestic law. It would be interesting to know whether this means that information has to be provided to the data subject even in such a case or whether this was neglected by the legislator. In the first case, it would mean that these domestic laws are stricter than the Directive and oblige the controller to provide information to the data subject even in the case of processing for scientific purposes.

In conclusion, it can be said that the exemption mentioned in Article 11(2) of the Directive concerning scientific research has been implemented by a large majority of the European countries and only a few domestic laws do not mention it. It is difficult to conclude that this means those domestic laws require the data

---

[99] Helena Moniz and Catarina Sarmento e Castro 'Report on the Implementation of Directive 95/46/EC in Relation to Medical Research in Portugal' in D. Beyleveld, D. Townend, S. Rouillé-Mirza, J. Wright (ed.), *Implementation of the Data Protection Directive in Relation to Medical Research in Europe* (Aldershot: Ashgate Publishing Ltd, 2004), 319–340.
[100] Vigdis Kvalheim 'Implementation of the Data Protection Directive in Relation to Medical Research in Norway' in D. Beyleveld, D. Townend, S. Rouillé-Mirza, J. Wright (ed.), *Implementation of the Data Protection Directive in Relation to Medical Research in Europe* (Aldershot: Ashgate Publishing Ltd, 2004), 289–305.
[101] Data Protection Act 1998, Chapter 29, Section 30(1), UK.

subject to be informed in all cases of processing for scientific purposes. However, a certain disparity can be seen between countries that outline particular situations in which the exemption to the right to information applies and concerning especially processing of medical data or medical research and other countries where the exemption provided in Article 11(2) of the Directive is not clearly mentioned.

Safeguards and other Means of Protection through the Standards of the Directive in Relation to Medical Research

Some safeguards or other means are outlined by the Directive to protect data protection standards when exemptions are made in particular cases. This section focuses on some of them that could apply to medical research. The prior checking requirement, the 'notification to supervisory authority' provision, the 'creation of public register by the supervisory authority' and the 'regulation of transfers of personal data to third countries' will also be analysed below in relation to medical research.

Prior Checking of Processing Operations for Medical Research

The prior checking of processing operations is mentioned in Chapter 10 of this volume in general terms. This section provides an overview of the countries that provide for prior checks of medical research processing operations. The relevant part of the Directive is Article 20, which requires that Members States shall determine the processing operations likely to present risks to the rights and freedoms of data subjects and organize the checking of these operations prior to the start of the processing. The question here is whether the domestic laws include any provisions concerning the need for prior checking in the case of processing for medical research. In Denmark, an authorization from the Supervisory Authority has to be obtained prior to the processing of personal data for medical research in the private sector. In France, processing undertaken for health purposes needs to be checked by an Ethics Committee, which gives an opinion, and then authorization is needed from the Supervisory Authority.[102] The European Report[103] adds that in Sweden 'prior checks have been stipulated with regards to processing sensitive data for research purposes without the consent of the data subject, unless the research has been authorised by an Ethics Committee' and in Germany 'processing of sensitive data and processing involving the taking of automated individual

---

[102] Bill of Law voted by the Senate on the 1 April 2003, on protection of individuals with regard to processing of personal data and modifying Law no. 78-17 of the 6 January 1978, Chapter 9, France.

[103] European Commission, *Analysis and Impact Study on the Implementation of The Directive EC 95/46 in Member States*, 3. Available online at http://europa.eu.int /comm/internal_market/privacy/docs/lawreport/consultation/technical-annex_en.pdf   (last accessed on 5 March 2004), 28.

decisions require a prior check.' In these examples, the type of processing operation concerned is broadly described as processing for medical research or health purposes. In other laws, provisions target the processing of genetic data. This is the case in Latvia, Luxembourg, Spain and Sweden. For instance, the Swedish law requires prior checking of the processing of data concerning a hereditary disposition derived from genetic investigation.[104]

To conclude on this matter, it should be noted that usually the laws provide prior checking in the case of the processing of sensitive data. This can be understood as covering in most cases processing for medical research where heath data are processed.

Exemptions from Notification to the Supervisory Authority Provided for Medical Research

One of the main safeguards on data protection established in the Directive is the notification of any automatic processing operation to the Supervisory Authority.[105] Such notifications enable the Supervisory Authority to be aware of the existence of such processing, to create a register in order to list them or even to exercise a prior checking of them. As for the other provisions of the Directive, this rule has certain exemptions. One of them is provided by Article 18(2), which could be interpreted as including an exemption from notification to the Supervisory Authority for processing for medical research purposes. Indeed, such an exemption is provided:

> where, for categories of processing operations which are unlikely, taking account of the data to be processed, to affect adversely the rights and freedoms of data subjects, they specify the purposes of the processing, the data or categories of data undergoing processing, the category or categories of data subject, the recipients or categories of recipient to whom the data are to be disclosed and the length of time the data are to be stored.

Analysis of the domestic laws of the countries surveyed shows that only a minority of them mention an exemption or a simplification of the notification to the Supervisory Authority that covers medical research. In Finland, Article 36 of the Data Protection Act provides an exemption from notification to the Supervisory Authority for processing made for the purpose of scientific research. However, the Supervisory Authority's interpretation leads them not to apply this exemption when the processing involves sensitive data, which means that most medical research registries are notified in Finland. In Greece an exemption is provided by Article 7 of the Data Protection Law for legal entities and health care institutions which provide health services and when the processing involves medical data. The

---

[104] Personal Data Act (1998:204) of the 29 April 1998, Section 10, Sweden.

[105] Directive 95/46/EC, Article 18(1): 'Member States shall provide that the controller or his representative, if any, must notify the Supervisory Authority referred to in Article 28 before carrying out any wholly or partly automatic processing operation or set of such operations intended to serve a single purpose or several related purposes'.

same exemption applies to medical services provided through a network. In the Netherlands, the law states that exemption from notification can be laid down by general administrative regulations. One of them, the Exemption Decree[106] provides exemption from notification, notably, for processing in individual health care and processing concerning research, each of them having a different regime of exemption. Medical research enters either in one or the other of these regimes of exemption. Finally, Sweden exempts processing made in the health care sector from notification to the Supervisory Authority.[107] This could concern certain cases of medical research.

Some countries have favoured simplifying the notification. For instance, Italy provides for a simplification for scientific research.[108] This results in giving less information about the processing but with the condition that the law and codes of conduct are respected.

In France, the law seems to be strict for processing carried out for the purposes of research in the health sector. Chapter IX of the Bill of Law states that each request for a processing for this purpose is submitted to the opinion of a consultative committee who are specialized in such matters. Then the Supervisory Authority must give its authorization to the processing. Thus, the French position is one not at all in favour of exemptions from notification to the Supervisory Authority for processing in medical research. Luxembourg's position is similar to the French one. Processing for scientific purposes must be prior authorized by the Supervisory Authority.[109]

Finally, it appears that the nomination of a Data Protection Official as provided for in the Directive allows the controller not to notify the processing. This exemption seems to apply to processing for medical research in such countries as Germany, Norway and Sweden.[110]

What can be summarized with regards to the domestic provisions concerning the exemptions from notification to the Supervisory Authority? Clearly, there is no homogeneous agreement in Europe, as only a few countries provide exemption from notification for medical research and two of them provide stricter regulations (prior authorization).

---

[106] Exemption Decree, 7 May 2001, The Netherlands.

[107] Personal Data Act (1998:204) of the 29 April 1998, Section 5(e), Sweden.

[108] Law n. 675 of the 31 December 1996 on the protection of individuals and other subjects with regard to the processing of personal data, Section 7(5-*bis*), letter c-*bis*, Italy.

[109] Law of the 2 August 2002 on the Protection of Persons with regard to the Processing of Personal Data A—Number 91, 13 August 2002, Article 12 which involves Article 14, Luxembourg.

[110] Dr Hermann Christoph Kühn 'The Implementation of the Data Protection Directive 95/46/EC in Germany' in D. Beyleveld, D. Townend, S. Rouillé-Mirza, J. Wright (ed.), *Implementation of the Data Protection Directive in Relation to Medical Research in Europe* (Aldershot: Ashgate Publishing Ltd, 2004), 121–140; Vigdis Kvalheim, n. 100 above; Professor Elisabeth Rynning, n. 61 above.

Special Public Registers held by the Supervisory Authority for Medical Research Operations

The Directive requires the publicization of all processing operations notified to the Supervisory Authority, according to Article 21. Logically, then, if processing operations have not been notified to the Supervisory Authority, they will not be publicized. This is noted because there are exemptions to the requirement to notify in certain situations. In the situation, for example, when the data controller has a personal Data Protection Official he or she does not have to notify, but must still maintain a register of processing operations according to Article 18(2), the details on which must still be accessible to any person on request (Article 21(3)). This is not the case for processing

> ...whose sole purpose is the keeping of a register which according to laws or regulations is intended to provide information to the public and which is open to consultation either by the public in general or by any person demonstrating a legitimate interest...(Article 18(3)).

They are firstly exempt from the requirement to notify (Article 18(3)) and also exempt from the requirement to maintain an independent register of processing operations (Article 21(3)), if the country chooses. If a country has, for example, established a cancer register by law, accessible to any person demonstrating a legitimate interest (for example, researchers), the controller of this register may not have to notify or keep a record of its processing operations (which, of course, have to be related to the keeping of the register). Indeed, in many countries, cancer registers and DNA databases have been established by law. It is therefore useful to know if any special provisions have been enacted relating to the publicization of the processing operations relating to these types of registers.

Generally, in answering this question many countries were unsure about the provision for such registers, underlining that perhaps these issues should be highlighted both within each country and generally in Europe. For example, Helena Moniz and Catarina Sarmento e Castro write in the report on Portuguese law:[111]

> There are various registers of health data, such as those held by the Cancer Institutes or the Institute of Medical Genetics, where there is not only a personal data base, but also an archive of slips of paper containing drops of blood from around 90 per cent of newborns from the last 26 years (since 1979). However, the existence of these bases has not been made public. Most members of the population are unaware of their existence.

This emphasizes that it could be important to create more public awareness of such registers and how data are used within them.

---

[111] Helena Moniz and Catarina Sarmento e Castro, n. 99 above, 339.

Many of those countries who did respond in relation to these questions outlined legal provisions for such registers, while in one country the practice was expounded. What follows is first a discussion of those countries responding with legal provisions in this area, followed by the country that responded about this issue in terms of practice, and a section addressing cancer registers more directly.

Legal provisions and practice for publicizing medical research registers In Germany there are specific laws in each state covering cancer registries.[112] As Dr Hermann Christoph Kühn outlines, '[t]hese registers are compelled by the various state acts to inform patients whose data is liable for registration (i.e. cancer patients) about the existence and the tasks of the register'.[113] In Italy, registers concerning rare diseases have been set up at the Italian Istituto Superior di Sanità on the basis of specific regulations. In Latvia several laws exist to regulate the establishment and management of public health registers and databases, which should be publicized as stated by these laws.[114] In Lithuania there is a separate law governing registers, the Law on Registers.[115] However, the Lithuanian report does not mention publicizing medical research or other related registers directly, so it is unclear whether there is an exemption for medical research and other related registers from the publicization requirements.

In Norway, there is an Act on Personal Health Data Filing Systems (also monitored by the Data Protection Official) which regulates the processing of health data within the Health Administration and Health Service. This includes provisions regarding national health registers, which constitute important registers for medical and health research.[116] The Data Protection Official's function includes keeping a systematic public record of every processing operation reported, including in relation to the aforementioned Act.[117] In Poland, Article 40 of the Act on the Protection of Personal Data[118] states that databases must be registered with the Inspector General for the Protection of Personal Data.[119] There are, however, exemptions from this which include medical records, if the records are to be used to prepare a thesis required to graduate from a University or be granted a scientific title, and those created for healthcare services. The Act does not focus directly on medical research, and is silent on whether, for example, therapeutic clinical trials can fall under the banner of health care.[120] In Portugal, the report states that when

---

[112] Dr Hermann Christoph Kühn, n. 110 above.

[113] Dr Hermann Christoph Kühn, n. 110 above, 134.

[114] Inga Cabe, n. 18 above.

[115] Asta Cekanauskaite and Professor Eugenijus Gefenas see n. 16 above.

[116] Vigdis Kvalheim, n. 100 above, footnote 7.

[117] Vigdis Kvalheim, n. 100 above.

[118] Act of the 29 August 1997 on the Protection of Personal Data, *Journal of Laws* of the 29 October 1997, No. 133, item 883 with later amendments, Poland.

[119] Dr. Paweł Luków 'Personal Data Protection and Medical Research in Poland' in D. Beyleveld, D. Townend, S. Rouillé-Mirza, J. Wright (ed.), *Implementation of the Data Protection Directive in Relation to Medical Research in Europe* (Aldershot: Ashgate Publishing Ltd, 2004), 307–318.

[120] Dr. Paweł Luków, n. 119 above.

creating a database for medical research, both notification and authorization is required, meaning that the processing operations should be published, but in practice they are not.[121] The Portuguese Supervisory Authority is considering whether to publish a register of all the existing medical research databases in Portugal, but whether it decides to go ahead is not a foregone conclusion.[122]

In Spain, the general provision regarding publicization is also applicable to medical research data, but registers are not mentioned specifically. In Sweden, there is specific legislation on health data registers, medical care registers and research registers for forensic psychiatry, which include provisions on the information that should be given to data subjects. Ordinance (2001:707, Section 7) on the Patient Register of the National Board on Health and Welfare contains a special provision according to which the Board shall ensure that the data subjects *and* the general public receive information concerning the registers. There are similar provisions in Ordinances related to other health data registers, such as the Medical Products Agency Register for Side-Effects from Medicinal Products (Ordinance 2001:710). In the UK, as in some other countries, the data controller must provide non-notified information to all persons who make a written request.

In Finland,[123] it is not required by law to publish processing operations, but many government-held registers, such as the cancer registry, have published their own, even on the Internet.[124] In Denmark, information about all research registers is publicly available on the Data Protection Authority's website.

There appears to be no provisions either in practice or law for the following countries: Belgium, Bulgaria, the Czech Republic, Greece, Ireland, Malta, Portugal (under consideration), Romania, and Slovenia.

In many countries therefore, there are specific practices for publicizing medical research registers—in some countries this is even on the internet. However, in some countries the practice is uncertain and no legal or other action has been taken. This issue needs to be more fully considered in these countries.

Cancer registers A few reports mention cancer registries specifically. The German report[125] contains an in-depth discussion on cancer registries in Germany generally. In 1994, Germany passed the 1994 Federal Cancer Register Act. This compelled each State to establish cancer registers and legislation, with the result that legislation can be different from state to state. The cancer registers all have a very high level of data protection, and operate a two-tier system of confidentiality. The data are first transmitted to a confidentiality agency to anonymize the data, and only a special agency holds the key to the anonymized data, which can only be used by people at the State cancer register, or at a central documentation centre at the Robert-Koch institute in Berlin. Provisions include that 'patients have to be

---

[121] Helena Moniz and Catarina Sarmento e Castro, n. 99 above, 339.

[122] Helena Moniz and Catarina Sarmento e Castro, n. 99 above, 339.

[123] Dr Lasse A. Lehtonen, n. 21 above.

[124] This web page details an example of some published research operations in Finland: http://www.stakes.fi/stakestieto/aineistot.asp (last accessed 15 Feb 2004).

[125] Dr Hermann Christoph Kühn, n. 110 above, 124–126.

made aware of the conditions under which their data will be registered and they must be informed about their right to refuse registration'.[126] These strict provisions are countered by the fact that generally informing can be done by leaflet. It is also questionable whether under existing legislation all cases are notified in Germany. There has been some recent discussion of provisions in relation to cancer registries in the UK, namely, Regulation 2 of SI 1438. The UK report contains a summary of these current regulations on providing information to cancer registries.[127] In general, there is also discussion on whether this legislation is in-line with requirements in relation to confidentiality and data protection. Hungary implemented Decree No. 24 of 1999 (VII.6.) of the Health Minister to regulate the National Cancer Registry. Physicians must notify *any* case of cancer to the National Registry.[128]

Derogatory Transfers of Data to Third Countries Provided for Medical Research

The Directive mentions in Articles 25 and 26 the regime relating to the transfer of data to third countries. This regime and its implementation in the surveyed countries has been analysed in Chapter 10 of this volume. This section specifically focuses on the exemptions to the Article 25 rules[129] provided by the countries concerning medical research. Article 26 of the Directive mentions several cases where the principle stated in Article 25 could be exempted, but none of them directly concern medical research. However, Article 26(d) states that the prohibition on transfer could be lifted where 'the transfer is necessary or legally required on important public interest grounds', and Article 26(e) lifts prohibition where 'the transfer is necessary in order to protect the vital interests of the data subject'. These reasons could be the legal basis used by the European countries to allow the transfer to third countries of personal data for processing for the purposes of medical research. Personal data used in medical research can hold considerable commercial value and it can be very tempting for a European country to transfer and sell such data to third countries even if these countries do not ensure an adequate level of protection to the personal data. The transfer of such data can also

---

[126] Dr Hermann Christoph Kühn, n. 110 above

[127] Deryck Beyleveld, Andrew Grubb, David Townend, Ryan Morgan, and Jessica Wright 'The UK's Implementation of Directive 95/46/EC' in D. Beyleveld, D. Townend, S. Rouillé-Mirza, J. Wright (ed.), *Implementation of the Data Protection Directive in Relation to Medical Research in Europe* (Aldershot: Ashgate Publishing Ltd, 2004), 403–428, 413–417.

[128] Professor Judit Sándor 'Protection of Health Care Data in the Hungarian Law' in D. Beyleveld, D. Townend, S. Rouillé-Mirza, J. Wright (ed.), *Implementation of the Data Protection Directive in Relation to Medical Research in Europe* (Aldershot: Ashgate Publishing Ltd, 2004), 157–174.

[129] Directive 95/46/EC, Article 25(1): 'The Member States shall provide that the transfer to a third country of personal data which are undergoing processing or are intended for processing after transfer may take place only if, without prejudice to compliance with the national provisions adopted pursuant to the other provisions of this Directive, the third country in question ensures an adequate level of protection'.

be very interesting from a research point of view and researchers can be attracted to exchanging personal data concerning the topic of their medical research. Thus, in order to provide protection to personal data which crosses beyond the borders of the European Union, the Directive provides the above-mentioned Article 25. It is possible that some of the European countries have interpreted these provisions as exempting certain processing made for the purpose of medical research, a position which will be discussed below.

It appears that only two of the countries surveyed have a provision mentioning the existence of such an exemption in this case. In Italy, Section 28(4) letter g-*bis* of the Data Protection Act states that the transfer of personal data to third countries is always permitted when the processing is carried out exclusively for scientific research or for statistical purposes if it complies with the codes of conduct and professional practice outlined in Section 31 of the law. However, no code of conduct on this topic exists in Italy for the time being. In Spain, one of the exemptions to the rules on the transfer of data to third countries states that these rules do not apply where '[t]he transfer is necessary for medical prevention or diagnosis, the provision of health aid or medical treatment, or the management of health services'.[130] Apart from this provision, no other country mentions medical data in particular. This provision does not mention the situation where processing operations are made for medical research but it can be assumed that medical research made for one of these purposes would benefit from this exemption. Italian and Spanish provisions do not seem to properly implement the Directive since they allow the transfer of personal data in cases that are not provided for by the Directive. However, Article 26(1) states '[b]y way of derogation from Article 25 *and save where otherwise provided by domestic law governing particular cases*, Member States shall provide that a transfer or a set of transfers of personal data to a third country which does not ensure an adequate level of protection within the meaning of Article 25(2) may take place on condition that:...' (our emphasis). Thus the Directive does not seem to be so strict concerning the exemptions the Members States can provide in their domestic laws on this issue. It is then difficult to conclude definitively that Italy and Spain do not implement the Directive well. However, we can conclude from this study that the actual provisions of Articles 25 and 26 of the Directive can allow the transfer of personal data for the purpose of medical research to countries which do not provide an adequate level of protection to data subjects.

Conclusion

Many areas are identified where further clarification is needed over concepts which relate and refer to scientific or medical research:

---

[130] Organic Law 15/1999 of 13 December on the Protection of Personal Data, Article 34(c), Spain.

-   Is pseudonymized or coded data personal data?
-   How would one define genetic information and protect it?
-   Are human biological samples personal data?
-   How is compatibility or incompatibility judged in relation to Article 6(1)(b) of the Directive?
-   Should the exemption to sensitive processing for medical purposes and treatment include medical research?
-   Should public interest cover medical research: or possibly just some aspects of it?
-   Which information provisions should scientific/medical research be exempt from?
-   Should there be some provisions for publicizing medical research registers?

Adequate implementation of the Directive   There were not many issues of inadequate implementation found in this Chapter, but it certainly raised a lot of questions and highlighted many areas that are in immediate need of clarification. The main issue of possible non-compliance is the situation where countries do not provide appropriate safeguards in relation to data protection principles in Article 6(1)(b) on further processing of data for historical, statistical or scientific purposes. In addition, some countries have interpreted the exemption from the prohibition on processing sensitive data, which refers to preventative medicine and medical diagnosis (Article 8(3)), to include medical research, even when this is not explicitly stated.

There are not many occurrences of non-compliance because many of the issues which affect medical research also affect data protection generally, and are covered in Chapter 10 and the conclusion. Another reason there are not many issues in the Directive *directly* related to medical research is because medical research itself is never mentioned within it.

Index

List of Cases